AF734819

Agency, Structure and the NEET Policy Problem

Also available from Bloomsbury

Agency and Participation in Childhood and Youth, edited by Caroline Sarojini Hart, Mario Biggeri and Bernhard Babic
Lost Generation?, Martin Allen

Forthcoming
Rethinking Youth Citizenship After the Age of Entitlement, Lucas Walsh and Rosalyn Black

Agency, Structure and the NEET Policy Problem

The Experiences of Young People

Ian Thurlby-Campbell and Leslie Bell

BLOOMSBURY ACADEMIC
LONDON • NEW YORK • OXFORD • NEW DELHI • SYDNEY

BLOOMSBURY ACADEMIC
Bloomsbury Publishing Plc
50 Bedford Square, London, WC1B 3DP, UK
1385 Broadway, New York, NY 10018, USA

BLOOMSBURY, BLOOMSBURY ACADEMIC and the
Diana logo are trademarks of Bloomsbury Publishing Plc

First published in Great Britain 2017
Paperback edition published 2018

A catalogue record for this book is available from the British Library.

ISBN: HB: 978-1-4742-7417-3
PB: 978-1-3500-9376-8
ePDF: 978-1-4742-7419-7
ePub: 978-1-4742-7418-0

Names: Thurlby-Campbell, Ian, author. | Bell, Les, 1942-author.
Title: Agency, structure and the NEET policy problem :the experiences of
young people /Ian Thurlby-Campbell and Leslie Bell.
Description: London, UK ; N.Y., NY : Bloomsbury Academic,2017. | Includes
bibliographicalreferences and index.
Identifiers: LCCN 2016054338| ISBN 9781474274173 (hb) |ISBN 9781474274197 (epdf)
Subjects: LCSH: Young adults–Employment–Great Britain.| Unemployed–Great
Britain. | Youngadults–Education–Great Britain. | Young
adults–Vocational guidance–Great Britain. | Occupational
training–Government policy–Great Britain. | Vocational
education–Government policy–Great Britain. | Social cognitive theory.
Classification: LCC HD6276.G7 T58 2017 | DDC331.3/40941–dc23
LC record available at https://lccn.loc.gov/2016054338

Typeset by Newgen Knowledge Works Pvt Ltd., Chennai, India.

To find out more about our authors and books visit
www.bloomsbury.com and sign up for our newsletters.

Ian would like to dedicate this book to his brother Samuel, his natural and spiritual family, his friends and colleagues, and all those giving their time and strength to ensure young people have hope and a future

Les would like to dedicate this book to his son Steven and daughter Georgina with best wishes for a brighter future for both of them and to his grandchildren Daisie, Lottie and Poppy

Contents

Abbreviations

BIS	Department for Business, Innovation and Skills
CCIS	Client Caseload Information Service
DfE	Department for Education
DWP	Department for Work and Pensions
EESC	European Economic and Social Committee
EET	Education, Employment or Training
EFSF	European Financial Stability Facility
EM	Engagement Mentoring
EMA	Educational Maintenance Allowance
EU	European Union
FE	Further Education
HE	Higher Education
IAG	Information, Advice and Guidance
LGA	Local Government Association
NEET	Not in Education, Employment Training
NEETs	Young people who are Not in Education, Employment or Training
OECD	Organisation for Economic Cooperation and Development
ONS	The Office for National Statistics
RPA	Raising of the Participation Age
SDG	Sustainable Development Goal
SEU	Social Exclusion Unit
UN	United Nations
UNECE	United Nations Economic Commission for Europe

1

How to Treat NEET: The NEET Policy Problem

Young people who are classified as 'Not in Education, Employment or Training' (NEET) have been the subject of ongoing policy action, research studies, social interventions, public debates and press headlines for almost two decades. The classification first appeared in the UK in 1999, but has gained widespread use in an international context as 'NEET' young people have become an international focal point of concern (e.g. Huang 2007; UNICEF Office of Research 2014). In 2015 the classification was adopted, with minor rephrasing, into the Sustainable Development Goals (SDGs) of the United Nations (UN). These replaced the UN Millennium Development Goals, and will guide the global development activities of the UN member states until 2030. Specifically, Goal Eight of the SDGs commits the 193 member states to, by 2020, 'substantially reduce the proportion of youth not in employment, education or training' and to 'develop and operationalize a global strategy for youth employment' (United Nations 2015). The five-year timescale set for these goals within the wider fifteen-year context of the SDGs typifies the sense of urgency that characterizes discussions about NEET young people.

Three key factors provide the impetus for this urgency. The first is the sheer scale of the issue. Where data are available, they tend to circumscribe NEET populations of disconcerting proportions. In 2009, the size of the NEET population in England rose above the symbolic threshold of 1 million young people aged between sixteen and twenty-four, and held there for several years. At its peak in 2011, the population approached 1.2 million, at which point almost 1 in 5 young people in England (19.4%) were NEET (DfE 2015a). By the following year in Europe, the NEET population across the twenty-seven EU member states had climbed to 14.6 million, a figure denoting almost 1 in 6 (15.9%) of the population between the ages of fifteen and twenty-nine (Eurofound 2014). The scale is even more challenging in some non-EU countries; for example, OECD

(Organisation for Economic Cooperation and Development; 2014) estimates of NEET rates for India and South Africa in late 2012 were 28.9 per cent and 31.6 per cent respectively for all young people aged sixteen to twenty-four. Although the NEET phenomenon (sometimes referred to in shorthand simply as 'NEET') is often associated with the concept of social marginalization, the 'margins' it is referring to are alarmingly large (e.g. Davidson 2009; Simmons, Thompson and Russell 2014).

The second factor is NEET's association with a long list of negative outcomes, both for NEET young people themselves and for society broadly (Eurofound 2015). Economically, at an individual level, NEET coincides with poverty, long-term and intergenerational worklessness, and 'wage scarring', where even long after finding work the wage levels of unemployed young people tend to lag behind those of others who were not unemployed, perhaps permanently (Gregg and Tominey 2004; Carcillo et al. 2015). This is reflected at the macroeconomic level in underproductive national economies, reduced tax receipts and increased state welfare costs. In 2012, for example, youth unemployment in the UK was estimated to have cost the exchequer £4.2 billion in welfare payments and £0.6 billion in foregone tax receipts, and the wider economy a further £10.7 billion in lost output (ACEVO 2012). There are also acute physiological and social associations. Physiologically, NEET coincides with poor physical and mental health, a higher prevalence of drug and alcohol addictions and heightened mortality rates (e.g. Vaughan 2009; Eurofound 2012). Socially, it is associated with crime and delinquency, and in more recent years even civil unrest, particularly following the 2011 riots in England, which were explained by the state and press as having largely been perpetrated by unemployed, less educated youth (e.g. BBC 2011; Isaac-Wilson 2011; Taylor, Rogers and Lewis 2011; Impetus 2014; Simmons, Thompson and Russell 2014). Eurofound (2015: 13) suggest that it may also be associated with political extremism, as NEET young people are 'more likely to accumulate traumatic experiences' that foster a 'resentment towards society … and lead some … to engage at the extremes of the political spectrum'. Although the number of NEET young people led in this way may be rather small relative to the overall NEET population, this observation nonetheless carries NEET discussions into some of the most fraught areas of current social and political affairs.

Given the first and second factors, it is unsurprising that successive national governments have pursued high-profile policy agendas and invested in large-scale programmes to reduce or completely eliminate NEET. This has been most conspicuous in the UK and Europe, where formal policy discussions about

NEET have been taking place the longest. However, despite all that has been done to address it, the scale, scope and seriousness of NEET in these nations has tended to persist (Eurofound 2012). For example, the combined 15- to 24-year-old NEET rate for EU member states was the same in 2013, at 13.0 per cent, as in 2002 when records for that particular statistic began (Eurostat 2016). The third key factor then is the persistence of NEET, and its seeming resistance to remedial action. The following discussions trace the development of concerns about NEET young people in the UK and internationally, the corresponding development of NEET policy and interventions and the establishment of these three factors as central features of ongoing NEET discussions. The discussions serve as a background to the central discourse of this book, which is concerned with understanding the roles that young people and the environments in which they live each have in creating and addressing the NEET problem.

NEET policy in the UK

Although it has roots in concerns about youth disengagement (in the form of youth unemployment) that go back almost four decades, NEET as a specific concept is a policy construct of the past twenty years (Simmons and Thompson 2011). The term originated in UK policy discussions, and was introduced into the public domain by the Cabinet Office's Social Exclusion Unit in 1999 (SEU 1999; Maguire and Thompson 2007; Toivonen 2008). It was foreshadowed by Istance, Rees and Willliamson's (1994) Status A and Status Zero, which essentially referred to the same demographic of young people (Furlong 2006), the latter designation particularly becoming a metaphor for those who seemed to 'count for nothing and were going nowhere' (Williamson 1997: 82). The term 'NEET' itself was, however, more specifically associated with a series of EU policy developments taking place throughout the 1990s and 2000s focused on improving social inclusion (Colley 2006). Pursuing social inclusion meant, in large part, raising employment levels, and investing into skills development, to make the European workforce more globally competitive. Its counterpart, social exclusion, which would become a central concept within NEET discourses, was correspondingly equated with being simultaneously unemployed and disengaged from skill-developing activities, that is, education and training (Colley 2006). From this perspective, education, employment and training (EET) policy were viewed as a whole.

The European policy developments were themselves linked to increasingly influential discussions about the knowledge economy, another concept often referred to in NEET narratives (e.g. UCU 2010; Simmons and Thompson 2011). This suggests the world economy is being increasingly driven by the supply of skilled workers, and that a competitively skilled workforce is more critical to a state's success now than at any time before (EU 2000; Stromquist and Monkman 2000; Waterman 2007; TLRP 2008). Positioned at the cusp of the present and future of the economy, and at the confluences of employment, FE (further education) and HE (higher education), young people inevitably became a focal point of policymakers' discussions. Those leaving school without qualifications were of particular concern (Colley 2006). They were thought to represent not only a failure of the state to respond to the demands of the knowledge economy, but also to be on a trajectory towards becoming the hard core of the future long-term unemployed, with all the economic and social challenges symptomatic of this group. This was compounded by the unqualified tending to become increasingly unemployable within a knowledge economy, heightening the sense of urgency felt by policymakers.

In 1997 the EU member states therefore committed jointly to an agenda formally obliging them to tackle youth unemployment (Miyamoto 2005; EU 2005). British policymakers were spurred further by comparative statistics showing levels of non-participation in education for school leavers in Britain were higher than in EU countries on average. Within two years the UK government's SEU (1999) published a report and initial policy response to these matters, introducing the term 'NEET' and thereby initiating the 'NEET' discourses. The EU discussions circumscribed some of the wider political, social and economic narratives of NEET, but the SEU report wove in a particularly pernicious-sounding domestic social narrative. This linked NEET to educational underachievement, school truancy and exclusion, generational poverty, poor health outcomes and criminality (SEU 1999; Rennison et al. 2005; Miyamoto 2005). NEET was established firmly as a UK policy priority with a view to reducing or eliminating it completely.

Systems were set in place for monitoring and reporting on NEETs prevalence, and an official statistical indicator for NEET was introduced alongside the more conventional youth unemployment indicator. These indicators differ in important ways, as NEET figures are not simply a subset of youth unemployment figures (Eurofound 2012). The youth unemployment indicator refers to young people who are unemployed but considered 'economically active', meaning they have looked for work in the past month and are able to start work in the next two weeks. This number can include individuals who are in education or training but are nonetheless looking for work. NEET excludes those who are in education or training, but does instead include young people who are considered 'economically inactive'. These include those that have either not looked for work in the past month or are unable to start work in the next two weeks (Lee and Wright 2011). Common to both indicators is the set of individuals who are unemployed, economically active and not in education or training.

This common set has in recent years gone from making up a slight majority of the NEET population to a slight minority, meaning that the two populations previously overlapped more than not, but currently do not (e.g. ONS 2014b, c). Even when they do mainly overlap, however, the differences between the two sets of figures, unless understood, can translate into some otherwise potentially misleading or confusing information. As Lee and Wright (2011) observe, not only can the number of NEET young people be higher than the number of unemployed young people (because of the inactive population), but this can be true even while the NEET rate is lower than the youth unemployment rate. This is because different denominators apply to each rate. Only young people working and available for work (i.e. the economically active) are included in the youth unemployment denominator, whereas the NEET denominator includes the total population for the relevant age group (Eurostat 2015a, b). Lee and Wright (2011: 5) therefore suggest that the youth unemployment rate can be 'artificially inflated by an increase in the amount of young people going into education' as many of these young people will cease looking for work, shrinking the denominator. Patterns in youth unemployment rates may be misleading for such reasons. Moreover, according to Bruno, Marelli and Signorelli (2013), NEET figures, by including the inactive group, are a more useful proxy than the youth unemployment figures for identifying the size of the group of youth that are genuinely marginalized. Although the inactive group is not entirely made up of young people that would necessarily be considered marginalized (e.g. those taking gap years to travel), it is known to include considerable numbers of those in the most challenging circumstances, including young carers, those with disabilities or health conditions and those 'pursuing dangerous and asocial lifestyles' (Simmons, Thompson and Russell 2014: 51). NEET figures may thus be thought of as describing a population with an overlapping but ultimately more acute set of circumstances than those covered by the youth unemployment figures.

The SEU report (1999: 9) articulated the 'four main elements' of the policy approach that would characterize the government's efforts to reduce the NEET figures until 2010 (i.e. throughout the New Labour government). These came to be expressed through a portfolio of initiatives with connecting aims (Maguire and Thompson 2007). This included the establishment of the Connexions service that provided IAG (information, advice and guidance) services through a network of personal advisors to enable young people to make better career choices. Financial support systems to encourage young people to participate in post-16 education and training were established, including the Educational Maintenance Allowance (EMA) and the Activity Allowance. A new support system was created for those most at risk of underachievement and disaffection, and included the provision of Engagement Mentoring (EM) services to support the disengaged back into EET (see also Colley 2006). Education and training pathways were made more diverse to meet a wider range of needs and interests (see also UCU 2010). A national minimum wage for sixteen- to seventeen-year-olds and the 'right to time off to train' for young employees were also introduced (Maguire and Thompson 2007). These 'flagship' measures all focused mainly on the sixteen to seventeen, sixteen to eighteen and sixteen to nineteen age groups, but young people of up to twenty-four years of age were in the scope of NEET policy, and were targeted through the New Deal for Young People 'welfare to work' scheme (Beale, Bloss and Thomas 2008). In 2009, the government's Future Jobs Fund created a temporary labour market that supported 105,000 unemployed young people to gain six months of paid work experience. This initiative treated the sixteen to twenty-four NEET bracket as a whole (Fishwick, Lane and Gardiner 2011). Despite over ten years of policy action, however, NEET remained largely 'intractable' (Sodha and Margo 2010: 13) and the scale and scope of the problem remained much as before. By this time, it had been noted that the NEET status of a young person in the UK might even be a 'matter of life and death', as a small research project conducted in the North of England found that more than one in seven long-term NEETs died within a decade of leaving school (Vaughan 2009).

The seriousness with which the NEET problem was considered was such that changes in law were pursued during this period. The Education and Skills Act (2008) included Raising of the Participation Age (RPA) legislation, which stipulated that young people would be required by law to continue to 'participate' in education or training until the age of eighteen. This was intended practically to eliminate NEET for the entire sixteen to seventeen age group. Participation was made achievable in several ways under the Act, including through full-time study, full-time work with part-time education or training, or an apprenticeship or traineeship. At the time of its passing, the legislation served only to heat up NEET discussions rather than ease them, as it was suggested by commentators that it might merely displace or transform the appearance of NEET for this age group rather than actually eradicate it (e.g. Hayward, Wilde and Williams 2008: 7; Wolf 2008; LGA and the Centre for Social Justice 2009a). However, the legislation was only scheduled to come into partial effect in 2013 (when the compulsory participation age would be raised to seventeen) and into full effect in 2015.

With a change of government in 2010 came, unsurprisingly, significant changes in approach. Connexions services were cut (Jayanetti 2010; UNISON 2011) and replaced by an all-age National Careers Service (NCS) which largely prefers to deliver IAG through telephone support and online materials, rather than face-to-face (Simmons et al. 2014). EMA was phased out (Wintour 2012). A headline £1 billion programme entitled the 'Youth Contract' was initiated in late 2011 and ran until March 2015 (HM Government 2011; DWP 2015a). The programme aimed to place 16- to 24-year-olds into sustained employment and training through increased numbers of apprenticeships and voluntary work experience opportunities, intensive support, guaranteed interview schemes and by providing wage subsidies to employers to employ the young (DWP 2013a; Mirza-Davies 2015). It also contained an element of 'NEET to EET' provision for 16- to 17-year-olds, modelled on the newly introduced Work Programme welfare to work service, for NEETs unable to access the Work Programme because of their age (Russell, Thompson and Simmons 2014).

The early results of the policy changes were far from encouraging. Data published in 2011 and 2012 put official figures for the number of unemployed young people at their highest since comparable records began in 1992 (1.04 million, ONS 2012), the then minister for employment referring to the matter as 'a social and economic timebomb' (House of Commons 2012: 7). Official NEET figures around the same time were 1.16 million (HM Government 2011). Employer take up of wage subsidies through the Youth Contract was less than 10 per cent of expected levels (Jozwiak 2013; DWP 2013b) and less than 5 per cent of the 10,000 sixteen- and seventeen-year-old NEETs accessing Youth Contract 'NEET to EET' provision had found EET placements lasting five months or more (EFA 2014). A seemingly unchanged youth unemployment figure of 1.04 million was evident at the time of the initial sampling for the empirical research study that features centrally in this book (ONS 2014a), with data at the time indicating only marginal year-on-year improvements in 'stubbornly high' NEET figures (Silvera 2014). During this period, social commentary on NEET had developed an even more alarmist tone, as unemployed, less educated youth were said by the state and press to be largely responsible for a period of rioting, looting and arson which took place across some of England's major cities in August 2011 (e.g. Isaac-Wilson 2011; Morrell et al. 2011; Cooper 2012; Simmons, Thompson and Russell 2014).

At this point the global economic crisis of 2008–9 and its subsequent recessionary effects had also loomed large in NEET discussions, and were absorbing much of the blame for the state of affairs. There were some good grounds for this. As was noted in a House of Commons (2012) analysis, youth labour market prospects may be 'ultra-sensitive' to economic cycles, and young people have historically 'tended to suffer disproportionately during recessions' (11). Accordingly, UK unemployment rates for 16- to 24-year-olds rose nearly twice as much as for the rest of the working population during the 2008–9 period, and youth unemployment accounted for nearly all of the increase in unemployment figures between mid-2009 and the end of 2011 (11, 172). Correspondingly, the number of NEET young people in England peaked in 2011 at almost 1.2 million, when almost 1 in 5 (19.4%) had become NEET (DfE 2015a).

However, it is important not to overestimate the relation of the recession to the long-term persistence of NEET. The concerns about NEET evidently preceded the economic crisis by many years, and as the same House of Commons (2012) analysis also notes, youth unemployment was already rising steadily from 2004, even when the economy was thought to be booming. The recession's effect, therefore, seems to have been mainly to accelerate, rather than create, a trend of increasing NEET figures. It seems clear from this that there are longer-term issues underlying the NEET problem, different and in addition to the cyclical ones imposed by the recession (e.g. Simmons, Thompson and Russell 2014), and these must be distinguished from any amplifying effects. Recognizing this is crucial for making sense of some of the more recent UK headlines and commentary about NEET at the time of writing, which have combined ongoing concerns about the NEET problem, with some limited signals of success in dealing with it, the latter mainly promulgated by the state.

Some of the marketed success can only be construed as such in comparison to the apparently acute failures preceding it. For example, take up of wage incentives through the Youth Contract were seen to increase considerably in the second half of 2013 and into 2014. This was seemingly due to a combination of generally improving conditions in the labour market as the recession's effects abated, and a delayed reaction to two widenings of the eligibility criteria for the scheme. Whereas initially only 18- to 24-year-olds participating in the Work Programme were eligible for the support, eligibility was first extended in July 2012 to include all 18- to 24-year old benefits claimants who had been receiving benefits for six months or longer in twenty geographic 'hotspots'. These were local authority areas with the highest rates of long-term youth unemployment, and consisted of locations predominantly in the Midlands, North of England, South Wales and parts of Scotland (HM Government 2012a). Eligibility was then extended again, to all geographic areas from December 2012 (DWP 2015a). Four times as many individuals benefited in the last year of the scheme as compared to the first. However, the scheme still fell hugely short of its intentions, ending slightly ahead of schedule to divert funds towards support for young people from Black, Asian and Minority Ethnicity (BAME) backgrounds, who had been gaining increasing attention as being disproportionately represented within the NEET figures (HM Government 2012a; Pickard 2014; Taylor 2015). In the final count, wage incentive payments were provided on behalf of only 36,740 young people, compared to an initial target of 160,000 (DWP 2015a). A further £50 million of the unspent Youth Contract funds were allocated to cities in England for the delivery of locally developed solutions to the NEET problem, including in Liverpool, Leeds City Region, Newcastle and Greater Manchester, in the hope these would be more effective than the nationally commissioned programme (e.g. HM Government 2013a; Mirza-Davies 2015). Whether this will be so remains to be seen.

A particularly mixed set of signals emerged from the data associated with the UK's economic recovery. In early 2015, official statistics showed the lowest unemployment rates nationally in six years for the overall population (DWP 2015b). This did not translate into an entirely better predicament for young people. Although unemployment rates for young people had improved year on year between 2013 and 2014 (from 20.1% to 16.9%), this improvement was far from equitable with the improvements seen for the population overall (ONS 2015). Rather, given that the unemployment rate for the population overall had dropped to 5.8 per cent, Boffey (2015) suggested that young people were actually in a position 'comparatively worse than at any point since 1992', since they were almost three times more likely to be unemployed than the rest of the population, the largest gap in more than 20 years. Nonetheless, a buoyant government announcement just days later claimed that the number of NEET young people was at its lowest level for more than eight years (HM Government 2015a), and a few months later, the lowest in a decade (HM Government 2015b). The contradictory timbre of these claims merits explanation.

Two key factors have enabled the UK government to make such positive statements about NEET figures. The first is the use of the recessionary period as a reference point. The recovery of the labour market as the effects of the recession have abated has impacted positively on NEET rates. However, the extent of this is more limited than headlines may first appear to suggest. Although the numbers of NEET young people reached their lowest for around a decade, the scale of NEET that had prevailed in the late 1990s and early 2000s and which had originally motivated NEET concerns continued to persist. Indeed, the 2014 UK NEET rate, as recorded in official European statistics, was considerably higher than for all years between 2000 and 2006 (Eurostat 2016). Therefore, if the longer-term trends of NEET were used as a reference point instead, these would indicate that the scale of the problem remained broadly as large as it had historically been. A December 2015 speech by the minister of state for employment seemed to recognize both the ongoing scale and urgency of the situation, emphasizing that '[w]e can never stand still when we know almost a million young people are not in education, employment or training' (DWP 2015c). Despite the headlines, the numbers of NEET young people, and the tone of policy concerns about them, remain much as they have been for nearly two decades.

The second key factor is the coming into effect of the RPA legislation. This legislation has naturally led to a reduction of the NEET population which, by force of law, should now comprise of young people in the eighteen to twenty-four age group rather than the broader sixteen to twenty-four age group. However, statistics continue to be routinely produced and reported against the latter. Figures thus show improvement on this basis alone, in a manner consistent with expectations of the legislation. Disaggregated data for the second quarter of 2015 showed that the size of the NEET population in the sixteen to eighteen age group had fallen around four times as fast as that in the nineteen to twenty-four age group, with the former reaching their lowest levels since records began in 2000 (DfE 2015b). The concentration of rate changes in this age bracket points towards an idea that the effects of the RPA legislation on NEET have been considerably more powerful than those associated with the labour market recovery. Indeed, it appears that this legally enforced reduction in NEET figures may be the only meaningful reduction in long-term rates since records began, once the temporary effects of the recession have been accounted for. Having therefore achieved some success in impacting NEET figures by power of law, and little success by any other means, policymakers remain challenged by questions of how to develop policy for the eighteen to twenty-four NEET group. If they are not going to drive this group into education, employment or training (EET) through the force of law, then other means will be needed.

The most recent policy drive has included an ambitious commitment to create three million apprenticeships by 2020, and a new volunteer mentoring scheme targeting those young people most likely to drop out or underachieve at the end of their schooling period (DWP 2015c; HM Government 2016). For now, the UK continues to have a comparatively poor NEET record in the international context, and still ranks lower than the OECD average for NEET levels, a fact opined by OECD officials to be a 'black spot' on its otherwise comparatively strong labour market record (Boffey 2015). The next section considers NEET policy development in this wider international setting.

NEET policy in the EU and beyond

The NEET policy problem is as fraught in Europe as it is in the UK. Cuzzocrea (2013: 3) posits that ongoing commentary 'about the rising numbers of NEETs across Europe, the conditions they face and their unpredictable future … illustrate … the seriousness of the situation of youth across the EU'. Frequent political disputes and tense public debates around youth education and employment policy are a corollary of this, and have noticeably impacted on some national social climates, perhaps most demonstrably in France, Greece and Spain (Eurofound 2015). In Spain, for example, a series of education and labour market reforms aimed at addressing the challenges linked to young people's education and employment has led to 'growing disagreements … and … has weakened social dialogue' (Eurofound 2015: 42–3). The broad economic, physiological and social narratives surrounding these debates are familiar, being very similar in tone and content to those in the UK. For example, at the macroeconomic level, the costs of NEET in the EU in 2012 were estimated to reach €162 billion in benefits, foregone earnings and taxes, equivalent to 1.26 per cent of EU GDP (Eurofound 2014). It has also likewise been observed that at an individual level in Europe, NEET is associated with the loss of future earnings, poor health, depression, alcohol and drug abuse, homelessness, crime and even premature death (Eurofound 2012). A couple of elements within the European NEET narratives, however, have a particularly strong emphasis.

The first of these pertains to the recession triggered by the global economic crisis, referred to monumentally as 'the Great Recession' in some Eurocentric publications (e.g. Coenen, Straub and Trabandt 2012; Eurofound 2015). Such labelling reflects the severity of its effects in Europe, even when compared with the UK. Indeed, Eurozone countries were among the hardest hit by the recession globally, with several, including Ireland, Portugal, Greece and Cyprus, requiring international financial rescue not to default on national debt repayments

(Donnan 2015; EFSF 2016). Unemployment rose sharply across Europe and the region was subjected broadly to a programme of government austerity measures, involving deep cuts to spending on public services and social security provision. As in the UK, young people were more affected by the economic and labour market changes than any other age group (e.g. Vuolo, Staff and Mortimer 2012).

The changes are also thought to have widened income inequalities by disproportionately affecting poorer people, and to have exacerbated existing social tensions. For example, a series of violent protests in Greece came to be interpreted as an expression of a 'collective sense of hopelessness' driven by the rising inequalities, in combination with a perceived longer-term oppression of marginalized groups by the state (Dalakoglou 2013: 33). As in the UK, young people were seen to be at the centre of the social unrest. Greece's 2008 riots were described as a 'revolt of schoolchildren and students' (Margaronis 2008) alongside unemployed and underpaid young adults, the lattermost belonging to a demographic that had become known as 'the €700 generation' on account of their worsening pay conditions during the crisis (Dalakoglou 2013). Similar troubles were seen across Europe more broadly, with 2009 'May Day protests and riots' on account of the economic crisis also being reported in Germany, Austria, Turkey and France (Samuel 2009).

The second element that is more strongly emphasized is the concept of social exclusion, which benefits from a stronger and more familiar frame of reference in Europe than in the UK. Indeed, the concept can be traced to a much earlier history in Europe. It originated in France, where it was first used to describe individuals who were excluded from the social insurance system, known domestically as *les exclus* (the excluded). These particularly included the disabled, lone parents and the uninsured unemployed. The concept quickly gained political traction, being considered more useful than the concept of poverty through its emphasis on social as well as economic disadvantage. Over time, it has to some extent replaced the concept of poverty in Europe's political narrative (Eurofound 2015). Its ongoing importance has been underlined by the relatively recent steps taken by the EU to quantitatively define, measure, monitor and address its prevalence.

In 2010, the EU's Employment, Social Policy, Health and Consumer Affairs Council (EPSCO) introduced an 'at-risk-of poverty or social exclusion' (AROPE) indicator, which supposes to measure the numbers and proportions of people at risk of poverty or social exclusion in the EU. The indicator takes its input from the EU-SILC (EU Statistics on Income and Living Conditions) survey, which collects data at the household and household member level on income, education, labour market participation, health, housing conditions, material deprivation and other complementary information. Three AROPE sub-indicators are derived from this. The most widely used of these is a relative component which produces an at-risk-of poverty rate based on comparative disposable incomes at a national level, where an income of below 60 per cent of the national median is taken as an indicator of poverty. The other two include a type of absolute measure of monetary poverty based on material deprivation indicators (such as the inability to keep the home adequately warm), and an indicator of exclusion from the labour market, which looks for 'severe low work intensity' wherein adults within the household have worked less than 20 per cent of their total work potential over the course of the year (UNECE 2013). The first of the sub-indicators – the at-risk-of poverty rate – has in particular been used to measure progress towards poverty reduction targets. Currently, the Europe 2020 strategy, adopted in June 2010, commits EU member states to reduce the number of people at risk of poverty or social exclusion in Europe by at least 20 million people over the ten-year period to 2020. However, these targets are now likely to be missed, as between 2010 and 2013, the proportion of people considered at risk of poverty or social exclusion grew from 23.7 to 24.5 per cent, the latter representing an absolute number of 122 million people (UNECE 2013; Eurofound 2015).

The precise meaning of these numbers and targets is uncertain because they are dependent on arbitrary thresholds (Bradshaw and Mayhew 2011). Nonetheless, AROPE data is useful for illustrating the relative predicament of populations over time, and for tracking trends in inequalities and the marginalization of certain groups or communities relative to the overall population. This usefully includes young people, as AROPE data for various NEET age brackets is readily available. AROPE figures thus sit alongside the NEET and unemployment indicators as a key measure of the effectiveness of Europe's youth policies (Eurofound 2012). The three indicators together convey Europe's serious long-term difficulties in developing effective youth policy. These have been particularly acute since the economic crisis. EU NEET rates for the fifteen to twenty-four age group rose considerably over the period affected by the crisis, from 10.9 per cent in 2007 to 13.0 per cent in 2013 (Eurostat 2016). Youth unemployment for the age group concomitantly soared from 15.6 per cent to 23.5 per cent over the same period. AROPE data for 2013 identified that the age group was comparatively the most at risk of poverty and social exclusion, with rates for the sixteen to twenty-four age group almost 4 percentage points higher than for the population as a whole, at 28.2 per cent (Eurofound 2015).

Youth education and employment policy thus remain at the top of the EU policy agenda, where they have long been (Eurofound 2015). This agenda has been articulated over the past two decades through a series of EU youth strategies, including most recently the EU Youth Strategy 2010–18 (European Commission 2016). The employment objectives of the strategy are being delivered practically through the Youth Employment Package (YEP). This encompasses a broad range of measures, including initiatives targeted directly at young people (such as skills training aimed at those with low qualification) and others aimed directly at the labour market including recruitment incentives, wage subsidies and the promotion of labour mobility across the EU (Eurofound 2014). A flagship initiative within the YEP, the Youth Guarantee, aims to provide all young people under the age of twenty-five with a 'good quality' education, employment or training offer within four months of their becoming unemployed or leaving formal education (Eurofound 2015). The approach is intended to prevent the damaging personal and social effects of long-term disengagement, and is based on previously established models in Sweden, Finland and Austria, where long-term youth unemployment is relatively low. It was adopted on behalf of all EU member states in April 2013, and each member state has since developed its own plan for implementing it. However, although the initiative is still in the early stages it is already subject to frequent criticism. This is often on the grounds of what it might mean to provide a 'good quality offer' (33). For example, there are concerns that the need to fulfil the Youth Guarantee may result in young people being channelled into vacancies that provide a poor or even negative experience of working life, or that are unlikely to offer them any kind of long-term progression. There are also concerns that the initiative is underfunded, despite a dedicated €6.4 billion Youth Employment Initiative (YEI) fund that will aid member states to implement it. The European Economic and Social Committee (EESC 2013), for example, has suggested that the '6,000 million euros earmarked … is not enough to cope with the magnitude of the problem and the urgent need to resolve it' (cited in Eurofound 2015). This remains to be proven, but for the foreseeable future, the NEET policy problem remains a major source of concern in Europe.

The discussion of EU NEET policy can be developed in two important ways to complete an introductory exploration of the international NEET policy context. The first is to observe that the use of the NEET classification has spread beyond the EU, most noticeably across the OECD, but also to some non-OECD countries. NEET data is now collated for all OECD countries (e.g. OECD 2015). However, it should be noted that this does not necessarily mean that the terminology has been adopted into mainstream domestic use in all of the OECD countries. Its usage appears to be rather limited in North America, for example, although Simmons and Thompson (2011) note that the NEET discussion nonetheless engages with ideas and debates that are highly relevant to current concerns in the country, as is reflected in other literature (e.g. Arnett 2000; Bynner 2005; Furstenberg 2010; Vuolo, Staff and Mortimer 2012).

The second way is to recognize the particularities of scale, context and policy applications associated with NEET at the national level, which are easily obscured in EU, OECD or global-level discussions. For example, NEET rates differ considerably across countries, and are not equally affected by changing conditions. During the period of economic crisis in the EU, some countries were clearly more severely affected than others. Those that had required financial assistance were noticeably among the worst affected. For example, NEET rates in the fifteen to twenty-four age group increased from 9.0 to 18.7 per cent in Cyprus, and from 11.3 to 20.4 per cent in Greece between 2007 and 2013 (Eurostat 2016). However, countries with initially low rates tended to be less affected; for example, rates in Norway went only from 4.4 to 5.6 per cent over the same period. Absolute numbers of NEETs also vary. In 2014, NEETs in Italy numbered almost 2.5 million. At the same time in Ireland, however, there were fewer than 80,000 and in Estonia only around 17,000 (Eurofound 2015).

Importantly, each individual country has its own particular ways in which NEET narratives have been contextualized, or have undergone 'indigenization', to use Toivonen's (2011) term. This is in respect of both how NEET is understood culturally, and responded to politically. The EU supports such policy differentiation through the Open Method of Coordination (OMC), within which individual nations are able to determine their own approaches to implementing EU policies. Cuzzocrea (2013) comments particularly on how this has been expressed in Italy which, she argues, serves as a useful example case within the EU rather than as an exception. Italy also serves as a particularly relevant case in the EU context as it will receive the largest YEI budget (€1.1 billion) under the Youth Guarantee framework (Eurofound 2015). The size of this budget reflects a couple of factors which relate to the particularities of the NEET context nationally.

First, this includes Italy's relatively high NEET rates. Even before the global crisis, the Italian NEET rate was among the highest in Europe. The crisis, however, pushed the rate up further from 16.1 to 22.2 per cent between 2007 and 2013 (Eurostat 2016). At this point, for early school-leavers, the probability of becoming NEET was higher than the probability of their finding a job

(Eurofound 2012). Second, it includes a deliberate decision by the Italian authorities to make all young people up to the age of twenty-nine eligible for the Youth Guarantee. This policy reflects a particularly delayed transition to adulthood for Italian young people; 'in Italy, the common parlance easily attaches the word "youth" even to adults in their late thirties or early forties' (Cuzzocrea 2013: 9). Combined with a sizeable overall population, these two factors mean that Italy has to address absolute numbers of NEET young people well in excess of two million disengaged young people (Eurofound 2015). The government's response has included a series of programmes aligned with EU policies but clearly contextualized for Italy, including *Diritto al futuro* (Right to the future), 'Italy 2020', *Salva Italia* (Save Italy), *Cresci Italia* (Grow up Italy), *Semplifica Italia* (Simplify Italy) and *Partecipiamo!* (Let's participate!) (Cuzzocrea 2013). Cuzzocrea also observes, at the cultural level, not only that 'use of the NEET classification is ... extensive in Italy, and has entered mainstream use' but that a 'popular version of the acronym' has also become common. This often ignores the last letter, such that 'it is often heard that NEETs are 'those not in employment or education'. She notes a similarity with Spain, where the term *ni-ni* is popularly used, again meaning 'not in employment or education' (11).

Beyond the EU, yet stronger forms of indigenization are noticeable in the Far Eastern countries. In Japan, China and Taiwan, energetic NEET narratives have developed, each communicating concerns about young people in particularly anxious tones. In these countries, the NEET phenomenon is often portrayed in terms of a moral panic (Toivonen 2011), in which young NEET people are seen as having failed to grasp the moral tenets held by the rest of society which would otherwise ensure their engagement. Huang (2007) reports, for example, that in China, young people in this group are known as 'drifters' and alarmingly even 'eaters of the elderly', in reference to their financial dependence on older family members. In Hong Kong, they are called 'the twice failed' referring to their apparent failure in both school and employment. For Huang (2007), some of the most cutting terms are used in Taiwan, where puns on 'NEET' produce terms such as 'wallowers' or 'the drowned'. In Japan, where press coverage on NEET dates to as early as 2004 (Nakamura 2004), young people are described as *hikikomori* (caged youth), referring to a stereotypical reclusiveness assigned to the group. These terms are translated by Taiwanese observers jokingly as 'home-squatting wastrels' and 'cocooned kids' (Huang 2007). In Japan, as in Italy, the term 'NEET' has been indigenized, in this case to *nitō*, using Japanese katakana syllables. Also as in Italy, the classification is applied to an extended age range, in this case officially 15- to 34-year-olds (Rahman 2006). This again reflects a lengthening transition into adulthood, driven in this case at least partially by an employment culture that favours older workers (Jō 2006; Honda, Asao and Gotō 2006); in challenging economic conditions, job protection policies have benefited older employees and made it difficult for younger workers to find jobs or to progress in their careers. This has lengthened the time typically lived within parental homes, and seemingly even caused some young people to decide that conventional career routes, a central element of Japan's conformist society, are not ones that they necessarily wish to pursue (e.g. Toivonen, Norasakkunkit and Uchida 2011). NEET young people are thus presently a source of considerable political, social, economic and cultural concern for Far East governments and societies.

Having established the scale and seriousness of the NEET policy problem in the UK and internationally, and the difficulties in resolving it, discussion now turns to the relationship between the NEET policy problem and the sociological concepts of agency and structure, in order to provide a framework within which to analyse the NEET policy issues in the UK.

NEET's 'vexed question'

A body of literature has developed in response to the policy challenges represented by NEET, and the difficulties in finding effective solutions to them. This literature seeks both to further understand NEET, and to critique and correct the policy and interventions used to address it. One outcome of this is that the demographics of NEET are now well known, as is alluded to throughout the above discussions. The likelihood of becoming NEET is clearly highest where young people have one or more of several relative disadvantages. Perhaps the most important of these is socioeconomic status, as young people from poorer backgrounds are consistently more likely to be affected, whether this is framed in terms of social class, or on the basis of poverty indicators (e.g. DfE 2011; Simmons, Thompson and Russell 2014). This holds true across the OECD countries (Carcillo et al. 2015). NEET is also known generally to be strongly correlated with lower educational attainment (e.g. Eurofound 2012; Siraj et al. 2014), although this does not hold true in all countries at all times; in 2011, the incidence of NEET was actually higher among young people with higher levels of education than those with lower levels in a number of OECD nations including Greece and Japan (OECD 2014), an observation perhaps best explained through particular labour market conditions within those economies. Other factors such as disabilities, ethnic minority backgrounds, caring responsibilities, leaving care statuses, immigration statuses, homelessness and criminal history are also known to be associated with a higher likelihood of becoming NEET (e.g. Eurofound 2015).

Understanding NEET's demographics, however, does not serve necessarily to explain its causes, nor offer a solution to it. Crucially from a policy perspective, knowing who NEETs are does not lead straightforwardly to what actions should be taken to address their situations. NEET occurs at a confluence of institutional responsibilities, most obviously including those relating to education and training systems and the labour market, but also perhaps including those relating to the welfare, social care, health and justice systems (Newton et al. 2014). Some research also associates NEET with complex interpersonal dynamics at the familial and neighbourhood levels, (Simmons and Thompson 2011). These together comprise a complex social topography within which the individual cases of NEET take place, and each part of this topography is potentially implicated in producing (i.e. causing) and addressing the cases. Then there are, of course, young people themselves, whose role in producing and addressing their own NEET statuses is perhaps the most contentious of all. These concerns are expressed collectively in what may be described as NEET's *vexata quaestio*, or 'vexed question' (Cuzzocrea 2013). The question asks to what extent young people find themselves NEET as a result of their own actions, relative to having this determined by the political, social and economic structures in which they live.

The policy implications of an answer are relatively intuitive. In simplified terms, if a young person's EET outcomes are primarily determined by their own actions, then policy approaches seeking to modify the thinking and behaviours of the young person are warranted. If instead their outcomes are primarily determined by the political, social and economic structures in which they live, then policy should focus on modifying these. To date, however, there is no consensus on what the contributions of young people or such structures actually are to producing or addressing NEET. The global economic recession may have diverted attention away from the debate around this question in recent years, by providing a temporarily convenient explanation for NEET's recalcitrance, but as the recession's effects abate the concerns circumscribed by the question are once again moving to the fore.

There is also evidence that the question is as relevant to praxis as to policy. For example, Colley's (2006) case studies show the interpretation of NEET young people's behaviours can be subject to ambiguity, so that where these behaviours appear to some practitioners to be wholly agentic, to others they reflect structural coercion. This leads to divergent views on how young people's individual's cases should be handled, with potentially life-changing decisions being made on their behalf as a result. This is developed further in the next chapter.

The 'vexed question' has classically sociological dimensions. It contraposes the role of the young person's agency (i.e. the personal and collective capacity of individuals to act and effect change) against the role of structure (i.e. the surrounding conditions that enable or constrain the use of agency) in determining their outcomes. This inquiry into the extent to which a phenomenon is attributable to the agency of individuals, as opposed to the environment they inhabit, is a form of sociology's structure-agency debate (Archer 1995). The literature review in the Chapter 2 shows that the broad NEET policy literature has often drawn on the concepts of agency and structure but without necessarily invoking them as such. It can be argued that where this happens, useful opportunities to progress the treatment of important social issues can be missed (e.g. Akram 2010). A natural course to take, therefore, is to position NEET properly within the structure-agency debate, and use this to address questions raised within the NEET policy literature. This idea is not new in itself. For example, Colley (2003) uses Bourdieu's concepts of field and habitus (from Bourdieu and Wacquant 1992) as a basis for analysing case studies of NEETs. Russell, Simmons and Thompson (2011) similarly use Giddens's (1984) structuration theory in an ethnographic study. Evans (2007) and Aaltonen (2013) use less familiar frameworks of agency and structure in other studies related to youth transitions. These and other studies thus constitute an important section of the NEET policy literature which does invoke such key concepts.

Coffey and Farrugia (2014), however, criticize how such studies have been carried out. They argue that conceptualizations of agency and structure are often politicized. This compromises the 'ethical commitment to critical research' (467) by obscuring potentially important narratives about young people and their relation to their environments. They also argue, crucially, that abstractions in the typical conceptualizations of agency and structure obfuscate the nature of the interactions that each has with the other, such that studies are incapable of discerning clearly between the roles of agency and structure in empirical youth transitions. Consequently, whether young people, or their environment, is responsible for a given set of outcomes ultimately remains unclear. These criticisms target contemporary youth studies as a whole, but apply meaningfully to NEET studies specifically, which have to date been unable to develop a clear distinction between the roles of agency and structure needed to address properly the *vexata quaestio*. It is broadly recognized that the relevant interactions between the young person and structures are actually complex and dialectical. Hence, neither agency nor structure is the sole determinant of outcomes. The literature shows a notable underdevelopment in the empirical understanding of the relative influences of each, the nature of the interactions and the ways in which these contribute to outcomes. Even determining when a young person's behaviours ought to be considered a genuine expression of their own agency, as opposed to being behaviours forced upon them by structural conditions, is noticeably problematic. Critiques of NEET policy by Colley (2006), Wolf (2008) and Sodha and Margo (2010) produce different perspectives on the role of young people in the determination of their outcomes, often with divergent implications for the means by which NEET should be addressed. To borrow the language of Coffey and Farrugia (2014), there is an epistemic 'black box' within NEET, the content of which is yet to be seen, and this must be elucidated in order to resolve the policy problem.

This book is a response to these several matters. It presents an empirical research study with three substantive aims. The first and primary aim is to progress empirical knowledge pertaining to NEET's *vexata quaestio* by 'opening' the epistemic 'black box', so that the interactions between agency and structure within NEET can be clearly understood. This is framed in terms of an investigation focused on NEET young people themselves, and the ways in which they exercise agency in determining their outcomes. The way in which this exercise is itself influenced by their perceptions of how agency and structure interact in their lives is also explored. The exercise of agency by young people, and the way in which this is influenced by their perceptions, is termed the function of personal agency. The investigation sets out to elucidate this function and its role in determining young people's outcomes. By this it aims to provide insight into how NEET policy and praxis might be improved. This is delivered ultimately through an original piece of empirical research, detailing the stories and perspectives of a diverse group of sixteen young people living in London, where the NEET classification was first introduced by politicians and policymakers to public policy discussions seventeen years ago. A central part of the book involves a detailed analysis of these young people's personal perceptions and experiences of becoming and being NEET. In this sense, the book is about much more than the NEET policy problem and the vexed question. It also very much about NEET young people, their lives and what they themselves have to say; the voices of NEET young people themselves are often silent in the policy debates, but they are brought to bear here. The findings of the empirical research, and the promise they hold for future improvements in policy and practice, are presented and then discussed in the later chapters of the book.

The second and third aims are subservient to the first. The second is to contribute to the theoretical treatment of NEET by locating NEET within a conceptual and epistemic framework that provides the resources necessary for elucidating the content of the 'black box'. Achieving this requires a conceptualization of agency to be defined and operationalized, by which it might be empirically identified and analysed, and clearly delineated from structure. This is developed in Chapters 2 and 3, predicated mainly on Bandura's (2001) agentic perspective on social cognitive theory. In Bandura's perspective, agency is 'temporally extended' through the four 'core features' of intentionality, forethought, self-reactiveness and self-reflectiveness. It is proposed that these four features can collectively be considered the signature characteristics of agency, and evidence of their exercise considered to be evidence of its exercise. A complementary framework for identifying and analysing the influence of structures on personal agency is developed largely by using Lopez and Scott's (2000) typology of structure and the NEET policy literature. It is intended that the consideration, critique and adaptation of the approach will support new and useful thinking about the theoretical treatment of NEET. The third aim is to situate the conceptual and epistemic framework within a methodological approach capable of supporting its effective use. The approach is set out in detail in the Chapter 4, to support analysis and replication of the study, and it is again intended that this will stimulate new thinking for researchers investigating similar problems.

Broad issues and value positions: How to treat NEET

A broad argument is sustained throughout the book that questions relating to NEET policy and praxis can be treated usefully by positioning NEET within the structure-agency debate. It is concurrently argued that the potential usefulness of this kind of treatment has not yet been fully realized insofar as studies have been unable to discern clearly between the roles of agency and structure in the determination of outcomes. Without clarity on this matter, research is unable to contribute authoritatively to discussions on key areas of NEET policy and praxis. On this basis, the study pursues a clearer understanding of the function of personal agency within NEET, and of the dialectical interactions in which it is involved. It also seeks to incorporate a sensitivity to the tacit concerns about, and conceptualizations of, agency and structure in the broader NEET policy literature, and so develop findings of practical relevance and utility to that research.

In doing so, the study holds to a basic value position that there is a complex and dialectical relationship between agency and structure. This is in contrast to reductionist positions which suppose that agency can be reduced to structure, or structure to agency, so that one is an epiphenomenon of the other. This position is generally consistent with contemporary sociological thought, as reductionist theories have become increasingly discredited (Akram 2010). This connotes associated value positions that the concepts of agency and structure are each ontologically and epistemologically valid. There are also ontological and epistemological value positions held in relation to the study's investigation into young people's perceptions. Ontologically, perceptual phenomena are recognized as real phenomena. This is in contrast to particular materialist reductionist positions, such as eliminative materialism (Churchland and Churchland 1998) which suppose these phenomena are illusory. Epistemologically, a cognitivist position on the investigation of perceptual phenomena is held. This is in contrast to behaviourist approaches which suppose that because perceptions cannot be objectively measured, they cannot be validly known (Schunk 2004). These positions are defended in Chapters 2 and 4.

The approach taken by this study also links it to other concerns within the NEET and broader educational and sociological literature. The links derive first from the observation that Bandura's (2001) four 'core features' are all centred within or are immediately derivative of the agent's thought life (thereby locating agency largely within perceptual activity) and the related idea that agency functions within a perceived structural context. Second they derive from the widespread idea that NEET is occurring in a sociostructural environment that differs significantly from that experienced by previous generations (Coleman and Hendry 1999; Miyamoto 2005). This difference is characterized by more sophisticated education and training frameworks, increasingly long and complicated transitions from school to work, and unique labour market conditions alongside broader societal change (e.g. Heinz 2000; Bynner 2005; Inui 2005; Miyamoto 2005; Colley 2006; Furlong 2006; Woodman and Wyn 2013).

Where such transformations are occurring in the educational system and labour markets, 'a limited understanding of how adolescents perceive these changes hinders educators in helping young people formulate effective strategies for coping with … transition' (Taylor et al. 1992: 177–8). This is not restricted to educators, and indicates that understanding how young people's perceptions are implicated in their outcomes may be important for praxis more widely. In an editorial on NEET Standish (2007: iv) insists that 'it is incumbent on us also to take seriously the ways in which our social world and our place within it are reconstructed, and hence to be alert to the new forms of disaffection – call this social exclusion if you will – that are perhaps increasingly underway'. He thus relates NEET, which is often associated with disaffection (Thompson 2011), to the ways in which young people perceptually relate to sociostructural changes. Nakamura (2004: 1), in a commentary on the emergence of NEET in Japan, notes that 'experts believe the problem might be related to psychological changes on the part of young people, though the specific causes have yet to be determined'.

Toivonen, Norasakkunkit and Uchida (2011: 1) raise the accompanying counterargument to this, suggesting rather that the observed behavioural changes in young people seem 'to be an outcome of labor market change rather than a psychopathology'. Honda, Asao and Gotō (2006, quoted in Ishiguro 2007) caution against relying on dominant NEET discourses to understand the nature of these changes in any case, suggesting that both political and popular motives can lead to serious gaps between the real images of youth who are categorized as NEET and the prevalent discourses that describe them. Simmons and Thompson (2011) also indicate that the real voice of NEET young people is mostly silent. By examining how the agentic behaviours of NEET young people are mediated by their perceptions, this study may contribute to the redressing of these issues by ensuring that these voices are now heard.

An outline of the study

Chapter 2 contains the first part of a literature review that establishes the theoretical dimensions of the study. It outlines the nature of the structure-agency debate, and posits basic dialectical definitions of agency and structure as a precursor to examining the debate's relevance to the NEET policy literature. Several aspects of NEET policy literature are reviewed. The nature of the research problem is established from Colley (2006) and further developed from Wolf (2008), the LGA and Centre for Social Justice (2009a) and Sodha and Margo (2010). The pieces are useful for framing the problem concisely, and on terms that do not overemphasize the importance of cyclical economic conditions. It is argued that the extent to which NEET young people are determining their own outcomes is empirically uncertain. It is shown that agency and structure are variously used to explain the same behaviours and outcomes of young people, and this problematizes NEET policy and praxis as is framed by the 'vexed question'. It is suggested that the way in which behaviours and outcomes are produced is a result of complex dialectical interactions, and it would be useful to develop a clearer understanding of what these interactions are, and how they contribute to behaviours and outcomes. The study thus sets out to examine empirically the extent to which young people's agency may be determining their EET outcomes, and to elucidate the nature of their interactions with NEET's structures. A topography of NEET, which outlines the agents and structures implicated in the determination of EET outcomes, is developed from the literature as a means of circumscribing the context in which the dialectical interactions take place.

Chapter 3 sets out to establish appropriate conceptualizations of agency and structure as a precursor to the empirical investigation. Historical conceptualizations of agency and structure in youth sociology, and the broader sociological literature are reviewed, from Coffey and Farrugia (2014), Parker (2000), Akram (2010) and Porpora (2013). The conceptualizations are seen to be problematized broadly by issues of abstraction and politicization, and it is argued that this makes them epistemologically unsuitable for use in addressing NEET's *vexata quaestio*. An original approach to conceptualizing agency and structure is instead developed from Bandura (2001) and Lopez and Scott (2000). Bandura's (2001) agentic perspective on social cognitive theory is used to conceptualize agency, and the function of personal agency is defined from this discussion. Lopez and Scott's (2000) typology of structure is developed into a suitable conceptualization of structure. It is proposed that the two can be used together to achieve the empirical aims of the study.

Chapter 4 develops the methodology. It defends the ontological and epistemological value positions associated with investigating perceptions and locates the study within the interpretive paradigm. The research objectives and questions are established. The research design, methodology and data collection process are outlined which, it is argued, coherently operationalize the study's conceptualizations of agency and structure.

Chapters 5 and 6 detail the empirical findings in two main sections. Chapter 5 presents findings on the relation of ten discrete elements of NEET's topography to the function of personal agency. Chapter 6 considers in detail the outworking of personal agency through Bandura's (2001) four 'core features' of agency. Common mechanisms that convey the influences of structures to young people as agents, and the perceptual factors that mediate their associated behaviours, are identified and discussed, and related to the determination of their outcomes. It is argued that the findings convincingly explain the function's operation in the lives of a diverse group of young people, and across a range of highly varied circumstances.

Chapter 7 presents a diagrammatic model of the function of personal agency in NEET. The model and findings are discussed in the context of the reviewed NEET policy literature, and their policy and praxis implications are explored. It is argued that the model and findings helpfully elucidate NEET's dialectical 'black box', and usefully account for a number of complex, heterogeneous and problematic dynamics within NEET. It is suggested that different theoretical approaches may sensitize investigations to particular dynamics within dialectically complex phenomena, and that the approach developed in this study is useful as one that can distinguish between agency and structure roles in relatively precise terms. Chapter 8 concludes the study. A summary of its purposes and achievements is presented, and some broader implications of the study are developed. The study ends with a discussion on the nature of the dialectical relationship between agency and structure, and a review of directions for future research.

Conclusion

Over the past two decades, the NEET policy problem has taken on increasing significance internationally on account of its scale, the seriousness of its impact on individuals and societies and the difficulties in developing effective policy solutions to it. These difficulties are in part expressed by what has been called NEET's *vexata quaestio* or 'vexed question' (Cuzzocrea 2013). This asks to what extent young people find themselves NEET as a result of their own actions, relative to having this determined by the political, social and economic structures in which they live. This book responds to the question, by developing and presenting an empirical study which investigates the function of personal agency in determining the EET outcomes of young people. The function of personal agency refers to both the exercise of agency by young people, and the way in which this exercise is influenced by their perceptions of how agency and structure interact in their lives. The study has three aims. The first and primary aim is to progress empirical knowledge pertaining to NEET's *vexata quaestio* by elucidating the interactions between agency and structure within it. The second aim is to contribute to the theoretical treatment of NEET. Previous studies have developed the relationship between NEET and the structure-agency debate, but their approaches have been problematized by conceptualizations of agency and structure that inhibit their capabilities to clearly delineate the roles of each (e.g. Coffey and Farrugia

2014). The third aim is to contribute to methodological thought and practice in NEET research by developing an original and effective approach to operationalizing distinct agency and structure concepts. These concepts are intended to bring greater clarity to the complex issues of policy and praxis that obscure the factors which lead young people to become NEET.

2

NEET's 'Black Box': Why Developing Effective NEET Policy Is Difficult

This chapter establishes basic definitions of agency and structure, and reviews the NEET policy literature to establish the nature of NEET's *vexata quaestio* and hence the issues that are central to this book. It is argued that NEET policy and praxis is problematized by a lack of clarity about the extent to which young people find themselves NEET as a result of their own agency, relative to having their outcomes determined by political, social and economic structures. Although there is a broad consensus that young people and their sociostructural environments each have contributing roles in the determination of outcomes, the relative influences of each, and the nature of the interactions between the two, are uncertain. The ways in which the uncertainties are interpreted can lead policy and praxis in different directions. Particular items reviewed include Colley (2006), Wolf (2008), the LGA and Centre for Social Justice (2009a) and Sodha and Margo (2010). This literature is used to circumscribe the uncertainties. It is also used to develop a topography of NEET in which the agents and structures implicated in NEET's production and transformation are identified, thereby circumscribing the contexts in which NEET's dialectical interactions take place. The selected literature is considered useful for framing the problem concisely, and on terms that do not overemphasize the importance of cyclical economic conditions such as the recent recession. This is increasingly important as the effects of the recession abate in the UK and internationally.

The structure-agency debate and NEET

The structure-agency debate has been described as '*the* central sociological problem' (Archer 1995: 1; emphasis in the original). It is concerned with the relationship between the individual and society, how each is influenced by the other and how the two interact to produce and transform social phenomena. These considerations are applicable to NEET, which might be described as the non-participation of individual young people in society's formalized educational, vocational or skill-developing activities, particularly where participation is considered normative and essential to both the individual and society (Fergusson 2013). It is useful therefore to position NEET within the structure-agency debate, as a means to treating its concerns. Akram (2010) suggests a failure to do this is problematic for social and political literature broadly, as invoking the debate can provide a way to respond to questions that may otherwise be difficult to identify or treat.

Three fundamental positions may be taken in respect to the structure-agency debate (Akram 2010). First, there is the intentionalist position, which emphasizes the importance of agency and denies the importance of structural influences in society. Second, there is the structuralist position, which emphasizes the importance of structure and regards the influence, and perhaps even existence, of agency as largely illusory. Third, there is the dialectical position which posits an interactive and mutually influential relationship between structure and agency, in which both are ontologically and epistemologically valid. Over recent decades, intentionalist and structuralist positions have been largely discredited, and dialectical positions are increasingly accepted (Akram 2010). The NEET policy literature reflects a broad commitment to a dialectical position. Consequently, the research problem that emerges from this review assumes a dialectical reality. The study itself is necessarily committed to starting from such a position.

Having established this, basic definitions of agency and structure can be posited. Neither is simply defined (Lopez and Scott 2000; Akram 2010) but within a dialectical model, agency is broadly considered to be the capability of an individual (or group of individuals) to act independently and intentionally to bring about outcomes through their choices and actions (Bandura 2001). Structure is counterpart to agency, and refers to encompassing conditions and patterned social arrangements which influence, direct or limit the choices and actions of agents (Barker 2003). While agency takes place within the context of structure and has capacity to influence it, structure shapes the choices available to agents, and the associated risks, rewards and efforts. This mutual influence is the basic quality of the dialectical relationship. The following discussion develops the relevance of the structure-agency debate to NEET policy and praxis. It establishes that there are uncertainties about the nature of the dialectical interactions that take place within NEET, and how these contribute to young people's outcomes.

While intentionalist and structuralist positions have largely been discredited, it will be shown that relatively intentionalist and structuralist perspectives on the determination of EET outcomes can exist within a broad commitment to a dialectical position. These perspectives are evident within the NEET policy literature, and highlight uncertainties about the young person's role within NEET.

The NEET policy literature

The NEET policy literature has its formal beginnings with the SEU (1999) report that introduced the term 'NEET' into the public domain and established it as a UK policy priority (Maguire and Thompson 2007). The scale and scope of NEET has remained largely consistent since this time, despite extensive policy action (e.g. Sodha and Margo 2010; Mirza-Davies 2014). This apparent failure of NEET policy has attracted criticisms, and it is this literature which is now the focus of this study. Four pieces of literature are examined, these being Colley (2006), Wolf (2008), the LGA and Centre for Social Justice (2009a) and Sodha and Margo (2010). These pieces are together useful for establishing the nature of the research problem under investigation. The timing of these publications also makes them useful since overemphasizing the effects of the recession can be avoided, and long-term issues can more easily be identified (Simmons, Thompson and Russell 2014).

These sources collectively convey the nature within the policy literature of several conflicting representations of the ways in which young people and their surrounding structures interact to produce NEET. These representations are reflected across the literature broadly and are typically associated with, first, central government policy narratives and mainstream public discourses which stigmatize the NEET young person's behaviours and attitudes (Thompson 2011); a modernized tradition of academic discourse that seeks to emphasize the role of sociopolitical structures in determining outcomes (Coffey and Farrugia 2014); a category of alternative academic opinion that emphasizes the self-determination of outcomes by young people (Heinz 2009; Coffey and Farrugia 2014); and the various contributions of policy think tanks and local political bodies which develop the range of possible emphases. The representations are associated with divergent policy responses. This altogether gives a useful indication of the parameters of the discourses associated with the research problem. The pieces also serve to establish that NEET is a problem 'entrenched … in a "triangle" between policy, research and practitioner' (Cuzzocrea 2013: 3), validating the linkages between policy, praxis and academic thought that run throughout the study. Most importantly, they can be used effectively to establish the character of what may be thought of as NEET's '*vexata quaestio* of how much responsibility lies with young people' in the determination of their outcomes (7).

A review of Colley's (2006) research serves as a foundation from which to establish the nature of the research problem. Colley is shown to develop a relatively structuralist perspective on the determination of EET outcomes, in which structural influences ultimately determine outcomes for NEET young people. She contrasts her own position with that of an implied position within EU and UK state policy literature, which is shown to be relatively intentionalist, that is, representative of a perspective in which young people are ultimately determining their own outcomes. The differing perspectives lead in divergent policy directions. It is argued from case studies presented by Colley that NEET's policy concerns are ultimately instantiated in the lives of individual young people, and that equivalent differences in perspective also problematize praxis. Possible difficulties in empirically identifying the role of young people's agency within NEET are also indicated. Hence knowledge of the role of agency is made unclear by dialectical complexity, but might usefully be elucidated by empirical investigation. Colley also contrasts the possible influences of close personal relationships on young people's outcomes, and the possible influences of certain types of organizations (e.g. government departments and employers). This highlights a distinction between two types of structure within NEET, and begins to circumscribe the topography within which NEET's dialectical interactions take place.

Wolf (2008), the LGA and Centre for Social Justice (2009a) and Sodha and Margo (2010) are reviewed to develop the context of the investigation further. Wolf (2008) is shown to develop a relatively intentionalist perspective in which young people are self-determining their outcomes, although not necessarily on the same basis as indicated within state policy narratives. The LGA and Centre for Social Justice (2009a) and Sodha and Margo (2010) are each shown to develop relatively structuralist perspectives which utilize the same distinctions of structure as Colley (2006). Where the LGA and Centre for Social Justice (2009a) emphasize the importance of personal relationships in influencing outcomes, Sodha and Margo (2010) instead emphasize the importance of organizations. These pieces are used to develop the topography further.

It may be noted again here that the concept of NEET – referring to individuals 'Not in Employment, Education or Training' – is ostensibly an amalgamation of otherwise historical phenomena, and has its roots in concerns about youth unemployment going back almost four decades (Simmons, Russell and

Thompson 2013). As such the NEET policy literature is preceded by a substantial body of earlier literature. However, agency and structure in the NEET policy literature, as they are being treated in this study, have a somewhat ambiguous relationship with their equivalents in the earlier literature. As Furlong (2006) notes, much is known about historical youth unemployment that ought not to be discarded. At the same time, however, the sociostructural environment has evolved such that earlier ways of thinking about it may not be suitable for what Furlong terms 'the modern age' (555). Coleman and Hendry (1999), Miyamoto (2005) and Toivonen, Norasakkunkit and Uchida (2011) corroborate the idea that the societal conditions in which NEET is taking place are markedly different from their historical equivalents. These conditions include more sophisticated education and training frameworks, increasingly complicated transitions from school to employment, and new labour market dynamics wherein the old employment/unemployment dichotomy may be obsolete (e.g. Inui 2005; Miyamoto 2005; Furlong 2006; Heinz 2009). The concept of NEET, and by extension its literature, is both symbolic and symptomatic of these differences. With sensitivity to the concerns developed earlier about young people's adaptation to changing sociostructural environments (e.g. Taylor et al. 1992; Standish 2007) it appears it is not judicious to carry forward observations from earlier studies unquestioningly. As such, this review focuses on literature directly related to NEET policy discussions, in keeping with an approach that pursues relevance and utility to contemporary policy activity.

NEET: A structuralist perspective

Colley's (2006) study builds upon an earlier study (Colley 2003) in which she utilizes Bourdieu's concepts of 'field' and 'habitus' as a means of articulating the interplay of agency and structure in school-work transitions and mentoring relationships. Although Bourdieu's concepts are not a specific feature of her later study, the concepts of agency and structure are explicitly referred to, and themes from the earlier study are developed in the context of NEET policy. This makes Colley's (2006) study the only one of the four pieces reviewed to refer explicitly to concepts of agency and structure, although all the pieces invoke the ideas associated with them.

Colley (2006) critiques the European policy documents and actions that induced the social exclusion and NEET discourses of the 1990s and 2000s, and the consequential use of engagement mentoring (EM) to reduce NEET. She then presents two case studies of NEET young people participating in an EM programme, to illustrate that EM does not work as envisaged by policymakers. In her critique, she argues EU policy constructed young people as the cause of NEET, and so targeted them in its actions. Social exclusion was associated with the values, attitudes and motivational characteristics of young people rather than the characteristics of the labour market and society, 'constructing them as a threat to society, rather than identifying ways in which society's systems might be a threat to disadvantaged young people' (4). In this way, EU policy is characterized by Colley as having a relatively intentionalist perspective on the determination of EET outcomes, that is, one in which young people's outcomes are largely self-determined.

The EU's pursuant policy actions focused on changing young people's vilified values, attitudes and motivations. EM, a form of one-on-one relational mentoring involving a responsible adult (usually a professionally employed, non-family member) and a young person, was used as one of the primary tools for achieving the changes. EM was extensively deployed by UK and European governments throughout the 2000s, and belief in its likely efficacy underpinned some of the most notable initiatives stemming from the SEU's (1999) publication. Colley (2006) suggests this belief was misguided, and that the evidence base for EM's effectiveness remained persistently slim despite numerous studies over several years. She posits serious doubts about neutrality in EM literature, citing a 'suppression of any negative evidence' and claiming 'it has become taboo to discuss its "dark side"' (3). She argues that EM is overused and overvalued, and that this is a result of the EU's errant portrayal of NEET as being driven primarily by the personal characteristics of young people. The use of EM, therefore, is ultimately based more on political expedience than on honest empirical evidence.

Instead, Colley (2006) argues more could be done to target labour market conditions, including through 'hard' policy interventions at the national level. She agrees with Philip, Shucksmith and King (2004) that mentoring can be useful as part of a range of interventions but not 'a magic bullet that solves all the ills of social exclusion' (Colley 2006: 12). She articulates her position in the words of Pawson (2004: i), arguing that 'close relationships … cannot sweep away the institutional and structural forces that hold sway over young people's lives' (Colley 2006: 12). Colley (2006) thus develops a relatively structuralist perspective on NEET, in which 'structural forces' are more powerful than young people in determining their outcomes. It is useful to note that Colley differentiates here between the influences of 'close relationships' and those of 'institutional and structural forces'. This actually suggests two distinct types of structural influence in NEET (on the basis of the definition of structure posited earlier).

These can be described as personal relational influences (in this case mentoring relationships), and organizational influences (associated here with the policies enacted by government, the education and training provision made available by providers and the labour market demands articulated by employers). These two distinct types of influence are broadly identifiable across the NEET policy literature and indicate a topography of NEET, which as a whole is implicated in the determination of outcomes. Colley's topography consists specifically of central government, education and training systems, the labour market, mentoring services and young people themselves.

Colley (2006) develops her arguments by presenting the empirical case studies, but by providing only two such studies, opens herself to the same charges she levels at other EM studies in regards to slimness of evidence. This is only partly mitigated by her careful use of the evidence to point towards further questions that support her direction of travel, rather than necessarily to bold conclusions. For example, she asserts that the use of interventions seeking to change the characteristics of young people to suit the demands of the educational systems and labour market 'begs a question that it simultaneously obscures: what should we be doing to change educational systems and the labour market to fit the needs, desires, and concerns of young people?' (12). So while Colley calls existing policy into question effectively, there is insufficient evidence to make her own positions conclusive. Her case studies nonetheless raise important questions about agency and structure within NEET.

Colley (2006) finds that the young people in her case studies exercise a sense of agency that in some ways negates or otherwise displaces the objectives of EM. EM formally aims to procure the attitudinal and motivational changes thought necessary to make the young people suitable for, and compliant with the demands of, the labour market. However, Colley finds that the young people bring their own personal agendas to bear on the mentoring process, shaping it to provide them with social and emotional support that they might not otherwise have. When the mentor seeks to enforce the formal objectives, this is met with resistance, subversion or disengagement by the mentee. Colley sees this as betraying a flaw in the model of agency underlying the EU policy design, wherein young people are portrayed as passive recipients of interventions. Her case studies demonstrate this flaw, and she finds that the exercise of agency by young people has significant impacts on EM's intended outcomes. This suggests that a failure properly to account for the exercise of personal agency by young people may lead to flawed policy and praxis. The prevailing exercise of agency by young people over the EM process does not however seem to translate into a similarly prevailing exercise of agency to achieve sustained EET outcomes. This raises questions about the effective limits of young people's agency within the context of NEET.

The case studies also highlight difficulties in determining how and to what extent personal behaviours and outcomes are rightly attributable to a young person's agency, and the precise way in which that agency relates to the influences of structures. In one case, a young person is viewed by an employment officer as clearly and wilfully exercising his agency to disengage from a work placement scheme and is accordingly fired from his job. The officer's conclusions are ostensibly reasonable given the young person's presenting behaviours of non-attendance and false excuses. His mentor however finds sociostructural issues in the workplace that may have been partially coercing his behaviours, and contests these as 'unfair' (Colley 2006: 10). In the eventual outworking of the case, Colley posits a complex dialectical interaction, but appears to side with the idea that state policy and labour market prerogatives (i.e. 'institutional and structural forces') are ultimately the determinant of disengagement for this young person. She concludes that 'the scheme's policy – and employer-driven prescriptions … resulted in his further exclusion from the education and training system – surely a failure snatched from the jaws of success' (11). Colley thus takes a relatively structuralist position on the case that supports her criticisms of the EU's policy constructions.

Crucially, the case shows that the identified contention between relatively intentionalist and structuralist positions at a policy level is reflected empirically in the interpretation of individual cases of disengagement, and in the praxis associated with them. Notwithstanding Colley's (2006) own conclusions, trying accurately to discern the role of the young person's agency in the case, relative to the influence of structures, is clearly difficult. The same behaviours and outcomes are variously attributed to either primarily agentic or structural causes by the different observing and practicing parties. The knowledge of the roles of agency and structure appears to be lost in a dialectical 'black box' (Coffey and Farrugia 2014: 461). As the attributions suggest divergent policy and praxis directions, this is clearly unhelpful.

NEET policy and praxis are therefore problematized by a lack of clarity on the roles of agency and structure within NEET. The problem can be framed in terms of a question that asks how the genuine exercise of agency by young people might be contributing to the determination of their outcomes, and how structures might be influencing, interfering with or overriding this agency. In order to understand this it is important to explore the lives of individual young people and the dialectically complex situations in which disengagement takes place. As Colley (2006: 3) suggests, policymakers, practitioners and researchers ought not just to be searching for 'what works' but also '"what happens" … and "how it happens"'. This requires the contents of NEET's dialectical 'black box' to be elucidated, and this may be possible through this book's empirical study.

NEET: An intentionalist perspective

Whereas Colley (2006) develops a view of NEET in which agency is important but ultimately of limited effect, and structure is the overriding determinant of EET outcomes, Wolf (2008) develops a contending view in which agency is the overriding determinant. She argues young people are very much in control of determining their own outcomes, irrespective of organizational behaviours. A number of clear statements support this. Wolf asserts, for example, that sixteen- and seventeen-year-olds who leave education 'have not been thrown out' and are clearly doing so of their own choice (12). She points to the breadth and diversity of post-compulsory learning opportunities available to them, and to the presence (at the time) of financial incentivization in the form of the Education Maintenance Allowance (EMA) suggesting 'if they are not in any form of education and training, it is because they really and definitely do not want to enter any of the programmes on offer' (12).

Wolf (2008: 15) finds it striking that large numbers of young people populate NEET despite the fact that the vast majority are eligible 'for cash payments, which they would receive simply for turning up … NEETs have made a very clear and definite choice to forego the income, as well as the education and training, they are being offered'. The characterization of the NEET status of young people as volitional constitutes a quite different position from that developed by Colley (2006). This position may be described as a relatively intentionalist perspective on the determination of EET outcomes.

Wolf (2008) bases an argument against the 2008 RPA (Raising of the Participation Age) legislation on her position. She argues that the coercive nature of the legislation unhelpfully negates the exercise of volition by young people, and that this is contrary to all knowledge about the links between motivation and learning. She sees the legislation as conveniently, and wrongly, alleviating the government of the need to improve the quality and attractiveness of EET choices, in order to persuade young people to enter EET of their own accord. She argues that the RPA legislation is flawed on both economic and social justice grounds, and should be abandoned in favour of investment into school literacy programmes, and more flexible access to FE. She thereby finds some common ground with Colley (2006), in agreeing that central government powers to effect structural changes are pivotal to addressing NEET, and does not argue for any interventions directly targeting young people's attitudes or other characteristics. This differentiates Wolf's (2008) intentionalist perspective from that implied in EU and UK state policy, as it is interpreted by Colley (2006). Some of Wolf's (2008) statements are noticeably two-edged however, and might also be useful for establishing an opposing position that fits with Colley's (2006) characterization of state policy.

By making it clear that a vast number of choices are available to NEET young people, and that they may not be satisfied with any of them, it may be alternatively argued that they have unreasonable expectations of society. Their NEET statuses are then essentially a product of their own idealism, and they are a generation quite in control of its own disengagement. This argument is not a major position in the UK NEET policy literature, at least in such explicit terms, but could become more so. Thompson's (2011: 792) suggestion that NEET narratives in official policy documents and the media have 'stigmatised … young people … as feckless' alludes to its underlying presence. The position is also implied in EU policy (Colley 2006) and is considered a major position in international NEET literature. It is particularly associated with state governments in Far East countries including China (China Today 2005), Japan (Inui 2005; Jō 2006; Honda, Asao and Gotō 2006) and Taiwan (Chen 2011) where the NEET discourse has been 'indigenized' (Ishiguro 2007; Toivonen 2011). Inui (2005), Jō (2006), Honda, Asao and Gotō (2006) and Chen (2011) all argue against such state policy positions, contending that structures rather than agency are primarily responsible for producing NEET.

Unfortunately Wolf (2008: 8) does not completely address the potential for her comments to be handled in this way, despite suggesting that NEET policy 'mis-conceptualises' the NEET group as 'a phalanx of … unemployable young people, mostly "hooded" … who do nothing but hang around, take and deal drugs, get pregnant, steal and fight'. Such images are harder to resist when NEET is characterized as volitional, and Wolf appears to accept that some young people may fit this image. Hence it may be affirmed that there are conflicting perspectives in the policy literature about the extent to which young people are determining their own EET outcomes, and about the proper directions that policy ought to take when this is accounted for. The topography of NEET developed by Wolf is consistent with that developed thus far.

This discussion might be developed usefully in two directions before the section is concluded. First, it may be demonstrated that the theory developed within the review thus far can be meaningfully related to real-world policy activity. It has been observed that Colley (2006), for example, develops a relatively structuralist view of NEET wherein structure is the prevailing determinant over EET outcomes, whereas Wolf (2008) develops a comparatively agentic view where agency is the prevailing determinant. Such differences may lead in divergent policy directions, and this is supported by a consideration of UK government policy actions since the NEET discourse began, as outlined in Chapter 1.

Under the direction of the Labour government (1999–2010) NEET policy responses primarily focused on providing Information, Advice and Guidance (IAG) and mentoring to young people through Connexions and complementary local services, broadening the range of education and training choices available, establishing financial support systems including the Educational Maintenance Allowance (EMA) and Activity Allowance (AA) to encourage young people to participate in post-16 education and training, and creating support systems for those most at risk of underachievement and disaffection (Maguire and Thompson 2007). Colley (2006) observed that these policies focused on changing young peoples' behaviours and attitudes, thus characterizing NEET as being driven by their exercise of agency, and offering an example of how policy may develop from a relatively agentic position on EET determination.

The change of government in 2010 resulted in a change in policy direction. Central government funding of Connexions services was cut, and EMA was phased out along with much of the rest of the previous government's approach (UNISON 2011). The £1 billion Youth Contract became the new flagship programme, focusing on placing young people into work and training through increasing the number of apprenticeships and pre-apprenticeships available, creating voluntary work experience opportunities and providing wage subsidies for employers to employ the young (DWP 2013a). The new set of policies clearly targeted the labour and training markets, suggesting that if more opportunities were made available then young people would fill them, reducing NEET figures. This provides an example of how policy may develop from a relatively structuralist view.

It is important to note that relativism rather than absoluteness is indicated in the differences between the positions. The Labour approach was indeed accompanied by some policy actions focused on the labour market, including the introductions of a National Minimum Wage for sixteen- to seventeen-year-olds, and the right to request time to train (Maguire and Thompson 2007). Likewise, under the coalition government, activities such as IAG and mentoring were valued and encouraged, but deemphasized in favour of actions focused on changing structural conditions in the training and employment markets. This reflects the underlying commitment to a dialectical relationship between agency and structure within NEET policy and discourse.

NEET: Personal relations and organizations

Colley (2006) and Wolf (2008) both argue that NEET may best be addressed by having central government policymakers effect structural changes, and this primarily in regards to education and training provision, and the labour markets. The LGA and Centre for Social Justice (2009a) however contest the effectiveness of centralized policy action, and emphasize the influences of young people's close personal relationships on the determination of their EET outcomes. They claim that NEET solutions are best driven by local government, in partnership with employers, community organizations and families, and firmly advocate the use of mentoring services coordinated by the local authority, since 'all the evidence suggests that the greatest influence [on the successful re-engagement of young people into EET] comes from families and informal relationships, and that the greatest impact of agencies may be through facilitating this' (24). 'Informal relationships' refers to mentoring relationships, and also those that young people may develop with staff or volunteers (i.e. youth workers) in informal environments such as youth and community organizations. By suggesting the greatest influence on the determination of outcomes lies not with young people, but with factors in their environment, the LGA and Centre for Social Justice take a relatively structuralist view. There are important differences however, from Colley's (2006) structuralist view.

The form of mentoring advocated by the LGA and the Centre for Social Justice, delivered through relationships but directed by the state, is precisely the type critiqued by Colley (2006). Despite the indication that 'all the evidence' points towards the efficacy of mentoring, the evidence presented is very slim, consisting of only a few ostensibly hand-picked case studies which lack sufficient detail to be convincing, and no referenced empirical research. This is nigh indefensible against Colley's observations regarding slimness of evidence. Potential biases are also apparent. The argument for localization and state-coordinated mentoring is clearly in the LGA's own interests, and they use it to recommend the reallocation of funding to local authorities (i.e. themselves) accordingly. This is consistent with Colley's doubts about neutrality, and supports her concerns about the evidence supporting the use of EM to address NEET.

The LGA and Centre for Social Justice (2009a) publication is also interesting because of the way in which it constructs the agentic role of individual young people. They are presented as often, although not always, exercising volition in disengagement, and not as passive recipients of interventions. While the overall perspective communicated is a relatively structuralist one, dialectical complexity is clearly recognized. Further, it indicates that while young people's exercise of agency may be constrained by persistent structural barriers, it may also be crucially shaped by the past and present influences of family and other close relationships. The evidence presented for this is again limited (two relevant references to empirical literature are given), but there is convincing evidence elsewhere to suggest that familial and other personal relationships do exert meaningful influences on the exercise of agency in processes of disengagement. Ross (2009: 36) finds, for example, that parental aspirations for their children have a statistically 'very strong association with their level of engagement'. Ross also finds that friends and peers may have an important influence.

The LGA and Centre for Social Justice (2009a) also assert that there may be a role for certain types of organization (particularly local authorities and schools) in influencing behaviours and outcomes. Like Colley (2006), therefore, they are seen to highlight two distinctive types of structure in NEET. Their discussion indicates that both may have a complex and important relationship with the exercise of agency, although relational influences are emphasized as more important. Thus, the review of the LGA and Centre for Social Justice (2009a) adds local government, the family and friends of young people, and youth workers to the topography of NEET.

Sodha and Margo (2010: 92) also support the devolution of responsibilities to the local level, arguing the capability of 'top-down levers' (i.e. central government policy) to address NEET has been overestimated. They critique NEET policy extensively, picking up on the economic narratives of NEET, and advocate systemic reform based on a principle of early intervention. The prima facie cases for early intervention and localized decision-making are convincing, and supported by extensive referencing. The calculations supporting their economic arguments are less convincing, involving numerous questionable assumptions. Of particular interest here, however, is the narrative that is developed by Sodha and Margo to justify their arguments.

Sodha and Margo (2010) present a narrative of disengagement which explains the behaviours and outcomes of NEET young people largely as the output of institutional and familial influences. This is used to support an emphasis on the capability of local institutions (mainly schools and local government services i.e. health and social services) to influence EET outcomes by delivery of a range of early interventions to young people and their families. This is clearly a relatively structuralist perspective, and again highlights distinctive roles within NEET for close personal relationships and for particular types of organizations. However, the emphasis on the importance of organizations, rather than close relationships, is the reverse of the emphasis developed by the LGA and Centre for Social Justice (2009a). The narrative also implies that young people are passive recipients of interventions, as Colley (2006) argues they are viewed by EU policy. Consequently, the capacity of young people to enable or subvert policy and praxis on their own account is largely undeveloped. Thus the underlying models of agency in NEET discourses are problematic.

Conclusion

The determination of young people's EET outcomes may be variously attributed to young people themselves and to structures within NEET, and this problematizes NEET policy and praxis. The problem can be framed in terms of a question that asks how the genuine exercise of agency might be contributing to the determination of young people's outcomes, and how structures might be influencing, interfering with or overriding this agency. The study sets out to address this question empirically, and to locate its answers in the lives of individual young people and the dialectically complex situations in which disengagement takes place. Two main types of structure within NEET are identified in the literature. One is associated with close personal relationships; particularly those young people have with family, friends and peers, and mentors and youth workers. The other is associated with certain types of organizations, particularly those pertaining to central and local government, education and training provision, and the labour market. The relative importance of each type is developed in various ways within the literature. Young people, and the relationships and organizations associated with the two types of structure, together outline a topography of NEET that is collectively implicated in the determination of outcomes. This topography circumscribes the complex context in which NEET's dialectical interactions are thought to take place. It is this complexity and the relative failure of policymakers to understand its nature that makes the development of effective NEET policy so difficult.

3

Finding a Better Lens: A Fresh Approach to Analysing NEET

It was established in Chapter 2 that this study sets out to examine empirically how the exercise of agency by individual young people might be contributing to the determination of their EET outcomes. It was indicated however that it may be difficult to identify the genuine exercise of agency in dialectically complex scenarios, where the same behaviours and outcomes may be variously attributed to agentic or structural causes. Any analysis of this topic, therefore, requires the use of a clear and operationalizable conceptualization of agency, and a complementary conceptualization of structure, by which the roles of each might be made empirically distinct. Prominent historical conceptualizations of agency and structure in the 'youth transitions' and broader sociological literature are now discussed, from Coffey and Farrugia (2014), Parker (2000), Akram (2010) and Porpora (2013). It is argued that the conceptualizations are problematized by issues of abstraction and politicization that make them epistemologically unsuitable for use in this study. Instead an original approach, developed from Bandura (2001) and Lopez and Scott (2000), is explained.

In Bandura's (2001) conceptualization, agency is 'temporally extended' through the four 'core features' of intentionality, forethought, self-reactiveness and self-reflectiveness. It is proposed that the four features can be identified empirically in sufficiently precise terms to enable the exercise of agency to be discerned within dialectical complexity. It is observed that Bandura's conceptualization associates the exercise of agency with individual perceptions, and the concept of the function of personal agency is established with reference to this. The typology of Lopez and Scott (2000) and their concepts of institutional structure and relational structure are used to frame the two distinct types of structure identified in the NEET policy literature. Institutional structure is related to the normative expectations that underlie NEET, and the ways in which these are reinforced through the activities of organizations. Relational structure is related to the potential influences of close relationships on NEET young people. The two concepts are collectively argued for as a suitable conceptualization of structure within NEET. The topography developed in the previous chapter is overlaid onto these conceptualizations to enable them to be operationalized. It is argued that this approach solves the problems of abstraction, politicization and polarization, and enables an empirical approach to data collection and analysis that is directly relevant to the discourses of the NEET policy literature, and is capable of addressing the research problem.

Conceptualizing agency and structure in studies of youth transitions

Coffey and Farrugia (2014) review the conceptualization of agency (and by extension structure) in the study of youth transitions. They find it to be highly problematic, arguing that 'the nature and conceptual meaning' of agency within youth sociology is 'ambiguous … a "black box" which while fundamental to youth sociology remains unpacked … a close examination … reveals considerable confusion as to just what young people's agency can be said to consist of, and what legitimate uses the concept can be put to' (461–2). They set the grounds for their argument by indicating a debate between youth sociologists about the natures of agency and structure. This involves what are essentially equivalents to the intentionalist, structuralist and dialectical positions on the structure-agency debate (Akram 2010). Coffey and Farrugia (2014) observe that researchers often contrast a conceptualization of agency developed from Beck (1992) with one developed from Bourdieu (1980). They suggest that Beck (1992) is often, and perhaps unfairly, used to represent an individualization thesis, which emphasizes the importance of agency in youth transitions and downplays the importance of structures. Bourdieu (1980) however is used, perhaps just as unfairly, to deny agents autonomy by arguing that what appears to be agency is in fact simply a reproduction of internalized structural conditions.

Coffey and Farrugia (2014) then discuss corresponding attempts to develop conceptualizations that find what they call the 'middle ground', in which both agency and structure are given appropriate causal power. This middle ground represents, in essence, a balanced dialectical position. One of the most notable, and widely regarded attempts is Evans's (2002, 2007) use of bounded agency, which posits a dialectical relationship between agency and structure, in terms broadly compatible with the basic definitions of each as posited earlier. This conceptualization, however, is beset with ambiguity and contradiction. It lacks precise definition and is variously constructed as: an inherent quality that young people possess; a set of feelings, emotions or attitudes that young people may or may not have; a form of class-based cultural capital; and sets of behaviours which go against the social status quo. Agency is invoked as 'a vague force … a catch-all … something mysterious which nevertheless does rather a lot of conceptual work' (Coffey and Farrugia 2014: 466). Evans's (2002, 2007) conceptualization is considered representative of a broader issue.

It is argued that the impreciseness, or abstraction, in these conceptualizations is such that 'the concept of agency has become so nebulous and contradictory that it is being used to explain itself' (Coffey and Farrugia 2014: 465). The explanatory power of these theoretical frameworks is, therefore, limited. Indeed, they even lose their distinctiveness from concepts of structure: 'The question as to which dimensions of a given transition pattern … represent agency … and which represent the structures that 'bound' this agency, remains ambiguous and, ultimately, unresolvable' (465). The output of their use is a conceptually 'mysterious black box … with unexaminable contents' (466). It is clear that this kind of conceptualization is epistemologically unsuited to the examination of agency in dialectically complex situations, and lacks the capacity to explore the problem being addressed by this study.

The literature's conceptualizations are also extensively problematized by politicization, insofar as they are reflective of politicized pre-commitments. This treatment of agency tends to involve 'certain kinds of identities and actions being defined in advance as agentic in accordance with the political commitments of the researcher' (Coffey and Farrugia 2014: 462). Sercombe's (2010) empowered agency is examined as representative of this issue. Although they consider Sercombe's empowered agency to suffer less from abstraction than Evans's (2002, 2007) bounded agency, it is more 'normatively charged' (Coffey and Farrugia 2014: 466), being concerned largely with a commitment to the political empowerment of young people. In Sercombe (2010), agency is associated with social change and 'resistance', while structure is associated with the reproduction of the social status quo. This is problematic in numerous ways. For example, where young people fail to exhibit 'resistance', their agency may fail to be identified. Young people whose actions are not considered 'emancipatory' are labelled as 'non-agentic, conditioned and structurally determined' (Coffey and Farrugia 2014: 468). Agency is thus identified in terms of a departure from norms, but this takes away the causal power of structure to induce abnormal behaviours, and may obfuscate the causal influences of structures other than those under consideration by the researcher.

This kind of conceptualization is often associated with a pre-commitment to identifying and criticizing the role of structures in the reproduction of social inequalities (Coffey and Farrugia 2014). The question emerges, therefore, about what happens when resistant or agentic behaviours seem to take the role attributed to structures in this reproduction (Raby 2005; Willis 1977). Raby (2005) argues that an 'ethical commitment to critical research' cannot 'define agency in advance as that which runs against existing structural patterns or the political status quo' as to do so 'erases forms of active subjectivity that do not conform to the ethical or political commitments of … research' (Coffey and Farrugia 2014: 467–8). It is clear that conceptualizations which fail to identify agency, or obfuscate knowledge of structural influences on the basis of politicized pre-commitments are also unsuited for use in this study.

Coffey and Farrugia (2014) posit that the development of new approaches to conceptualizing agency that resolve these conceptual, normative, ethical and political challenges is an important frontier for youth research. They conclude that 'a more robustly defined and carefully theorised conceptualization of agency … will strengthen the work of those … seeking to analyse young people's lives and improve the social conditions they face' (473). Their critique sets the platform for the pursuit of an 'ultimately more useful account of agency which is better able to respond to the complex challenges of theorising and researching youth' (473). This study pursues such an account, and so requires such a conceptualization.

An examination of the youth transitions literature beyond that directly discussed by Coffey and Farrugia (2014) seems to support their arguments. Definitions of agency as resistance clearly permeate the literature. Simmons, Russell and Thompson (2013: 19) in one instance separate the two concepts with only punctuation, suggesting 'agency/resistance finds expression in avoidance and self-exclusion'. These definitions do also indeed appear to predispose studies to particular portrayals of young people. Aaltonen (2013), for example, in a study of agency among Finnish ninth graders, uses a conceptualization developed from Lister's (2004) typology of agency as it is 'practised by people in poverty' (Aaltonen 2013: 378). The use of Lister's (2004) typology presupposes the roles that agency may take by allocating its use to four categories, specifically 'getting by' (coping and managing), 'getting back' (resistance and rule-breaking), 'getting out' (pursuing change) and 'getting organised' (entering collective political action) (Aaltonen 2013: 378). This conceptualization is clearly politicized in the manner indicated by Coffey and Farrugia (2014). Aaltonen's (2013) approach appears particularly to risk the reproduction of antisocial stereotypes of young people by predisposing data analysis to pick up on antiestablishmentarian attitudes and behaviours, requiring Aaltonen to resist this stereotyping in her conclusion.

The defining of agency in terms of resistance may thus have a recursive effect, wherein discussions that highlight the pernicious nature of structures that are to be 'resisted', also reinforce images of misbehaviour and delinquency, even if they are explained away (Raby 2005). Young people and the structures may both be endowed with a certain limited character in relation to one another. Crucially, the narratives that emerge from this, and other approaches that broadly seek to criticize structural conditions, may be somewhat removed from the lived experience of young people as agents within those structures. Thompson (2011: 790) notes, for example, that participants in a study by MacDonald et al. (2005) express '"bemusement" at the idea that they might be socially excluded'. This is often explained as representing an 'epistemological fallacy' (Furlong and Cartmel 2007) wherein young people 'are somewhat blind to the existence of structural constraints arising from gender, ethnic or class divisions' (Aaltonen 2013: 387) that may shape their exercise of agency. In any case, the distance between the narratives and young people's self-awareness indicates that these approaches may obscure self-perceptions held by young people that might account better, or at least differently, for their thoughts and behaviours.

Problems of abstraction are also evident. In the aforementioned study Colley (2003) utilizes Bourdieu's concepts of 'field' and 'habitus' to articulate the interplay of agency and structure in school-work transitions and mentoring relationships. She refutes the idea that field and habitus can be used to delineate clearly between agency and structure. Although she sees the concepts as a 'distinct theorization of the articulation between structure and agency', she argues 'it would be incorrect to see field as a representation of structure, and habitus of that as individual agency ... *both* express the dialectical relationship between structure and agency' (14, italics in original). Colley's treatment of Bourdieu's concepts is fair, and so it is easy to see how this theorization is unable to demarcate the exercise of agency in dialectically complex situations. Such approaches tacitly embrace the loss of a distinct notion of agency within dialectical complexity, and so can only aim to achieve something markedly different than this study aims to. On this basis, it is necessary to look beyond the prominent conceptualizations of agency and structure in youth sociology. The historical conceptualizations of agency and structure in the broader sociological literature are now reviewed, from Parker (2000), Akram (2010) and Porpora (2013).

Historical conceptualizations of agency and structure in sociology

In his discussion of Giddens's (1973) structuration theory, Parker (2000) suggests the prominent conceptualizations of agency and structure in sociology have been historically politicized, and are now problematized by a polarization of academic positions, and a possible dependency on high levels of abstraction. Parker traces the politicization to a focus in earlier sociological theory on providing conceptual resources for understanding the sociostructural changes associated with industrialization, and modernization processes more generally. He suggests the resulting theories resembled systems functionalist approaches (Parsons 1971) and supported the social and political philosophies of modernism and scientism that were dominant at the time. Although these acknowledged the importance of agency (Parsons conceptualized the populations of societies as 'actors' free to make choices about desired ends and means to achieve them) the role of agents was seen as largely determined by society's needs. The autonomy of agents was so reduced or highly constrained by the 'necessary' structure of modern society that agency seemed to be more an expression of structure than actually of agency.

When social and political enthusiasm for modernism and scientism gave way, it came with an increasing willingness to challenge authority and orthodoxy. This predicated the rise of New Liberalism and accompanying historical phenomena including the civil rights movement, the beginnings of the modern feminist and environmentalist movements and American dissent against the Vietnam War (Boydston et al. 2001). Prevailing functionalist models could neither predict nor account for this civilian assertiveness and radicalism. This triggered a period of 'intense social theoretical activity motivated by moral and political interests' (Parker 2000: 10). New theory had to engage more deeply with the conceptualization of agency, and account more adequately for its ability to transform social structures. A variety of burgeoning positions emerged, whose only basis for unity was 'in their preoccupation with conflict and opposition to orthodoxy' (11). These included highly relativistic postmodernist positions (e.g. Lyotard 1979) that underpinned some social and political activism whereby, to employ Akram's (2010) terms, newly conceived intentionalist positions were competing against the orthodox structuralist positions of the functionalists.

Parker (2000) argues that the appeal of Giddens's (1973) structuration theory was that it offers a means of reconciling the competing positions by positing a structure-agency duality where both structure and agency are located or embodied within the agent. This appealed to those wanting to appear sensible to both orthodoxy and unorthodoxy, and helped complete a spectrum of positions with which people of differing sociopolitical interests could align. Parker (2000) thus makes the case that the conceptualization of agency has been historically politicized or, in Coffey and Farrugia's (2014: 466) terms, 'normatively charged'. He indicates, however, that overly agentic or structuralist views are not largely supported any longer. Rather contemporary debate centres on the way in which structure and agency are related within a dialectical relationship.

Parker (2000) discusses the two dominant positions around which this debate centres. There is, first, Giddens's (1973) duality, which Parker (2000) also associates with Bourdieu (1979) and his concept of habitus, wherein structure and agency are co-located within the agent. This is contrasted with dualism (e.g. Mouzelis 1974; Archer 1995) where structure and agency are considered to exist separately, represented by systems and people respectively. Both have different implications for the nature of agency, and the debate is polarized. Parker (2000: 5) suggests trying to articulate the precise natures of agency and structure in theories of duality is highly problematic, positing that neither Giddens nor Bourdieu has 'entirely escaped the charge of obscurantism'. This indicates that the theories suffer from an impreciseness that problematize their use to discern clearly between agency and structure, as was already indicated from Colley's (2003) discussion of Bourdieu's concepts, and as is also argued by Willmott (1999). Parker (2000) leans strongly towards dualism, arguing that it can be better related to a number of historical cases. However, from Parker's discussion, it is quite unclear how agency and structure might be usefully defined from a theory of dualism.

This overall problem is underscored by Akram (2010), who critiques conceptualizations associated with both duality and dualism, highlighting some of their common grounds, as well as issues that problematize their collective empirical use. Usefully, Akram posits the idea that across the contemporary literature, agency is considered to have a number of key inherent qualities, normatively considered to include intentionality, reflexivity and strategy. Beyond this, however, there is little more that may be considered solid ground; 'much of the literature' tends to use concepts of agency of structure without 'clarifying how they are used' (6). The literature can 'neglect to specify in sufficient detail how structure and agency refers to the empirical questions at hand and, thus, structure and agency debates are used as an overarching conceptual framework, without really interrogating how they relate to the empirical phenomena they represent' (6). This equates to an issue of abstraction, which in turn seems to stem from the way the concepts are typically constructed.

Akram (2010) convincingly highlights the delicate nature of the ontologies on which the conceptualizations normally rest. Maintaining the ontologies while also defining the concepts so as to make them coherently operationalizable seems to be difficult. The result is a conceptual inconsistency between the theoretical and empirical aspects of studies. Akram argues that a 'theoretically sound concept of agency is clearly important … but it is equally important to develop methodological concepts to enable the use of theoretical concepts in empirical research … and … it is very important to have consistency amongst these concepts' (12–13). She notes there is a 'fundamental problem of translating theoretical concepts into their methodological equivalents' (155), and to illustrate this she considers the methodology in one of Bourdieu's (1999) last empirical studies, and finds confusion and ambiguity in how habitus is handled.

Although the scrutiny in this instance is again directed towards a theory of duality, Akram (2010) does extensively discuss Archer (1995) who is associated by Parker (2000) with dualism. Specifically, Archer is often associated with the concept of analytical dualism, which accepts an ontological interdependence between structure and agency, but posits that to understand the nature of their interactions, they must be analysed separately (Willmott 1999). This study could be said to be in pursuit of such an analysis. However, an exploration of Archer's (1995) morphogenetic approach to such analysis, and Akram's (2010) and Porpora's (2013) discussions, do little to clarify further what 'agency can be said to consist of' (Coffey and Farrugia 2014: 462) or how the dialectical 'black box' might be elucidated.

Porpora (2013: 26), writing in a recent publication edited by Archer herself, asserts that 'although some have sought to provide what they call morphogenetic explanations for some aspect of social life, I believe such effort … is misguided … the morphogenetic approach does not explain anything in particular'. Rather, it seeks to establish, as a fundamental principle, that structure, culture and agency must all be accounted for in any properly explicated explanation of social change. It does not seek to specify what each is: 'Any particular social change will need to be explained by the particular structures, by the particular cultures, and by the particular agents involved … the morphogenetic approach does not say anything about these' (26). Such an approach is not useful for the development of the clear conceptualization of agency and structure that is required here.

Arriving at suitable conceptualizations of agency and structure for this study is thus clearly problematic. There are particular issues of abstraction, politicization and the polarization of academic positions that affect the prominent conceptualizations in the youth transitions literature and in the sociological literature more broadly. The first two issues have been seen to problematize the epistemological aims of the study. The third issue, at the very least, requires an account to be given as to the necessity, rationale and implications of taking a position that is considered to be polarized. It is proposed that these issues are not intractable and can be resolved by conceptualizations of agency and structure developed from Bandura (2001) and Lopez and Scott (2000) respectively. These are now argued for in turn.

Bandura's agentic perspective on social cognitive theory

Bandura (2001) presents what he terms an agentic perspective on social cognitive theory. Within it he develops a typology of agency which distinguishes between three modes of agency: personal, proxy and collective. Personal agency denotes the direct exercise of agency by an individual. It is distinct from proxy agency which is the exercise of agency through others, and collective agency which is the exercise of joint agency by two or more agents acting as a group. The type of agency that this study focuses on is clearly recognizable as a form of Bandura's personal agency. Bandura also posits that agency is constituted of four 'core features'. These are intentionality, forethought, self-reactiveness and self-reflectiveness, each of which is now considered in turn.

Intentionality refers to the idea that agency is expressed through things agents do intentionally. Indeed, it is central to the definition of agency; Bandura (2001: 2) succinctly conceptualizes agency on its terms, saying 'to be an agent is to intentionally make things happen by one's actions'. It is 'the power to originate actions for given purposes', and an intention is a mentally held 'representation of a future course of action to be performed' (6). The intent to perform is important, as a passive expectation of a future occurrence is not considered agentic here. Also, whether or not actions result in the intended outcomes is largely immaterial, as the use of agency often results in failures and unintended or undesired outcomes.

Forethought is the mental process of anticipating the likely consequences and outcomes of particular courses of action. It is used by the agent to project the likely results of various conceivable paths of action or inaction, and to select those most likely to produce desirable outcomes and avoid undesirable ones. Through it the agent constructs short-, mid- and long-term plans that take into account imagined or expected environmental conditions that may support or hinder the carrying out of the plans. Self-reactiveness is the activity of self-regulation in the execution of a plan. It is temporally situated within the process of performance, and involves the self-monitoring and self-adjustment of affects, thoughts and actions to influence events in line with goals, and personal values and standards.

Self-reflectiveness is a para- or post-situational self-evaluation of motivations, thoughts and behaviours. It differs from self-reactiveness in that it is temporally situated outside the moments of performance. It is metacognitive and involves panoramic assessment of one's environment, understanding, values, goals, behaviours and the outcomes that are produced by their interactions. Self-reflecting agents weigh the adequacy of their predictive and operative thinking, comparing actual outcomes to intended ones, and seek understanding of why intended outcomes were or were not achieved. Through it, agents may make changes to their values, goals and behaviours in order to increase the likelihood of obtaining desirable outcomes in future instances, and avoiding undesirable outcomes. Agents may even decide that once desirable outcomes are no longer so and vice versa.

It is argued that Bandura's (2001) conceptualization of agency is suitable for use in this study. It fits the broadly accepted criteria for concepts of agency, as its four features align well with the three normative qualities of agency discussed by Akram (2010). Intentionality is common to both; self-reactiveness and self-reflectiveness are clearly related to reflexivity; and forethought is akin to strategy. It is thus well positioned in regards to the broader consensus on the nature of agency, and contains the necessary conceptual elements to link it analytically and discursively to the wider literature. It is also clearly committed to a dialectical position. It recognizes that the choices and actions of agents are constrained by their environment, but nonetheless ascribes autonomy to those agents, and recognizes their capacity to act upon their environment. Crucially, it manages this with a relatively low degree of abstraction, and without any noticeably problematic commitments to politicized or polarized positions.

It achieves this by approaching agency from a primarily cognitive, as opposed to sociological perspective. Whereas sociological approaches are in many senses obligated to develop the role of society (i.e. structure) in tandem with the role of the agent, the cognitive approach is not so obliged. The first requires considering the role of the individual in the context of society, but the second requires considering the role of mind and affect in the context of the individual. The 'frame' of the conceptualization is therefore in the agent rather than in the structure. Agency is thus defined without overprescribing the agent's relationship to wider society. The inability to define agency without such overprescribing has characterized the conceptualizations reviewed throughout this chapter, and has in some cases entailed politicization and polarization. In other cases, it has entailed abstraction through a loss of precision in the boundaries of agency, wherein agency appears to occur not on distinctive terms, but within a rather indeterminate space that overlaps with structure. This produces, as has been seen, an epistemological and analytical zone which is justifiably termed a dialectical 'black box' (Coffey and Farrugia 2014: 461).

On this basis, Bandura's (2001) conceptualization presents a compelling opportunity to operationalize agency coherently. The four features – intentionality, forethought, self-reactiveness and self-reflectiveness – are defined as essentially cognitive phenomena, having the mind of the agent as their definitive site of occurrence. They are thus located in a particular, and ostensibly investigable, context. They have potential for empirical identification insofar as each is a recognizable phenomenon. Each is also relatively precise, insofar as it has a clearly defined nature, and is at least notionally distinguishable from the others, and from other cognitive phenomena. It thus provides a possible solution to the difficulty of empirically identifying the genuine exercise of agency in dialectically complex situations. It also offers the potential for consistency between the theoretical and methodological representations of the concept, as the same definitions for each feature seem applicable at both levels. This suggests a low degree of abstraction in the conceptualization. It is proposed therefore to use the conceptualization to operationalize agency for the study, on the basis that where the exercise of agency is genuinely occurring these definitive features of agency should be evident, and where it is not occurring they will not be evident. A methodology to support this is developed in the following chapter.

Defining agency as cognitive in nature has some important implications. It connotes particular ontological and epistemological value positions in regards to research into perceptions, as are defended in the following chapter. It also accentuates the importance of perceptual factors in the exercise of personal agency. As Bandura (2001: 3) argues, to 'make their way successfully through a complex world full of challenges and hazards, people have to make good judgments about their capabilities, anticipate the probable effects of different events and courses of action, size up sociostructural opportunities and constraints, and regulate their behavior accordingly'.

The exercise of personal agency in a given environment might then be said to be mediated at least in part by the agent's perceptions of how agency and structure interact to determine outcomes in that environment, where 'perception' is the organization, identification and interpretation of sensory information in order to represent and understand the environment (Schacter, Gilbert and Wegner 2009). This notion of the role of the perceptual in determining the behaviours and EET outcomes of young people is consistent with the concerns of Taylor et al. (1992), Nakamura (2004), Honda, Asao and Gotō (2006) and Standish (2007) developed in Chapter 1.

The function of personal agency in NEET might therefore be considered to consist of two key dimensions. First, the exercise of personal agency is under consideration as a mediator of young people's EET outcomes. Second, it is recognized that this exercise may be mediated by personal perceptions of the roles of agency and structure in determining EET outcomes (i.e. the roles of environment and self, and where these perceptions include the evaluation of challenges, hazards, personal capabilities, the likely results of particular courses of events and actions, sociostructural constraints and opportunities, and how personal behaviours are to be regulated). The way in which its exercise mediates outcomes, and the way in which its exercise is itself mediated by perceptions may be jointly referred to as the function of personal agency. The empirical examination of this function is central to this study. Discussion now turns to the pursuit of a complementary conceptualization of structure, which is developed from Lopez and Scott (2000).

Lopez and Scott's typology of structure

Lopez and Scott (2000) discuss the historical conceptualization of structure in sociology. They echo issues identified by Coffey and Farrugia (2014), Parker (2000) and Akram (2010), suggesting the 'actual uses of the concept … are strikingly nebulous' (Lopez and Scott 2000: 1). This indicates high degrees of abstraction. They also identify polarized academic positions. They argue there are two main branches in the historical conceptualization of structure, which they represent using the terms 'institutional structure' and 'relational structure'. The two have been largely and quite unnecessarily presented as dichotomous, with the proponents of each seeking to reduce the other to an epiphenomenon. Difficulties in satisfactorily reconciling them and a general failure to accept both as useful have led to what Lopez and Scott (2000) refer to in the synopsis of their book as a 'plague of confusion'. They conclude that the two should instead be treated as complementary, as each yields valuable analytical perspectives. They also develop an idea of embodied structure which features in the more recent literature; while this is not clearly distinct from the two main concepts, it is potentially a way to reconcile them. The three elements of the typology are now considered in turn, in order to assess its usefulness as an analytical tool in this study.

The concept of institutional structure is traced back to Durkheim's (1898) 'collective representations' and considered to be represented most clearly in the work of Parsons (e.g. 1971) and structural functionalism. Although it was the subject of sustained criticism, it is still an important element of contemporary discussion and is now associated with 'neofunctionalists' such as Alexander and Colomy (1985) and Luhmann (2012). 'Institutional structure' is defined as 'comprising those cultural or normative patterns that define the expectations which agents hold about each other's behaviour and that organize their enduring relations with each other' (Lopez and Scott 2000: 3). It refers to social norms that are in some way formalized or otherwise regularized (i.e. institutionalized) across sections or the whole of society, and which are not dependent on the ongoing conformity of any particular individual to give them their perceived validity (Jarvie 1972). Economic behaviour such as the five-day working week, social behaviour such as marriage and cohabitation and features of social etiquette like queuing or table manners may all be classified as institutions. The expectation that young people ought to be in EET – which drives NEET discourses and policy activity, and shapes the relationships young people have with the state and wider society (Fergusson 2013) – can be understood as a form of institutional structure.

The concept does not refer directly to institutions in the bureaucratic sense. Bureaucratic institutions are nonetheless pivotal to the production, transformation and maintenance of countless instances of institutional structure, insofar as they set, adjust and enforce norms. For example, government departments, courts, banks and employers propagate and govern norms and expectations relating to the payment of taxation, the behaviour of employees within the workplace and the limits on the legally acceptable treatment of one person by another. Institutional structure may therefore be set inside or outside the context of the bureaucratic institution, and may be used to theorize widespread societal behaviours. This type of structure is thought to exert a regulatory influence on agents by conferring upon them social roles or 'positions' that come with sets of 'role expectations'. These are expectations of attitude and behaviour that define 'what are felt to be, in the given society, proper, legitimate or expected modes of action or of social relationship' (Parsons 1960: 7–8, quoted in Lopez and Scott 2000). These perceived expectations may be internalized and re-enacted by the agent, externalized in the interactions of others with the agent, or both. The use, for example, of rewards (such as social approval or the conferring of honours or privileges) and sanctions (such as social disapproval, financial penalty or the threat of physical punishment) are themselves social institutions which reinforce role expectations.

Relational structure is also traced back to Durkheim (1895), but this time to his idea of collective relationships. It is held to be: 'the social relations themselves, understood as patterns of causal interconnection and interdependence among agents and their actions, as well as the positions that they occupy' (Lopez and Scott 2000: 3). Whereas institutional structures are societally embedded so that they are beyond dependence upon any given individual, relational structures depend on the 'actually existing relations' (Radcliffe-Brown 1940: 2) between individuals. The most basic relational structure is therefore the dyad, consisting of two persons (i.e. persons A and B) who have direct interactions with one another, and exhibit some degree of causal interdependence. These structures are typically amenable to classifications that socially locate each person in relation to the other in a recognizable and useful way. Examples of such classifications include mother-son, manager-employee or friend-friend. Dyadic relationships can be complex, and may consist of intricate patterns of co-operative and antagonistic behaviours. This complexity may increase where dyadic relationships form along several lines, for example, where a manager and employee may also be friends. The next most basic relational structure is the triad, consisting of three persons (i.e. persons A, B and C) who have direct interactions with one another. The triad may be conceptualized as comprising three interdependent dyads (A-B, A-C and B-C) of similar or differing classifications, and exhibits a corresponding increase in complexity. The triad enables social phenomena not possible within a dyad (e.g. the forming of cliques). The introduction of fourth, fifth or sixth persons further increases the complexity and relational possibilities. These additional persons may or may not interact with all the other persons within the group, and two triads may become linked by a new dyad forming between single members of each.

Larger relational structures may be classified in terms of relational groupings, which are collections 'of individuals who stand in regular and relatively permanent relationships' (Nadel 1957: 146, quoted in Lopez and Scott 2000) and who may be socially connected through shared 'sentiments or emotional tendencies' (Lopez and Scott 2000: 45). Groupings may occur as specific types of social formations, of which the nuclear family or household, extended family and neighbourhood community are some of the simplest examples (Weber 1920). Within a typical society, each individual is commonly part of several relational groupings, linking them together in ways that are causally interdependent. The whole society is networked, so that every individual is connected to every other through a relatively small number of interconnections (Barabási 2003). By theorizing how this networking gives rise to larger-scale social phenomena, relational theories have been used to explain intermediately scaled phenomena such as the corporation or church, and large-scale phenomena such as class systems. NEET, which may be associated with identities derived from family and neighbourhood relationships, and with class-based inequalities (Simmons and Thompson 2011: 6–9), might also thus be explained in terms of relational structure.

Lopez and Scott (2000) consider that embodied structure neither fits neatly into the two main conceptualizations, nor is it properly distinct from them. Rather, it is constructed by them as a potential solution to the institutional-relational dichotomy. The central tenet of the concept is developed from Gidden's (1984) structuration theory, and suggests that by necessity all structure, whether institutional or relational, depends upon the thoughts and activities of human beings for production and transformation. Essentially, structure is therefore embodied within the human being, whether individually or collectively. The human is the intersection and common component of both institutional and relational structure, and an opportunity for their reconciliation. Lopez and Scott (2000) acknowledge the concept is underdeveloped and is neither as clear nor as robust as are the two main conceptualizations. Partly for this reason and partly because it was found to be empirically unhelpful, embodied structure features no more in this study.

Lopez and Scott's (2000) typology is useful for developing a conceptualization of structure for this study that resolves the issues of abstraction and polarization. This is partly because Lopez and Scott's institutional structure and relational structure can each be related, in reasonably straightforward ways, to one of the two distinct types of structure identified in the review of the NEET policy literature. Institutional structure can be related to the concept of organizational influences, which was associated with central and local government, education and training providers, and employers. These groups of organizations are each involved with the production (or perhaps reproduction) of particular sets of norms, role expectations and patterned conditions that may be reflected in wider society, and in their own organizational behaviours. These norms, expectations and conditions are represented by central and local government policies, education and training frameworks and labour market demands respectively. The idea of institutional structure thus represents the nature of the organization's own activities (as might become regularized as normative patterns of behaviour acted out by their representatives e.g. civil servants, teachers, managers and recruitment staff), and the ways in which they influence patterns of thought, behaviour and interaction in society more widely. Lopez and Scott's idea of relational structure can be similarly related to the concept of relational influences, which was associated with young people's family, friends and peers, and mentors and youth workers. This is suitable insofar as these influences are thought to be mediated largely through personal relationships that are amenable to classification (e.g. father-son, friend-friend and mentor-mentee) or otherwise through relational groupings (e.g. being part of a neighbourhood peer group).

The degree of abstraction associated with this approach is relatively small, insofar as the conceptualization of structure is related closely, in commonly recognizable and meaningful ways, with empirical settings and entities. Although the empirical 'structures' and the theoretical constructs to which they are being linked can only imperfectly represent each other, the conceptualization is far from nebulous. This supports the pursuit of consistency between the way the conceptualization is represented at theoretical and methodological levels. Overlaying the topography of NEET onto the conceptualization (i.e. associating institutional structure with central and local government, education and training providers, and employers, and relational structure with family, friends and peers, and mentors and youth workers) effectively concretizes it for operationalization, and at the same time allows the investigation to retain a clear relevance to the context of the research problem.

By positioning this conceptualization of structure with the conceptualization of agency developed from Bandura (2001), which represents the role of the young person themselves in NEET, every element of the identified topography of NEET is clearly accounted for. The topography, which circumscribes the contexts within which NEET's dialectical interactions are thought to take place, is represented within a viable conceptual framework by which those interactions might be examined. The topography, in this way, becomes a framework for coordinating data collection and analysis. This is developed further in the following chapter. There are other advantages to using Lopez and Scott's (2000) typology. As a typology it accounts for a rich heritage of sociological thought and provides analytical and discursive links to this work. It also enables the study to avoid commitment to one or the other of the polarized positions associated with the two main historical types of structure. The approach is further strengthened by recognizing the interpretive factors that underlie the conceptual construction of the topography as it has so far been developed. These interpretive factors might be termed 'situational and perceptual dualities'.

Situational and perceptual dualities

The alignment of the elements of the topography with the concepts of institutional and relational structure, and personal agency, is useful but not absolute. Particularly it might be noted that there are overlaps between Bandura's (2001) 'modes' and Lopez and Scott's (2000) 'types', whereby a single element of the topography might take on both structural and agentic characteristics. For example, Ross (2009) finds that parental aspirations for their children are significantly related to their post-school choices. Using Bandura's (2001) 'modes' of agency, these might be recognized as instances of either proxy agency or collective agency, where the former denotes exercise of parental agency over the young person and the latter the joint exercising of agency together with the young person. However the influence of the family has already been associated with Lopez and Scott's (2000) relational structure. Both Bandura's (2001) and Lopez and Scott's (2000) designations are valid in this study, and so the property given to the family (or other elements of the topography) by this overlap may be described as a situational or perceptual duality, as its effective designation appears to depend on both the nature of its interactions with a young person in a given situation, and the way in which these are interpreted.

The idea of duality here is distinct from Giddens's (1984), which argues that structures require agents to recall and propagate their norms and patterns, and are therefore agent-dependent. Structure and agency are thus a duality, being internally related. Whereas Giddens's duality is essentially ontological, here the focus is at the level of the situational and interpretive. An overlap might also be identified in respect to institutional and relational structure, insofar as relational interactions between a young person and their family (e.g.) may well reflect norms and expectations held by wider society. It was decided therefore that despite the usefulness of the classifications, the data collection and analysis processes ought not to seek to constrain how a given element might be interpreted, but rather to let this emerge wholly from the data.

Conclusion

Suitable conceptualizations of agency and structure for this study are developed respectively from Bandura's (2001) 'agentic perspective' on social cognitive theory, and Lopez and Scott's (2000) typology of the historical conceptualization of structure. Each conceptualization avoids issues of abstraction, politicization and polarization, and has the potential to be operationalized in a way that affords the study conceptual consistency across its theoretical and methodological aspects. Together they offer a means of empirically determining the function of personal agency in dialectically complex scenarios, and of elucidating its interactions with the structures of NEET. The conceptualizations are concretized for operationalization by overlaying them with the topography of NEET developed in the first part of the literature review. The following chapter develops the methodology that supports their empirical use to address the research problem.

4

Opening the 'Black Box': A Methodology for Empirical Investigation

This study empirically examines the function of personal agency in determining the EET outcomes of young people. It has been established that the investigation will use conceptualizations of agency and structure developed from Bandura (2001) and Lopez and Scott (2000) respectively in order to achieve this. Discussions of the nature of the research problem and a review of Akram (2010) have identified the importance of maintaining conceptual consistency across the theoretical and methodological aspects of the study. This chapter develops a methodology to achieve all of this. The methodology is set out in detail in eight main sections. This is done to support readers' analysis of the findings and to enable other researchers to replicate the study wholly or partially.

The first section defends ontological and epistemological value positions underlying the empirical investigation of perceptions, which are intrinsic to the concept of the function of personal agency. The second section develops these positions to show from Cohen, Lawrence and Morrison (2011) that the study sits within an interpretive research paradigm. The third section develops the research aims, objectives and questions from the output of the literature review, on terms that retain the integrity of the conceptualizations of agency and structure. The fourth section argues that a research design consisting of interviews and a short survey is most suited to the epistemology suggested by the conceptualizations and the constraints of the research project. The methodology is developed with reference to relevant literature and the outcomes of a pilot.

The fifth section discusses the sampling approach. Several key considerations are discussed including selecting an appropriate age bracket and geographic scope, and accounting for 'NEET churn' (Furlong 2006: 555; Maguire and Thompson 2007) wherein a tendency for NEET young people to move rapidly in and out of NEET can problematize sampling. Details are presented of a sample of sixteen young people who are or have been NEET. The sixth section discusses strategies for establishing validity and reliability, from Charles and Mertler (2002) and Creswell (2003). The seventh section discusses ethical considerations, and the potential vulnerabilities of participants are accounted for with reference to BERA (2011) guidelines. Finally, data analysis is discussed, and the approaches to coding and extracting meaning from the data are developed from Pole and Lampard (2002).

A defence of research into perceptions

The concept of the function of personal agency recognizes the role of perceptions in mediating agentic behaviours. However, there are ontological and epistemological challenges to the empirical investigation of perceptions. Ontologically, their nature and existence come under attack from materialist reductionism, particularly in its extreme form of eliminative materialism (e.g. Churchland and Churchland 1998). The arguments of material and eliminative reductionists centre on the basic materialist assertion that there is no form of reality except physicality. They attempt to extend this without limit to every facet of human life and experience, including essentially psychological phenomena such as perceptions.

In their stronger forms, which Menuge (2004) collectively refers to as Strong Agent Reductionism (SAR), they deny the existence of intentionality, which covers the category of psychological phenomena including such things as beliefs, values, attitudes and perceptions. It should be noted that the definition of intentionality here is different from that of Bandura (2001) which is associated with the more conventional idea of human intention. Menuge (2004) points out that the belief that there is no such thing as intentionality is of course an instance of intentionality itself. Hence the SAR argument is guilty of being a *reductio ad absurdum*, falling foul of its own logic. Notwithstanding the logical fallaciousness that derives from such a position, it is evident that this research could not be conducted from the viewpoint of the eliminative materialist. Such positions are rejected outright for the purposes of this study, and almost certainly most other educational or sociological research studies.

At an epistemological level, the debate over whether or not psychological phenomena can be known so as to qualify them as valid objects of empirical investigation is represented in the disputes between behaviourist and cognitivist schools of thought (Schunk 2004). Behaviourist philosophy asserts that although these phenomena do exist, and so are valid ontologically, they are not valid objects for empirical study as their properties cannot be ascertained or quantified using any objective instrument. Instead they may only be inferred from the physical behaviours of agents, which in any case are only responses to material or external stimuli. Schunk suggests this position derived from the desire of behaviourists to gain psychology acceptance as a true science among the physical and natural sciences. This entailed employing a strictly positivist paradigm, giving no credence to those things which are by nature unable to be subjected to material quantification.

Cognitivism in contrast emphasizes the role of thought processes, including those classifiable as perceptions, in determining agents' behaviour. It asserts that although they are not subject to material quantification, they can yet be identified, assessed and measured. Furthermore it contends that they are completely indispensable in any comprehensive theory of psychology, behavioural or otherwise. As Bandura (2001) asserts, a purely behaviourist view of human activity, which characteristically makes little or no recourse to the role of cognition in determining behaviour, is empirically untenable. The strength of cognitivist arguments has been historically demonstrated in superior explanations of observable behaviours, and successful experimentation involving the use of data collection tools to measure psychological phenomena. This led to an overturning of the dominance of behaviourism in what has been termed by some as 'the cognitive revolution' (West, Farmer and Wolff 1991). Modern psychologists thus tend to refer freely to processes and states of mind in the development of psychological theory and in the design of experiments. This study clearly holds to a cognitivist epistemology, and rejects behaviourist epistemology. This connotes the positioning of the study within the interpretive research paradigm, which is now developed.

The research paradigm

Cohen, Lawrence and Morrison (2011) discuss two main research paradigms: the normative and interpretive. The normative paradigm is associated with an objectivized, positivistic viewpoint, and the use of methodologies akin to those applied in natural sciences. In contrast, the interpretive paradigm is concerned with understanding the subjective world of individual human experiences. The paradigms are broadly associated with the pursuit of quantitative and qualitative data respectively. Mixed methodologies are considered a possible third paradigm, but Cohen, Lawrence and Morrison suggest that it is too early to commit to a firm position on this. This study is clearly aligned to the interpretive paradigm, as it seeks to understand the subjective worlds of young people, and how their individual perceptions and choices determine their life outcomes. Qualitative approaches are able to probe 'issues that lie beneath the surface of presenting behaviours and actions' (219).

The two paradigms are differentiated not only by the qualitative/quantitative distinction, but also by different conceptions of human activity which may be described by the terms 'behaviour' and 'action' (Cohen, Lawrence and Morrison 2011: 17). 'Behaviour' is linked with the normative paradigm and represents a 'stimuli-response' view of human activity that is essentially behaviourist in the sense discussed and rejected earlier. 'Action', however, is linked to the interpretive paradigm and is considered to be 'behaviour-with-meaning' or intentional behaviour. This behaviour is not rooted in external stimuli as much as it is in perceptions, and the direction of self towards intended outcomes. 'Action' therefore is a concept of human behaviour congruent with the conceptualization of agency employed within the study. This affirms the positioning of the study within the interpretive paradigm.

The research aims, objectives and questions

This study has three interrelated aims, as are presented in the introductory chapter. The first and primary aim is to contribute to NEET policy and praxis discussions by developing an empirical understanding of the function of the personal agency of NEET young people in determining their EET outcomes. The second aim is to contribute to the theoretical treatment of NEET by positioning it within a conceptual framework that enables the roles of agency and structure within it to be discerned in dialectically complex situations. The third aim is to contribute to methodological thought and practice by situating this framework within an approach that provides consistency across the theoretical and methodological aspects of the study, thus enabling the framework's effective use.

The corresponding research objectives are:

1. To examine the nature, extent and efficacy of the exercise of personal agency by NEET young people to determine their EET outcomes.
2. To examine perceptual factors that mediate the exercise of personal agency by NEET young people.
3. To identify how policy and practice for NEET might be improved by accounting for the function of the personal agency of young people.

The research questions used to direct the data collection and analysis processes were derived as cleanly as possible from the objectives, and aimed to clearly operationalize the concretized conceptualizations of agency and structure. They are:

1. In what ways do NEET young people exercise intentionality, forethought, self-reactiveness and self-reflectiveness in their pursuit or otherwise of EET?
2. How do young people perceive the roles of: national government, local government, education and training providers, employers, mentors and youth workers, parents and families, friends and peers, and young people themselves in determining EET outcomes?
3. Can meaningful relationships between young people's perceptions of the roles of agency and structure within NEET, their exercise of agency and their outcomes be established?

The following sections develop the data collection and analysis processes. No predictions were made of what would be found. As Cohen, Lawrence and Morrison (2011) note, theory in the interpretive paradigm should not precede research but be derived from it.

Research design, methodology and data collection process

The research design consisted of interviews and a short survey. Both were carried out with the same sample. Interviews were used to collect the most voluminous part of the data. Interviewing is an established and tested means of data collection, and perhaps the most common of all research methods (Pole and Lampard 2002). Interviews are particularly suited to the need to obtain data on perceptions. Although there are several means of obtaining qualitative data on social perceptions, including ethnographic and a wider range of observation-based methods (Charles and Mertler 2002), the direct nature of the interview affords an opportunity to prompt directly for and access specific information on what is happening within a participant's mind (Patton 1980: 196). This is a crucial quality for this investigation, given that agency is defined on essentially cognitive terms. Such information may not necessarily become available through observation-based or other qualitative approaches even over a protracted period of time. Interviewing is useful for collecting data on, for example, present constructions of events, reconstructions of past experiences, and motivations (Lincoln and Guba 1985). Silverman (1993) adds that interviews can be deployed for exploring present or previous behaviour, and for eliciting reasons and explanations. These uses are clearly conducive to the purposes of the investigation.

It is also observed that NEET young people are by definition more conspicuous by their absence than presence in the typical settings of educational research. They may thus be less likely than their EET counterparts to see through educationally or vocationally related commitments. This presents a critical risk to research designs which rely on protracted or repeated access to them (Simmons and Thompson 2011). The focused and relatively intensive nature of interviewing provides an opportunity to collect substantial quantities of relevant data in a short time frame, and makes the most of potentially one-off opportunities to collect data. Similarly, NEET young people may also be less likely to produce or have produced the kind of documentary records (i.e. diaries, journals, blogs) that might otherwise provide useful data, and this is unfavourable towards methodologies that might require them. On the basis of all this, it is argued that a semi-structured, interview-based methodology is suited to the epistemological requirements of the study. This allows richer data to emerge than a fully structured interview, while keeping the research design practical in terms of the time demands made upon participants (Pole and Lampard 2002). The semi-structured interview is flexible enough to allow respondents to project their own ways of defining the world, another important quality for this study (Silverman 1993).

Each participant was interviewed once. Interviews were not time limited, but participants were told to expect them to last from around an hour to an hour and a half each. They were scheduled according to the availability of both researcher and participant, and took place during office hours or in the early evening. They were conducted one-to-one (except in the pilot, where a mentor accompanied the interviewee as required by a specific organizational safeguarding policy) and face-to-face. With the exception of the pilot, all interviews were conducted on the premises of the mentoring and training organizations through whom the sample was accessed. The pilot interview was conducted in a private area within a restaurant. The face-to-face approach allowed the researcher to observe and respond to non-verbal communication cues such as body language and facial expression. This can be helpful for facilitating an effective interview and gaining a better understanding of the data (Mason 1996; Pole and Lampard 2002).

Interviews were recorded digitally using two audio recorders (one acting as a redundancy) and under guarantee of confidentiality to the participant; Cohen, Lawrence and Morrison (2011) distinguish between confidentiality, which involves withholding participants' real names and other identifying characteristics, and anonymity, where identity is withheld because it is genuinely unknown. The purpose of the confidentiality guarantee, and preference for one-to-one interviews, was to encourage openness and honesty from participants. These provided the chance for them to communicate their thoughts and experiences without having to consider how these might be responded to by others such as peers, parents or workers with whom they may have to interact post-interview, or by those who later read the study.

As Miller and Dingwall (1997) indicate, the formality or unnaturalness of an interview situation may unsettle some participants, and as Maxwell (2005: 93) stresses, the researcher has to find a culturally appropriate and culturally sensitive way of gathering data. It was intended therefore that interviews be informal and conversational in style, and carried out in such a way as to minimize the sense of disruption to the young person, relative to their normative expectations within the interview environment (i.e. the premises of mentoring and training agencies). In practical terms, this was reflected particularly in the choice of clothing worn by the interviewer (i.e. jeans and sports shoes) and the choice of language (i.e. colloquial) used.

The specific questions asked of participants were largely straightforward derivations of the research questions (again supporting the coherent operationalization of the conceptualizations of agency and structure) and were organized into two sets. The first was concerned with the young people's EET/NEET history from the time of leaving school to present, and their exercise of the features of agency – intentionality, forethought, self-reactiveness and self-reflectiveness – in their pursuit or otherwise of EET outcomes along this history. The second was concerned with their perceptions of the roles of agency and structure within NEET, as they are represented within the topography. The data from the interviews was supplemented by further material collected by the short survey.

The initial purpose of the survey was to support an evaluation of data validity and reliability. The survey covered essentially the same content as the interviews, but in a different and more concise format. It was for completion at the end of the interview, and was designed to add only a short amount of time to the process. The use of surveys to capture data on perceptions has been an important part of methodology for several decades. Although they are often associated with the normative paradigm, de Vaus (2003: 5) contests the idea that questionnaires are unsuited for use within the interpretive paradigm, and asserts that in their case the 'distinction between quantitative and qualitative is … unhelpful and misleading'. He suggests instead that they may be used wherever structured approaches to data collection might prove useful, as is the case for this study.

There are standard approaches to survey design, and the most established of these includes the use of Likert Scales (de Vaus 2003). Critics of these scales point out that although they do not force respondents into giving yes/no answers to items on which they may not have an absolute opinion, they still present a relatively limited range of choices that force respondents to approximate their exact thoughts. Ray (1980) examines this, and in mitigation finds increasing the number of options on a scale (e.g. from five to ten) improves its reliability by allowing finer approximations. However, scales with too many options may reduce usability. The survey used in this study contains eleven items based on the Likert Scale. The first seven are asked using conventional (i.e. numbered) Likert Scales and seek to identify the level of importance in determining outcomes that young people ascribe to each element of the topography. The scales provide eleven options, that is, 0 at one end and 10 at the other, with nine equally spaced divisions between, where 0 indicates 'no importance' and 10 'absolute importance'. The final four items seek to identify young people's perceptions of their own exercise of agency. The numbers (i.e. 0 and 10) are replaced by opposing statements (labelled A and B) relating to their self-perceived degree of use or non-use of intentionality, forethought, self-reactiveness and self-reflectiveness. The use of statements rather than numbers on survey scales has precedents in the use of semantic differential scales, which are deployed similarly to Likert Scales to explore opinions, attitudes, values and perceived meanings, that is, perceptions (de Vaus 2003). This approach is useful in situations where it is not intended to communicate that one end of the scale is 'better' than the other. The interview and survey methods were trialled in a pilot.

Piloting does not guarantee, but does increase the likelihood of the successful implementation of a research design (van Teijlingen et al. 2001). The pilot was carried out with one participant and was generally successful, yielding a high quantity and quality of rich data that was ostensibly relevant to the research questions. Nonetheless, some minor changes to the opening, interviewing and survey completion processes were made as a result. The planned opening process for the interviews involved friendly introductions followed by an explanation to the interviewee of the research purposes and processes. This was to be followed by a point-by-point review of the consent form, which participants would then be asked to sign if they were happy to participate. Audio recording was to be started after signing, and with the participant's awareness. This process was found to be largely suitable, and was developed by introducing two questions at the beginning of the interview. These questions were asked immediately after recording began, and were intended to put interviewees at ease with the recording in motion. They were: 'What is your favourite colour?' and 'What is your favourite food?' The interviews then transitioned into the originally intended questions. The questions about national and local government however, were subsumed into one. This was to improve the flow of questioning, and not to seem by repetition to emphasize falsely expectations of data about government. During the completion of the survey, it was noticed that the participant made a number of interesting and potentially useful statements. It was resolved as a result that audio recording would not be discontinued until surveys had been completed, and that participants would be invited to comment on their thought processes while they completed the survey.

Once the piloting process was complete, the problem of selecting a representative sample for interview from the NEET population was addressed. Sampling from a NEET population is far from simple. The age range and geographic scope generate the first set of issues to be discussed here. The issue of 'NEET churn' (Maguire and Thompson 2007) is then considered, which relates to the propensity of young people to move fluidly in and out of the NEET category. The problems this causes for research, and typical approaches to accounting for it are critically examined before presenting the approach developed for this study. The sample size, sources and method are then discussed. Finally, data on the sixteen young people that participated in the study are presented.

Sampling: Age range and geographic scope

NEET research is problematized by a multiplicity of age conventions within NEET policy and literature. According to the UK Department for Education (DfE 2014), the most authoritative data on national NEET figures is that published in the Participation Statistical First Release (SFR). SFR data covers the 16–18 age group. Its use however is limited as it is released only annually and cannot be disaggregated to subnational levels. The DfE therefore also uses data from the British Office for National Statistics (ONS) which collects NEET data for 16- to 24-year-olds in its more regular Labour Force Survey (LFS). This information is more flexible and is used by the DfE (2016) to produce NEET figures for eight age brackets (16, 17, 18, 16–17, 16–18, 16–24, 18–24 and 19–24). The DfE also utilizes data from a third source, the Client Caseload Information Service (CCIS) databases maintained by local authorities (DfE 2016). CCIS data covers the 16–19 age range. If commissioning activities are considered, even more age brackets are evident. A 2014 procurement by the London Enterprise Panel (LEP) sought to commission NEET services for the 15–19, 16–24 and 15–24 age brackets (London Councils 2014), and local authorities often seek to make NEET projects accessible to 25-year-olds (e.g. LGA and Centre for Social Justice 2009a). In the international environment the situation is even more complex. Official EU NEET data is publicly available for the 15–17, 15–19, 15–24, 15–29, 15–34, 18–24, 20–24, 20–34, 25–29, 25–34 and 30–34 age groups (Eurostat 2016). Some of these age groups are particularly relevant to policy in specific countries and contexts. For example, the EU Youth Guarantee generally targets young people under 25, but several countries have tailored their national Youth Guarantee programmes to also offer support to young people of up to 29 (European Commission 2014), including Italy. Beyond the EU, in Korea and Japan, the term 'NEET' is officially applied to 15- to 34-year-olds (Cuzzocrea 2013).

Defining an age group for a NEET sample for research is thus problematic, and there is no perfect solution. For this study, it was observed that Wolf's (2008) comments regarding the volition of NEET young people (which partly uphold the tension developed between the 'intentionalist and 'structuralist' views of EET determination developed in the literature review) were primarily applicable to those for whom further education remained free, that is, the 16–19 group (CAB 2013). However, as relevance to future policy discussions was sought, the impact of RPA legislation coming into effect around the time of sampling (i.e. October 2013) was also taken into account. In 2013 this increased the 'compulsory participation' age from 16 to 17, legislatively displacing the lower end of the NEET bracket by one year, and indicating 17 may have been a more relevant lower bound for imminent NEET concerns. It then increased again to 18 in 2015, ostensibly displacing NEET by two years (Wolf 2008). The primary NEET concern of the future may thus well be the 18–21 age group. It was proposed then to set 21 as the upper bound. The study therefore focuses on the 17–21 age group.

NEET in the UK is clearly a national phenomenon and some studies, typically quantitative pieces using central government datasets, sample at this level (e.g. Ross 2009). This was impractical for this study given its aims, so consideration was given to sampling at a local level. There are arguments in favour of this. Maguire and Thompson (2007) comment that the characteristics and circumstances of young people who are NEET, the proportion of young people who are NEET and the composition of the NEET group varies between localities (see also LSC 2006; Sachdev, Harries and Roberts 2006; LGA and Centre for

Social Justice 2009b). Variations in local labour market conditions may create meaningful differences in the barriers faced by young people (Ashton, Maguire and Garland 1982; Ashton and Maguire 1988; Bynner 1991). Evidence of local variation has persisted, and this has been indicated in the UK in more recent years by the government's identification of twenty geographic NEET 'hotspots'. These were local authority areas given priority in NEET policy interventions, and consisted of locations predominantly in the Midlands, North of England, South Wales and parts of Scotland (HM Government 2012a). Similar variations within countries are recognized across the EU broadly. Italy, for example, shows wide differences between the south and the centre-north, with NEET rates in 2010 of 26.7 per cent and 14.9 per cent respectively (Eurofound 2012). Such variations are thought to reflect varying local levels of growth, industrial structure and skill composition of the workforce (Eurofound 2015).

It can be recognized in the above that much of the official UK NEET, labour market and other potentially related data is organized by local authority area. This study chooses therefore to sample at the local level, as defined by local authority boundaries. Although the study does not immediately seek to exploit the official data, beyond what is useful for examining the representativeness of the sample, it gives recourse to do so later if desired. Specifically, participants were sought from three local authority areas in London, including Southwark (for the pilot), Hackney and Hounslow. NEET rates for these areas at the time of sampling were 7.7 per cent (Southwark), 7.0 per cent (Hackney) and 4.4 per cent (Hounslow) (DfE 2013a). The choice of areas was pragmatic, and predicated on existing professional relationships conducive to accessing a suitable sample. The disadvantage of local sampling is a possible limitation on the generalizability of findings beyond the local areas. The benefit is that it offers the potential for generalizability within the local areas and some relation to other potentially meaningful local data. However, establishing the sample even within a localized context was made more complex by NEET 'churn'.

Sampling: Handling NEET 'churn'

The issue of 'NEET churn' (Furlong 2006; Maguire and Thompson 2007) relates to an observation that the NEET population tends to be highly dynamic, and includes substantial numbers of transient NEETs who come into it only to leave it again in a relatively short time. This problematizes sampling by highlighting a dimension of heterogeneity in the population as 'churners', who may have been EET the month before and are about to become EET again, may arguably be different in important ways from those who have been NEET continuously over a protracted period, that is, 'long-term NEETs'. Long-term NEETs are typically considered the most problematic, and often become a specific focus of discourses (e.g. Mirza-Davies 2014: 6). Researchers may often wish to differentiate between NEET 'types' (Maguire and Thompson 2007), sometimes with an implied value that longer-term NEET samples are more valuable (Furlong 2006). NIACE (2010) differentiates between 'young NEETs' and 'recent young NEETs', for example, and Rossiter (2009) sets 'sustained NEETs' into their own category. This kind of approach is not adopted in this study for several reasons.

It is clear that the boundaries derived to distinguish between types of NEET young people are difficult to defend critically. For example, young people may move between categories overnight, but is not clear how they become qualitatively different in doing so. The boundaries have also often been arbitrary, although it is noted that there is now a quasi-official definition of 'long-term' as longer than one year (e.g. Mirza-Davies 2014). Restricting the sample to particular types may create unnecessary access problems, on both numerical and procedural levels. Appropriate samples may become harder to find, and place more strain on the relationships being used for access. There is particularly a risk of undertaking a 'wild goose chase' in pursuit of long-term NEETs. Newton (2009) found that because of churn, 17 per cent of young people were NEET between the ages of sixteen and eighteen (with roughly 10 per cent being NEET at any given time), but only 1 per cent were NEET at sixteen, seventeen and eighteen. It should be recognized, however, that the proportion of young people that remain NEET long term varies by location and over time, so this aspect of the design could be dealt with quite differently in a future international context. Over 60 per cent of Italian NEETs, for example, were found to have remained NEET from year to year between 2007 and 2009, and this proportion was understood to be increasing at that time (Eurofound 2012).

Perhaps most importantly, limiting the study to long-term NEETs might obscure some of the richest data. There is no substantive reason to conclude that the function of personal agency for those in churn is less interesting than for long-term NEETs, especially as 'churners' make up such a substantial part of the NEET population. Furthermore, classifying NEETs by length of disengagement may marginalize the investigation of 'repetitive churners', that is, young people who repeatedly go in and out of EET but never show up formally as long-term NEETs. As Furlong (2006) suggests, NEET discussions may systematically overlook this group's vulnerabilities. Sampling from this group might therefore yield useful insights into a relatively under-examined cohort of NEETs. It may also be particularly interesting because the interview design then affords the study an opportunity to examine multiple instances of engagement and disengagement in the life of a single participant, through the sequential discussion of their EET/NEET history.

Taking this approach also offers a potential boon for sampling by indicating that young people might make for suitable participants regardless of which side of the churning cycle they are on, that is, participants may be EET at the time of sampling as long as it may be shown that they can provide data on relevant NEET experiences. This broadens the population of potential participants – perhaps by around 70 per cent if Newton's (2009) figures are used as a rule of thumb – and so reduces risks related to sample unavailability. It was proposed therefore not to restrict or differentiate participants by length of their disengagement, or to exclude those who may be in EET at the time of sampling due to churning. Rather NEET churn was accounted for through the sequential discussion of EET/NEET histories as is provided for in the interview design.

Sample size, method and sources

Patton (1990: 184) argues that 'there are no rules for sample size in qualitative enquiry' and decisions should reflect what one wishes to know, the purposes of the research, what will be useful and credible and what can be done within the resources available, for example, time, money, people and support. It was proposed, due to the need for relatively in-depth interviewing, and practical constraints upon the study and the researchers, to establish a sample of fifteen young people. This is undoubtedly a small number relative to the NEET populations of the targeted boroughs at the time; sixteen to eighteen NEET figures for Hackney and Hounslow were 530 and 330 respectively at the end of 2012 (DfE 2013a). This leaves concerns about generalizability, which is desirable for developing the relevance of findings to the populations from which samples are taken, and wider populations. Some mitigation for these concerns was thus sought through the sampling method. Probability sampling and non-probability sampling methods were both considered.

Probability sampling is preferred by some researchers for its protection of sampling from researcher biases, and its potential for supporting generalizability (Pole and Lampard 2002). It was found however to be highly impractical for this study. Probability sampling requires access to a truly random sample 'where every element (e.g. person) in the population of interest has a known non-zero chance of being included' (Pole and Lampard 2002: 34). NEET defies such access. The most detailed record of the UK NEET population is held in the CCIS databases (DfE 2010) but even these are incomplete; 8.3 and 7.0 per cent of young people between sixteen and eighteen had an unknown EET status in Hackney and Hounslow respectively at the end of 2012 (DfE 2013a), near the time of sampling for the study. There is then no means of obtaining a truly random sample. Furthermore, accessing the CCIS database is highly problematic. Stringent data protection protocols surround it, and all access to persons on the database has to be mediated through the local authority. Transitional problems in the handover of the database to local authorities from the Connexions services, and organizational restructuring associated with public sector funding cuts, made it impractical to secure stable local authority support for this study despite efforts. Any sampling based on the CCIS database was deemed not viable. Similar challenges would be likely to problematize NEET sampling internationally. Eurofound (2015) considers that the proportion of unemployed young people not registered with public employment services may be as high as 37 per cent in Belgium and 60 per cent in Estonia. In Bulgaria, it is suggested that only about 34,000 young people aged fifteen to twenty-four were registered as unemployed in March 2014, while the overall number of NEETs in the country was estimated to be more than 175,000 (Eurofound 2015).

For this study, therefore, a purposive sampling approach was taken, which is often used in qualitative research and can achieve representativeness, a key contributory factor to generalizability (Cohen, Lawrence and Morrison 2011). The overall sample sought to reflect the key demographic variables normatively associated with NEET data in the CCIS database, that is, age, gender and ethnicity (DfE 2013b). Although such an approach might not achieve numerical representativeness, as probability sampling is expected to, it does seek to ensure that as much of the relevant population as possible is represented to some degree. Samples of NEET clients were sought through three local mentoring and training agencies (one in each of the Southwark, Hackney and Hounslow local authority areas respectively) in receipt of state funding to support NEET young people in their respective areas. The agencies are unnamed in the study as a safeguard to confidentiality. Access was based on existing professional relationships between the researchers and managers within the agencies. All data was collected over a fortnight. In pursuit of the desired sample, the agencies were asked to provide samples from both genders, across the ages within the seventeen to twenty-one bracket, and from as wide a range of ethnicities as available. It was recognized that an ideal sample might not be achievable by this means, and was subject to practical constraints acting upon the agencies.

Details of the sample

A total of sixteen young people participated in the study, including the pilot. Pilot data is included in the findings as it was found to be relevant and useful, and the changes made to the methodology on the basis of the pilot were not sufficiently substantive to warrant its exclusion. The sample was diverse in terms of gender, age (within the determined age bracket) and ethnicity, and achieved a limited representativeness of the populations from which it was drawn, in line with the expectations of the approach. Seven interviewees were male and nine female. This was crudely proportionate to the overall gender balance of the sixteen to twenty-four NEET population nationally (DfE and BIS 2014). Hackney, however, had a noticeably contrary local gender balance at the time, where NEET males outnumbered NEET females on a ratio of 7:6 (Team Hackney 2014). The equal balance of Hackney males and females in the sample meant that a crude proportionality to that population was maintained nonetheless. At least two participants (including one of each gender) were of each of the five ages within the bracket.

White British, White Irish (Traveller), Eastern European, Black Caribbean, Black African, Bangladeshi and Mixed White/Asian ethnicities were represented in the sample. This provides representation of half of the groups in the CCIS Ethnic Code system, excluding catch-all codes. The non-represented groups are Gypsy/Roma, Mixed White and Black Caribbean; Mixed White and Black African; Indian; Pakistani; Chinese and Arab (DfE 2013b). None of the non-represented groups make up more than 5 per cent of the total sixteen to twenty-four population in the selected boroughs, with the exception of the Indian and Pakistani populations in Hounslow, which make up 16 and 7 per cent respectively, according to the most recent census data at the time of sampling (ONS 2011, cited in GLA 2014). Data to identify whether or not these groups were at all present in the local NEET populations was not readily available. The sample included a rich mixture of NEET 'types', including a small number who had been 'long-term NEETs', that is, NEET for over a year (by Mirza-Davies 2014 definition), a majority of 'repeat churners' who had (or had also) been in and out of NEET multiple times and a remainder with singular experiences of NEET of less than a year. This data is detailed in Table 4.1.

Table 4.1 Participant demographics and EET histories

Name	Gender	Age	Ethnicity	Borough	EET History
Anthony (Pilot)	Male	17	Black African	Southwark	FE – 1 month NEET – 11 months FE – 3 weeks*
Brian	Male	20	White British	Hounslow	FE – 10 months NEET – 2 months FE – 1 year NEET – 3 months FTE – 2 days NEET – 2 months FTE – 1 month NEET – 5 months VT – 6 weeks NEET – 2 weeks PTE – 3 months*
Caroline	Female	17	White British	Hounslow	FE – 5 months NEET – 2 months VT – 6 months*
Darren	Male	19	White British	Hounslow	FE – 4 months NEET – 7 months VTE – 3 months NEET – 1 month FTE – 1 month NEET – 6 months VT – 4 months*
Elaine	Female	19	White British	Hounslow	NEET – 2 weeks FE – 11 months NEET – 13 months VT – 3 months VTE – 2 months App/FTE – 5 months NEET – 3 months*
Fiona	Female	21	Black African	Hounslow	FE – 1 year FE – 1 year NEET – 5 months FTE – 6 months NEET – 6 months FTE – 7 months NEET – 5 months VT – 6 months NEET – 3 months*
Gina	Female	20	White British	Hounslow	FE – 9 months NEET – 4 months FTE – 2 years NEET – 2 weeks VT – 3 months NEET – 3 months FE – 9 months PTE – 4 months App/FTE – 2 days*

Name	Gender	Age	Ethnicity	Borough	EET History
Hannah	Female	18	Black Caribbean	Hackney	FE – 8 months NEET – 5 months FE – 7 months NEET – 5 months VT – 3 weeks*
Ishmael	Male	18	Bangladeshi	Hackney	FE – 10 months NEET – 2 months FE – 10 months NEET – 1 month VT – 1 month*
Jeanne	Female	17	Black Caribbean	Hackney	DNFS NEET – 3 months FE – 6 months FTE – 4 months NEET – 7 months App/FTE – 4 months NEET – 2 months VT – 3 weeks*
Kevin	Male	20	Eastern European	Hackney	DNFS NEET – 40 months VT – 3 months App/FTE– 1 month*
Lisa	Female	21	White British	Hounslow	FE – 2 weeks FE – 1 year NEET – 18 months FE – 3 months NEET – 6 months FTE – 1 month NEET – 3 months VT/VTE – 6 months*
Megan	Female	18	White Irish (Traveller)	Hounslow	FE – 1 year NEET – 6 months FTE – 4 weeks NEET – 6 months VT – 5 weeks*
Neil	Male	21	Black Caribbean	Hounslow	FE – 2 years NEET – 3 months FTE – 4 months NEET – 2 months FTE – 14 months NEET – 5 weeks VT – 1 months*
Orlando	Male	17	Mixed White/Asian	Hackney	NEET – 9 months VT – 6 months*
Pam	Female	18	Black Caribbean	Hackney	FE – 10 months NEET – 3 months VT – 1 month*

Note: The following abbreviations are used in the table to describe the EET histories of the participants: App – Apprenticeship; DNFS – Did Not Finish School; FE – Further Education (Sixth Form or College); FTE – Full-Time Employment; NEET – Not in Education, Employment or Training; PTE – Part-Time Employment; VT – Vocational Training; and VTE – Variable-Time Employment. The length of time the participant spent in a given EET status is denoted alongside it. An asterisk denotes the participant's EET status at the time of sampling.

In accordance with the confidentiality provisions, pseudonyms are used to represent the participants. This has been done by listing participants in order of interview date and time, and allocating a common name to each that results in an alphabetized list of names with respect to gender conventions. Hence, the first interviewee has the pseudonym 'Anthony'.

Validity and reliability

Charles and Mertler (2002: 155) posit that validity is concerned with whether 'data are, in fact, what they are believed or purported to be'. In qualitative research the concept of validity is usually concerned with establishing whether 'a given information source is *authentic*' (157, italics in original). This study is therefore concerned with whether or not the data gathered on young people's perceptions and exercise of personal agency is genuinely what it purports to be. It was partly for this purpose that an interview-based design was favoured. Agency is defined for this study in essentially cognitive terms. It is situated within the minds of young people and may not be directly observed, and so there is no more authentic source of data available than the young people themselves. There is also no certainty that the sought data would ever surface except for direct prompting. The directness of the interview and survey methods proposed therefore offer the best available means to obtain valid data.

This does not of course connote unquestionable validity. Oppenheim (1992), for example, suggests validity in interview and survey data specifically relates to the honesty and commitment of interviewees and the depth and richness of their responses. Validity may therefore be compromised if interviewees provide inaccurate, dishonest or exclusively superficial information because of fear, mischief or otherwise. As Cohen, Lawrence and Morrison (2011) note, subjective reports in whatever form can be incomplete and misleading. Participants may not want to expose their true perceptions for personal, social or other reasons, and may, for example, over-report socially desirable behaviours and under-report socially undesirable behaviours, causing data to falsely reflect social norms (de Vaus 2003). With younger interviewees, greater than usual care may be needed to avoid using leading questions, as they may be particularly susceptible in this area (Krähenbühl and Blades 2006). Ultimately, the honesty of participants cannot be guaranteed, but reasonable efforts can be made to remove the incentives to be dishonest.

Creswell (2003) posits eight primary strategies for establishing qualitative validity. Seven of these were utilized to support validity in this study. First is the triangulation of data, which involves checking for integrity of data across multiple sources. Three sources were used for this including the interviews, the surveys and the managers of the agencies through whom samples are accessed. In regards to the last, basic details of proposed participants (i.e. gender, age, ethnicity and an outline of their NEET history) were provided by the managers prior to interview, to qualify the participants' inclusion within the sample. It was not proposed to present this data formally except where it might identify concerns about the integrity of data provided by participants (as it is otherwise made redundant by the same). Second is the use of member-checking, which involves checking the researcher's comprehension of participant responses with them to confirm accuracy. It was proposed to do this as part of the interview process in two ways, which may be labelled as conversational and summative. Conversational member-checking involved checking and clarifying participant responses as they were made during the interview. Summative member-checking involved making summarized understandings of participant responses at pertinent points during interviews and asking participants to confirm or reject their accuracy. Third and fourth are the use of rich thick description and presenting negative or discrepant information when conveying findings. A commitment was made to both these.

Fifth is clarifying researcher bias. As Cohen, Lawrence and Morrison (2011: 225) develop from Preissle (2006), 'Qualitative enquiry is not a neutral activity, and researchers are not neutral; they have their own values, biases and world views, and these are lenses through which they look at and interpret the already-interpreted world of participants'.

One researcher carried out the interviews for consistency. This researcher managed and participated in the delivery of NEET reduction services within the Croydon, Greenwich and Southwark local authority areas between 2007 and 2011. The researcher retains professional relationships gained within the field and benefits from a first-hand understanding of praxis issues in working with NEET young people. The researcher is now involved with tendering for NEET services (among other services) being procured by central and local government. It is inevitable that the experience of working within the field has shaped this researcher's views of NEET. This is almost certain to have influenced the manner in which the investigation is undertaken and the way in which data is interpreted, probably in unintended and unidentifiable ways (Onwuegbuzie and Leech 2007). Pinpointing the extent to which this has affected the study is not possible, but there is a commitment throughout to making the reader aware of the assumptions, methods and data being used. There are no obvious professional or financial interests to be gained by the researchers from the study, other than those that may reasonably and fairly be gained by developing a better empirical understanding of the problem. Prior to the study, the researchers did not hold any definitive conscious position on the function of personal agency in determining the EET outcomes of young people.

The sixth and seventh of Creswell's (2003) strategies are 'peer debriefing' in which informed others ask questions of the study in order to enhance the way in which it presents and accounts for data, and 'external auditing' which involves the review of the research by persons new to the researcher and project. These were provided for kindly through the support of other academics working in related fields. The strategy that has been excluded is prolonged time in the field, as it is already established earlier that the research design seeks to avoid dependence on repeated or protracted access to NEET young people.

Charles and Mertler (2002) suggest that reliability is distinct from validity and is concerned with the consistency and stability of responses. Arriving at an objective standard for establishing the reliability of qualitative data is difficult (Pole and Lampard 2002), but it is widely held that checking for consistency across multiple sources of data is the key. The means proposed above for triangulating data are, therefore, also useful for establishing reliability. Responses to the short surveys were therefore examined for consistency with those given in interviews. Demographic information, and outline information on the NEET history of participants received from the agency managers were examined for consistency with information given by participants.

Ethical considerations

At the most basic level, ethical research should be of benefit to those being studied (Creswell 2003). With reference to Taylor et al. (1992) and Standish (2007) as discussed in Chapter 1, this study stands to benefit young people by developing insight into their relationship with important aspects of society. This may be useful in the hands of policymakers, practitioners and researchers who aim to improve outcomes for them. The following ethical considerations also pertained to the study, with reference to BERA (2011) ethical guidelines. Young people participated on the basis of voluntary informed consent. Creswell (2012) advocates the use of an informed consent form to facilitate this. This provides documentary evidence that consent was obtained, and of the way in which it was informed. A consent form was developed and used in accordance with BERA (2011) guidelines and Creswell's (2003) discussion of appropriate content.

The social exclusion narrative of NEET, as developed in the introductory chapter, suggests a possibility of young people disclosing 'harmful' information (Creswell 2003: 65). Creswell's two examples of harmful disclosure include a student disclosing information on parental abuse and a prisoner disclosing information about a prison escape. Creswell posits the ethical code for researchers in such cases is to uphold participant confidentiality. However, because of possible links between NEET and criminality, there was a possibility of participants disclosing information on intended criminal acts. BERA (2011) guidelines and the safeguarding frameworks surrounding professional engagement with young people in the youth sector create an expectation that such disclosures be reported to the relevant authorities. This expectation was accepted and communicated to participants as a caveat to the observation of confidentiality. It is noted the potential impacts of this on data collection are not ideal, and may have prohibited some participants from being as completely open and honest as they may otherwise have been, to some extent negating measures to achieve this.

Practical measures to uphold participant confidentiality included the use of pseudonyms for individuals to protect identities (Creswell 2003), and protecting data at all times from being viewed by unauthorized persons. The latter included protecting digitally stored (soft) information with passwords, and protecting paper documents by use of secure storage equipment. It was also noted that some participants might be considered 'vulnerable' by BERA (2011) definitions. A commitment was thus made to a careful focus on ensuring no interactions occurred between researcher and participants that might have endangered, harmed (whether physically, mentally or emotionally) or in any other way created a detriment or potential detriment to them or other parties. In practical terms this required careful observation of participant comfort during data collection and maintaining sensitivity when discussion entered into personal areas (Berry 1999).

Data analysis

The purpose of data analysis is to organize, account for and explain data, making sense of participants' definitions of data and noting patterns, themes, categories and regularities (Cohen, Lawrence and Morrison 2011). A substantial volume of data was collected. The data was rich, and participants were generally very comfortable in conversing about and disclosing personal information. Over 90 EET/NEET transitions were observed. Interviews lasted on average for an hour and fourteen minutes, giving a total of almost twenty hours of audio data, in addition to a completed survey for fifteen participants, and a partially completed survey for the remaining participant. The data from interviews was transcribed verbatim, and in full by the researchers. Transcribed data totalled around 113,000 words. The transcripts were the primary source of data analysis. The use of the transcripts was supported by the continued use of the audio recordings. As Kress (2010: 97) points out, there can be important information conveyed by the spoken word that is lost in the printed word, such as the clues about an interviewee's cognitive and emotional states expressed through tone of voice and pace of speech. Continued use of recordings can thus remove the need for developing textual conventions for notating these expressions (see Cohen, Lawrence and Morrison 2011: 537–8). Hesitations, pauses and silences were denoted by the use of dots (. . .) in the transcripts. The content of the transcripts was then coded.

Pole and Lampard (2002) argue that the basis of all qualitative analysis is effective coding. Maxwell (2005: 95) suggests coding is organizational, substantive (descriptive), theoretical and thematic. It is to be aimed that the integrity, that is, wholeness, of the data is preserved, rather than fractured during coding (Cohen, Lawrence and Morrison 2011). Coding of the interview data was done in two stages. It was first coded and analysed in respect to each of the identified elements of the NEET topography (government, education and training providers, employers, mentors and youth workers, parents and families, friends and peers, and young people) and each of the features of agency (intentionality, forethought, self-reactiveness and self-reflectiveness). The richness of the data was evident, with a single paragraph of transcribed text possibly containing references to several or all of the features, and several of the elements. The second stage involved identifying and coding for themes and patterns in the data, relationships between the sets of codes (Bogdan and Biklen 1992) and how these all related to EET outcomes, with the overarching intention of addressing the research questions. The findings are presented in the following chapters in the form of a structured discussion that reflects the coding approach, and makes every effort to 'ground' claims demonstrably within the data (Pole and Lampard 2002). The presentation of the findings is structured according to the initial rather than secondary coding in order to retain as direct a relation as possible to the research questions.

The survey data was examined with the primary intention of establishing the extent to which it supported validity and reliability claims. The responses to the survey did not appear to the survey did not appear to provide otherwise useful information unless contextualized by the discursive data associated with them. The survey responses are therefore not extensively discussed in the findings as standalone data, but are rather referenced on a number of occasions where this is useful to develop broader arguments.

Conclusion

The function of the personal agency of NEET young people was investigated through a qualitative research design consisting of semi-structured interviews and a short survey. The design clearly operationalizes the conceptualizations of agency and structure developed in the literature review, supporting the achievement of conceptual consistency across the theoretical and methodological aspects of the study. The method was developed to mitigate risks to data collection and quality by incorporating a number of specific measures to procure participant openness and honesty, including a guarantee of confidentiality. It was piloted with one young person, and a small number of changes were made as a result. A probability sampling approach was rejected as impractical, and a purposive sample was sought instead. A diverse sample of sixteen young people of both genders, between seventeen and twenty-one years of age, who were or had been NEET, was obtained from across the three London local authority areas of Southwark, Hackney and Hounslow. White British, White Irish (Traveller), Eastern European, Black Caribbean, Black African, Bangladeshi and Mixed White/Asian ethnicities were represented in the sample. Almost twenty hours of interview data was collected, in which over ninety EET/NEET transitions were observed. Seven of Creswell's (2003) strategies for establishing data validity were utilized, and were seen to overlap with appropriate strategies for establishing reliability. The interview data was transcribed, coded and analysed together with the survey data. The findings are presented in the following chapters.

5

Structure, Agency and Lived Experiences within the NEET 'Black Box'

This chapter and Chapter 6 present the findings of this study. The findings together account for the function of personal agency, and the nature of its interactions with NEET's structures, in over ninety highly varied EET/NEET transitions. This chapter discusses young people's perceptions of the roles of each element of the NEET topography in determining their outcomes. Two further elements are also introduced to the topography and discussed subsequently, these being media and celebrity influences, and faith and religion. Several themes that collectively detail the function of personal agency, and the nature of its interactions with NEET's structures are developed. These include: the inseparability of EET from the wider life of the young person; a distinction between the hard and softer influences of structure; the idea that instability and crisis often precede and compound disengagement; the young person's limited capacity for agency; the prioritization of intentions; the shaping of patterns of agentic behaviours throughout the life course; the mediation of structural influences to young people through the discursive environment and agentic modelling; and the perceived primacy of agency in determining EET outcomes. The data analyzed in this chapter has been organized to support the treatment of the themes, and is examined in the following order: parents and families; education and training providers; mentors and youth workers; friends and peers; employers; government; young people; media and celebrity influences; and faith and religion. Each is discussed under a single subheading except for parents and families which is treated under three subheadings because of the volume of data being handled.

Parents and families: The impact of intractable circumstances

The data showed clearly that parents and families have a crucial influence on the exercise of agency by young people and the determination of their outcomes. This influence is manifold, and perhaps the most comprehensive of all within the NEET topography. This is detailed here in several stages, beginning with a discussion of the observation that instability or crisis in the family was often found to be a trigger for the young person's disengagement. Anthony, Jeanne and Kevin all provided powerful cases to this effect.

Anthony was a seventeen-year-old who had been on the verge of becoming long-term NEET. Having been perhaps just days shy of a year as NEET, he had returned to college three weeks prior to interview. He had dropped out of college at the start of the previous academic year mainly as the consequence of his father's unexpected death. The death had a major emotional impact on him. He explained, 'For someone to go, it's like you break down.' The sense of bereavement was only part of a wider impact however. Anthony had lived with his dad and younger brother in a single-parent family. Following their father's death, the two siblings had moved to the 'infamous' Aylesbury estate in Southwark (Fletcher 2008: 1; Lees 2009) to live with their grandmother. Anthony assumed an increased sense of responsibility for his brother, and the new home came with tensions. His grandmother was trying to cope with the loss of her son, and was finding it difficult to relate to the boys. Anthony expressed frustration at this, saying:

> My grandma ... needs to realize that although she's lost her son, we also lost our dad. It's deep ... sometimes she goes on as if she doesn't care. So if you don't care, what am I meant to do? He's not here right now, what am I meant to do? Am I meant to go and die for you to care then?

The situation led Anthony into a time of deep self-reflectiveness which he linked directly to his disengagement from EET. He said:

> When my dad passed away, it took time for me to think whether or not I was up for college. It took me so long ... to think if I was going to fit into college at this time. I was thinking am I really ready for it? I began to look at things differently.

It took Anthony many months, and a lot of thinking to answer his questions.

Jeanne also experienced sudden family crisis, when her mother who lived in Jamaica contracted an illness that had brought her close to death. This was happening just as Jeanne's GCSEs were about to begin. Her grandmother broke the news to her. Jeanne said, 'My head just went … I didn't know what to do.' She sought advice from family and close friends. She was advised to see her mum in case the worst happened. Jeanne explained her father had died when she was six years old, and she did not know her mum very well. She was close to being orphaned, but at the same time she had her exams to think about. It took her three days to reach a decision. She explained:

> I had a choice, but I had to think a lot … She could die … I had to make that choice and go to Jamaica to see her … I didn't want it to be too late.

She felt extremely stressed about her exams, and asked her teachers if she could do them on her return. She was told this would not be possible. She said:

> I was on the plane literally crying … 'oh my God, I'm going to miss my GCSEs, I'm not going to have no life anymore. Everything is over for me, but I … have to support my mum'.

By the time Jeanne returned, the exam period had finished and she found herself scrabbling to find a place in FE.

Kevin was doing well in school until Year 11. He had also found regular weekend and holiday work in a local games store. Suddenly his parents announced they were divorcing. Kevin chose to stay with his mum and younger sister, but further disruption ensued when three months before his GCSEs, his mother decided to move the family to her homeland Poland to help her get over the separation. This was a huge surprise to Kevin. His initial reactions were angry. He said:

> You know the first thing that came to my head? I served five years in school … bloody hell … I did five years, why not just wait the extra three months …? I worked my head off to get to where I am … why not just wait another three months then do what the fuck you like.

He confronted his parents about their timing. He said they 'understood where I was coming from' but nothing changed. Like Anthony he asked questions of his family:

> My GCSEs were around the corner and I didn't get to do it because [of] their little bullshit at home … Why does it have to affect me?

Like Anthony, he also felt it necessary to assume greater responsibility for his family. He explained:

> I started to think … I've got to be the man of the family now. I've got to … not only take care of myself, I've got to take care of my mum and my little sister.

Kevin did not stop aspiring to work or be educated, but nonetheless left his school and job for Poland. He returned to the UK a year later as a NEET, and remained NEET for over two years.

These cases introduce a number of key ideas that run throughout the data. Instability and crisis often precede disengagement. These are often not directly related to the EET circumstances of the young person but nonetheless impact on them. In this way, EET is inseparably linked to the wider life of the young person. Circumstances may occur in their wider life which influence their EET decision-making and which might be reasonably considered by them to be intractable (in these instances bereavement, family illness and parental divorce). These and other such circumstances may be thought of as 'hard' influences of structure, that is, those which set the conditions in which agency must be exercised.

Such circumstances do not negate a young person's agency, but rather force upon them a prioritization of intentions. In all three cases the young people were engaged with, and continued to be concerned about education at the point of crisis, and demonstrated exercise of all four core features of agency towards it. Ultimately however they all decided to prioritize their obligations to family over those to EET. Within this there is a suggestion that young people have a limited capacity for agency. The agency they might exercise in pursuit of EET appears to be subsumed into a total capacity for agency. Anthony, for example, doubted his capacity to engage with EET effectively while expending his efforts on caretaking family issues.

These ideas continued to co-occur throughout the data. Fiona was a softly spoken 21-year-old with aspirations to work in the local airport. She benefited from a comparatively stable family environment. She nonetheless postponed job searching for a few months and lost focus on the possibility of going to university when her infant sister was diagnosed with diabetes. She resumed job searching once her sister started attending school. She said, 'I was more focused on looking after my sister, because I believe family is first.' Intractable family circumstances clearly have a meaningful impact on the exercise of agency by young people, and the determination of their EET outcomes, seemingly in quite definable ways.

Parents and families: The impact of relational fallout versus supportive relationships

In the cases discussed, the circumstances of family crisis were clearly beyond the young persons' control. There were however cases of familial instability caused by relational fallouts in which the young person was potentially implicated. Hannah was doing moderately well in school until she fell out with her dad 'halfway through Year 11'. She explained that they were not 'seeing eye to eye … and he … kicked me out'. She went to live with an older sister but this was violently disastrous. Hannah claimed:

> It was ridiculous, police was getting involved, that's how bad it was. My sister bruised my body up, my face, like literally. I'm not saying that I don't defend myself.

She went from there to live with a friend until her friend's mother was no longer willing to support her. The instability caused her to underperform in her exams, and contributed to her eventually becoming NEET. She said of her exams:

> I just didn't feel prepared, so I was nervous, frustrated. A lot was going on in my brain and … to be honest I didn't want to go in for my exams. I just wanted a breather, a break … I wasn't ready for it. I think [because of] the situation between me and my dad … I just couldn't care less about what was going on education wise.

Relational fallouts pushed several young people into leaving home and looking for their own places. However, instability was apt to continue in their new homes and have similar impacts, even in the absence of relatives. Hannah eventually obtained her own place in a hostel, but domestic difficulties continued to impact on her EET. She ended up failing to complete a hair and beauty course at one point, noting, 'I was in rent arrears so … it may sound like I'm making excuses but my mind was not there.' Hannah was subsequently NEET for five months.

Lisa's account was not entirely unlike Hannah's. Lisa had been adopted as a child and had experienced sometimes difficult relationships with her adoptive family and a number of foster carers before finding her own place. She was NEET for around eighteen months at one point. Although she initially described this as a time of gathering her thoughts, self-reflecting and developing her intentions, she went on to describe housing related problems that were clearly implicated in her prolonged disengagement. She had been living in a hostel, sharing facilities with seven or eight other girls. She was living in fear of several of them, including one she had previously had run-ins with at a shared foster home. She said:

> They all ganged together against me, and for about 6 months I was trapped … When I'm using the bathroom and stuff, I'd actually ring the staff downstairs to make sure people had gone out before I left my room, because I didn't want to

be caught on the hallway. So I'd get a text first thing in the morning, telling me who's gone out and who's still in, and if all 3 of them had gone out I'd quickly have a bath, go to the shop, get what I needed from the shop, make some food and go back into the bedroom. It got to the point where my dad even had to buy me a personal microwave because I didn't want to come out of my room. So basically I lived in a room. That was it. So I was doing all my cooking, all my washing up in there.

Eventually a violent assault took place and Lisa was badly beaten up. She explained:

I got beaten up really, really bad in the hostel after 6 months of telling my social workers that I'm being bullied in this hostel, I need to move … For the last 6 months that I was in the hostel I was basically like a caged animal. I wouldn't come out of my room, I wouldn't do anything … My eye was out, my lips were out, my nose was out … both sides of my lips were popped. Both of my eyes were bloodshot and just bruised and fucked. I had lumps all over my head and my stomach.

She called a previous foster carer for help, who agreed to move her out of the hostel in contravention of social services protocols. Lisa felt that her life would have been at risk otherwise.

She said, 'Social services didn't authorize it but I'm still doing it. I'm taking you out of this situation, because if not you'll be dead by next week.' It was true, I would have been dead if she hadn't come.

She stayed with the foster carer for six months before moving to a flat. When the flat was burgled, Lisa was again in fear and petitioned the local authority until she was given a more secure place. Although she was still a 'repeat churner', she had found frequent temporary jobs since moving into stable accommodation and had not come close again to being 'long-term NEET'.

Occasionally, the interaction between family relationships and fallouts, and a young person's EET status was more direct. After being thrown out of college at one point, Jeanne secured an immediate job opportunity with an uncle, working in his Caribbean restaurant. She found herself working from 6 am to 11 pm several days a week, but for only £50 a week. She declared, 'It wasn't enough for me. I think it's because [it was] the family business he thought … she's family, she wouldn't really care.' She claimed that to endure the long hours of work she would 'drink 10 Red Bulls a day just to stay awake'. This eventually became dangerous. In a moment that apparently combined extreme fatigue with some degree of frivolity, in which she recalls having mixed her Red Bull with brandy, she momentarily lost consciousness while descending a steep staircase and narrowly avoided serious injury. She remained working, but was eventually asked to take a week off by her uncle, so that her auntie's sister could work in the shop instead. Her uncle offered her £25 for the week. Her temper reared its head for a moment, and this led to a fallout and a loss of the job. Jeanne said, '[He was] only giving me £50 a week already. That's not enough, but to drop it down to 25, he's trying to take the piss', even though this was money offered to her to not work. She explained her being upset was 'because he's the one who told me to take the week off. It's not like I asked him to. And so we had an argument about it'. She decided to quit. Jeanne became NEET for several months, describing this as a time of socializing with friends, being at home and smoking.

In these cases, instability and crisis in the young person's wider life is again associated with disengagement, and not only as a precursor but also as a compounding factor. The inseparability of EET from the young person's wider life is again implied. Relational fallouts are associated with difficult if not intractable living circumstances. In these circumstances there is again evidence of a prioritization of intentions towards resolving relational, financial or domestic security issues, and these seem to take precedence over EET concerns. A limited capacity for agency is again implied.

Not all the young people became NEET because of such issues; six out of the sixteen reported home or family life crises that directly triggered their disengagement. Rather, some had very supportive and stable families. This was associated with a more consistent prioritization of EET intentions, and rather different drivers of disengagement. Darren was a 'repeat churner' with very supportive parents who showed a persistent (if somewhat unhurried) pursuit of EET. His most recent return to NEET had come when a temporary job reached its end, and his previous return had come when a zero-hour contract became exactly that. Darren's parents were more than willing to support his 'churning', and provided him with moral and financial support while he looked for something stable.

A supportive family could also open up job opportunities. Darren reported that a job opportunity at Sega had come because his dad 'knows someone higher up'. A temporary job in the Post Office had come through his dad directly, who was a manager at Royal Mail. Darren explained, 'He basically helped me with that, got me into the interview, and helped me to put the application in.' Likewise, when asked about how she had obtained a work trial at a pub, Elaine explained, 'Literally … my friend's nan's boyfriend hooked me up.' It was conversely found on occasion that highly supportive families could contribute to disengagement, even for the same young people. Elaine was close to leaving a job she did not like and a large pension payment to her parents tipped the balance. She claimed:

> My mum said don't worry about going back, you don't need to worry about money for the moment … Just find something you actually want to do.

Elaine didn't go back, and had unhappily now been NEET for several months as a consequence.

In a somewhat more dramatic case, Jeanne found a seemingly supportive family coercing her out of an unhappy job situation. After several months in NEET Jeanne had decided to go to Connexions, who helped her to find work at a local nursery in support of her longstanding intention to work in childcare. Everything seemed to be going well for the first two months, but then started to deteriorate. She had begun to feel that

> because I was the youngest there, everyone used to basically treat me like a slave. Like, I'll clean up after[wards] … from top to bottom. The boss' daughter that used to work there … used to just sit down and be like 'do this, do that, go upstairs and do this'. She wouldn't do anything at all. So then, I just had enough … I was like … let me complain … to the boss. The boss … she just went mad. She was like 'how "the f", why "the f" are you lying, my daughter does "f-ing" help you'… it was just unexpected … I was like 'is this really happening'?

Jeanne went home in tears. She recounted:

> My nan was like … why are you crying? I told her the story, she told my aunty, my aunty went there. She went mad, and she and my boss nearly had a fight.

Her aunty made her leave the job. She was at home for another month before returning to Connexions.

Relational and financial support was not only important when it flowed from parents to young people, but also in reverse. In several instances, young people felt they could help address domestic financial needs by finding work. Kevin was once told by an employer to return to college as his lack of qualifications was preventing him from getting a job. Although he would have liked to, he felt unable to because he needed to generate income for his family. Kevin linked this to family health; his mum had a medical problem preventing her from working. His desire to help was reflected in a prioritization of intentions towards work over those towards education. Kevin explained how compelling this motivation was even in the face of his frustrations and failures to find work. He said he would think:

> Fuck everything … maybe I should just get the fuck out of this house, vanish on my own … but … even though I was angry I knew I can't leave my mum here. That was the only thing holding me there man … I knew I had to stay … no matter how angry I was. I knew I had an objective … No matter what happens at the end, I will know it's worth it. And that's actually family man.

Whether for better or worse, the relational, domestic and financial stabilities associated with parents and families are important 'hard' influences in the life of the young person. These stabilities may be disrupted through death, bereavement, divorce, illness, financial crises or relational fallouts. The typical response of young people in such circumstances is to prioritize intentions towards resolving these disruptions, often but not always at the expense of EET.

Parents and families: Shaping the exercise of agency

These 'hard' influences can crucially determine the priorities towards which agency is exercised. Parents and families were also found to have 'softer', but not necessarily less powerful, influences on the way in which it is exercised. These influences were found to not only bear on immediate processes of EET decision-making, but also on underlying patterns of agency which develop throughout the life course and are then implicated in later decisions and behaviours. These patterns often surfaced in narratives of independence, and more rarely, dependence. Lisa spoke of maintaining a good relationship with her adoptive father, although they no longer lived together. He was wealthy and had encouraged her on several occasions to take up a part in his business. Lisa maintained this as an option but was deferring it indefinitely, claiming 'I kind of want a career of my own'. She asserted a learned independence from her adoptive parents, who had often left her at home while they both worked late. She said:

> Since an early age I've fended for myself so I'm half-street, half-posh … by the time I was nine I knew how to switch the washing machine on. I knew how to cook my own dinner … I didn't have a choice. Otherwise I'd be starving.

Lisa continued to express this learned independence in her current decision-making.

Pam similarly displayed a learned independence in EET decision-making that had been shaped within the family. One day during the college exam season, she felt she was unlikely to pass the year and decided she would be leaving. She thought it through and decided on an alternative plan that same day, before telling her mum in the evening what was going to happen. She immediately signed up with an apprenticeship provider, while still doing her exams, knowing it would take 'a few months' for an opening to materialize. She thus found herself NEET but not without direction. When asked about her thought process in all of this she explained her mum had

> grown us up as independent basically. That's what she's always tried to do. So if I come to her with … a question, she would say look it up. That was always her answer.

This independence was associated with Pam's decision to move out at eighteen:

> Now that I have my own place, I'm good … because when I was at my mum's … you're still depending … But being by myself … it's all me. Do you know what I mean? If I want to go here, go there. If I need to do this, just strategize everything. So it's alright.

Caroline, who displayed a strong sense of learned independence, captured a key underlying notion when she said the influence of parents and families on young people is '50/50. It depends what kind of person you are, whether you need their support or not. If you're independent then probably zero, but if not then…' In Caroline's case, it even appeared that some of her decisions had been made for the very purpose of underlining her independence, rather than because of any other personal benefit. In this way, it was shown that young people may use EET choices as a tool of deeper personal intention rather than for the sake of EET itself.

Ishmael, on the contrary, showed a rare level of parental dependence. His first college had been picked jointly with his mum. After this college had closed unexpectedly, his second was picked by his mum alone. As he described it, '[T]o be honest I never picked that, my mum did … she found about them and yeah, they accepted me.' The pattern of allowing others to make choices for him continued into other environments. When asked how he selected his current course, he claimed that 'the manager … just done it for me'. When asked about whether he was happy with other people making choices for him, he said, 'Depends. I'm alright as long as I'm doing something.' Highly independent participants tended to give lower scores on the survey for the importance of parental influences.

In between narratives of independence and dependency was suppressed independence. This could hinder the development of clear intentionality and other agentic traits. For example, Hannah had felt like she couldn't develop a sense of what she wanted to do while living with her dad:

> I don't think I had any goals or any achievements I wanted to achieve because … it was either his way or no way. He'd sit there and listen to what I had to say, but … he'd say you're in the wrong basically.

When she did finally have independence, she said, 'My focus wasn't education anymore.' This meant partying and 'wild living' until she eventually felt that she had the space and need to develop clear intentions for her life.

The 'softer' influences were found to be mediated through two key mechanisms. The first involved discursive interactions between the young person and family. These were strongly associated with young people's EET motivations. They could act both as motivators for specific actions, and as pivots for broader motivational dispositions. Gina and Elaine faced discursive pressures to find work. Gina explained:

> I'll be … sitting at home and my dad will come in and [say] 'you haven't done anything.'… Obviously you got earache after a while, so I'm like if I find a job they'll get off your back.

Elaine echoed 'they're in your ear constantly if you don't have a job' but also recollected how she had left a job on her mum's advice. She recounted how:

> She told me not to bother going in. I was like … 'I'm going to lose my job, and you're going to moan about me not having money'. She's like 'no, no I won't', so I didn't bother going in, and then I lose my job and she's moaning about me. Argh, it's confusing.

Megan, who had once been at loggerheads with her mum over EET, explained how a single discursive interaction could trigger a major shift in attitude. She said:

> She tried to kick me out the house plenty of times … to get a job … One day something did hit me. I couldn't afford to go out with my friends one night and they all had money … I went to my mum 'can I have some money?' And she said 'no, prove me wrong. You find money and then I'll give you money.' It changed my opinion. I found a job. Now I'm eager, so eager.

Although Megan had lost that job, she was continuing to express an enthusiasm for work through the pursuit of a vocational qualification that she hoped would take her into the catering profession.

The quality of family discourses seemed to be a proxy for the quality of family relationships and their corresponding motivational effects. Fiona, who described her mum as a best friend, stated her number one motivation in pursuing EET was to make her mum proud. Similarly, Neil, who found frequent comfort and companionship in talking to his sister, mum and dad, described family as 'one of my main incentives in life'. Gina underlined the correlation:

> If … they want you to do good, it makes you want to do something with your life [but] if they're not really bothered … then you're not going to be.

Hannah related a decline in the quality of discourse with her dad to a decline in motivation for learning. She said:

> My dad always used to motivate me. I used to be happy, bubbly … but when I was going through my situation with my dad … education was the least of my worries.

She concluded, 'If at home's good, then [the young person's] mindset will most probably be good.' Discursive interactions are thus implicated in the production and transformation of relational stabilities, and of the motivational states of young people.

The second mechanism involved the modelling of agentic thought and behaviour. Such agentic modelling provided young people with examples of how to respond to challenges and opportunities. Neil found out that he would be made redundant from his sales assistant job. His family not only empathized discursively, but modelled resilience to him. His dad recounted a redundancy experience '10 or 11 years' previous, his sister a more recent experience and his mum explained she was also facing potential redundancy. Their examples convinced Neil that staying positive and looking ahead to new opportunities was the best way to handle the situation.

The influence of models was related to the degrees to which young people identified and enjoyed positive relations with them. Ishmael's uncle was a particularly inspiring model to him. He said:

> I want to be like him, because he was like me once upon a time, a bit before. He was bad and that … All of a sudden … he changed his life so quick, so nice, now he's got a degree and … a good job and he's living his life.

Ishmael's cousin however was a frustration. His cousin had become local Young Mayor the previous year, and was held up to him as an example by his dad. Ishmael said:

> Obviously I like him as a cousin, but I feel like hitting him because … my dad keeps on talking about him. My dad's telling me to be like him, and I … get angry and start shouting.

Elaine's brother was at the same time inspiring and frustrating.

> He's doing well with himself, I'm not, there's a big difference. It just makes me feel like shit. He's coming in with bags of stuff, his phone, argh everything, and I'm sitting there like 'damn'.

She did nonetheless aspire to follow after him by finding a good job.

Models could also provide examples of what not to be like. Caroline felt her stepdad was such an example for her and her seven siblings. She explained that he had suddenly turned up in the home one day, and she and her siblings were told by her mum, '"There's your dad, get on with it" … I didn't even know the geezer.' This situation developed negatively:

> He'd been in our lives for like 4, 5 years and then he got sent to prison, lost his job and everything … that and everything onwards, bad influence … Mum can't work … but he chooses not to.

She wanted to be nothing like him. She eventually fell out with her mum and stepdad and left the family house.

Like discursive interactions, agentic modelling was implicated in the shaping of patterns of agency over the life course, as well as in influencing its immediate exercise. When Pam told her mum that she was not returning to college an argument ensued. Pam reminded her mum that she herself had worked her way to a professional management position with little or no further education. She recounted days of visiting her mother at work after secondary school, and helping her out with administrative tasks. She explained how this had influenced her own view of how to achieve success in employment, and had been a major factor in her decision to take her current course, an apprenticeship in business administration. Again, such modelling could be for better or for worse. Orlando claimed that during his primary school years:

> My parents never told me to do homework because they were kind of lazy … And I was … lazy. So I've never really done homework … my whole life. It sounds … stupid, but it's true, and then I took that attitude to secondary school … I'd not been doing work for years. I just couldn't stop it.

He felt this laziness had contributed to him failing his GCSEs and becoming NEET immediately upon leaving school.

Parents and families influence not only the immediate exercise of agency by young people, but also the shaping of unique (i.e. heterogeneous) habitual patterns of agency that develop throughout the life course. These influences are mediated in two key ways. These are first through discursive interactions.

These interactions are crucially implicated in young people's EET motivations, and in the production and transformation of relational stabilities. It will be developed that the interactions with parents and families are part of a wider discursive environment which has a powerful influence on the function of personal agency. Second, these are through agentic modelling. This modelling provides patterns (and anti-patterns) for thinking and behaviour, and for responding to challenges and opportunities. The strength of its influence is related to the degrees to which young people identify with and positively relate to models.

Education and training providers

Experiences in school were also heavily involved in the shaping of habitual patterns of agency. This was most pronounced in the accounts of Brian, Caroline and Lisa who each reported experiencing long-term bullying. In accounting for their EET decisions they would often refer back to these experiences, and the way in which they had dealt with them was often reflected in more recent decision-making. Brian's experiences had left him with a strong sense of vulnerability to peers. As a result, his EET decisions seemed often to revolve around his assessment of the friendliness of a given environment. New opportunities would typically be met with apprehension and followed by a period of gently developing friendships before settling in. He said of his current training course:

> At first, I didn't really want to come back ... because I was too nervous and didn't know anyone. But then I became close to my group, and then I looked forward to coming in every day.

He gave a very similar account of his settling into the workplace where he was currently working part-time.

Caroline, who happened to be Brian's girlfriend, recounted years of bullying and shyness before a major turning point. She claimed, 'I started going out with Brian in Year 10 ... and it built my confidence up.' Her change in confidence was dramatic. For the bullies, it was 'a completely different day!' She felt it was time to turn the tables around. She explained:

> I was sitting in one of my English lessons and one of the girls was walking past and trying to take the piss and I told her to 'shut the fuck up'. Everyone turned around ... like, 'oh my gosh, she's retaliated'.

A fight ensued. This moment marked a watershed in the way that Caroline dealt with life challenges. She was adamant she would never go back to feeling oppressed. She said:

> I couldn't wait to leave [school] and do my own thing. I don't like being told what to do, being controlled by anyone or anyone thinking they over rule me. I don't like it. I like being top dog.

She declared further that no one, including Job Centre Advisers, parents or training providers could coerce her against her will. She said, 'I'm learning what I want to learn at my own pace … But being forced to do something, I'm just not going to do it.' This sentiment was evident in her ongoing approach to EET.

Lisa had responded fiercely to perceived bullying from the start. When the story of her adoption found its way into her primary school's rumour mill (i.e. discursive environment), she explained, 'I basically punched up the girl who spreaded it in the playground. Actually booted her … So I got excluded.' Lisa was diagnosed with an emotional and behavioural disorder (EBD), and fell into a pattern of moving from school to school as a result of similar incidences. In one episode she was being called names, and after involving a teacher found nothing had changed. She recounted:

> So I was like 'well fuck this, call me an Oompa Loompa one more time!' He said it, I picked up a plank of wood – I was in DT at the time – and … went 'smack' in his head. Knocked him out … [The] headteacher came and tried to … restrain me … so I ended up punching her in the face and knocking her out … I didn't get charged for assault or anything – I got lucky – but they ended up kicking me out.

She was placed in a 'boarding school in Sussex' where she also complained of bullying and ran away 'about sixty times'. She said, 'When you ran away you were literally on the M25. So there's me running up and down the M25, trying to get home.' Her adoptive parents found her unmanageable when she 'just refused to go' to school anymore, and aged fourteen she went into foster care, eventually going through several homes, and to yet another school. The chaotic 'short stay' pattern continued into her EET life; she had 'churned' through at least ten courses and jobs since leaving school. The six-month period of variable-time employment indicated in Table 4.1 was actually made up of a spate of different temporary posts. In a somewhat different example, Anthony explained how his school's failure to address issues of local violence had nurtured a learned sense of independence for him and his peers. He said:

> At that time there was a lot of killing going on, beefing … Teachers didn't even sit down and explain [it] to the students … Students would … think they have to do stuff for themselves.

This appeared to mean taking rather serious issues relating to local violence and crime into their own hands.

The quality of relationship implied in discourses with adults in the learning environment exerted meaningful motivational influences on young people, just as it did within the home. Elaine claimed never receiving positive affirmation from teachers had a profound effect on her. She said:

> It affected my attitude towards school really badly, so I didn't want to be there. So I fucked about in the classes [and] distracted all the other kids so they got sent out [with] me.

She suggested her teachers had 'favourites' that would receive help, whereas they were 'rude to me to the extent of [saying] you're a little bitch and I don't want to talk to you … I just rebelled'. She claimed to have 'settled down a bit in Year 11 [when] one of my teachers told me I was good … But … it was too late'. Jeanne expressed similar sentiments when she claimed to have hated school because 'the teachers … never understood me at all'. She continued:

> I can barely understand myself, so I expected them to understand me so I can understand myself. But it wasn't working so I went a different way, instead of their way.

She further suggested that

> teachers need to be a bit more understanding … because [when some students] don't pass their GCSEs or anything like that, it's because the teachers don't exactly encourage them. Because when I was in school, teachers were [saying things] like 'you're not going to get nowhere in life, you're just worthless'.

Both conveyed sadness over what could have been a better school experience.

Caroline underlined the idea that the exercise of agency in learning environments may vary as a function of the perceived quality of relationships. She believed that colleges did better than schools because

> they know how to work with young adults … how to handle people, and that's why you don't get so many people being kicked out for misbehaviour and stuff.

She recounted not liking college much however because 'I didn't get on with my tutor'. Comments of this nature were common, and reflected a strong tendency for the influences of schools and colleges to be perceived in relational terms; participants rarely spoke of schools or colleges in the abstract, but rather focused on their relationships with individual staff. As Pam articulated it, 'I would say schools do help, but I don't think it's the whole school … it's teachers that show a bit more interest in the students.' She suggested that positive discursive interactions with staff could increase student motivation considerably.

Educators appeared to exert considerably more influence through discursive interactions than through agentic modelling. There were however some clear cases of the latter. Neil wanted to get into an HR career. He said:

> I thought it would be hard work to get into. That's what my teachers say … If you don't get in the first time, you might get in the second time, the third time, the fourth time.

He explained that his teacher had been in the same position as him but had gotten his breakthrough into HR on his sixth try. Neil said, 'If you don't get it the first time don't beat yourself up about it. Second time, still don't beat yourself up about it.' He was currently preparing for his third attempt.

A final key theme under this heading was the sentiment that education often failed to be relevant, particularly insofar as it did not prepare young people for 'life'. This sometimes meant getting into EET. Brian said, 'At school we have to do GCSEs and things we'll never use' and argued that qualifications did not necessarily lead to jobs. Gina similarly opined that 'you could be unemployed and have every single qualification, or you could have no qualification and be employed'. Lisa concurred, claiming 'somebody … I know with a law degree is working in McDonalds'.

More often, however, this related to personal unpreparedness for difficult circumstances, that is, relational, financial and domestic crises and instabilities. Caroline explained:

> School didn't teach you half the shit you need to know … You have to learn it by yourself … how to budget money … how to look after yourself. If … you … get kicked out of your house, everything that your mum … or your dad was doing for you, you have to do that by yourself and no one's taught you how.

Fiona said similarly that 'not a lot of them tell you how it is … they don't tell you how it could be, what could happen, how it would feel if you weren't going to get a job', and also that schools should 'tell you how it is … after you finish your education, so you would be prepared for it'. Kevin vented:

> The Pythagoras Theorem? Man, where am I going to use that? Personally I don't give a fuck about Pythagoras's Theorem, it's just useless to me, I don't remember when was the last time I used it. It's not life. It's nothing to do with life.

Orlando commented, 'I just didn't like doing work at school … I don't think the work was that relevant, and I was like what has it got anything to do with?' These comments reflected the persistent tendency of the young people to see EET and wider life concerns as an inseparable whole. They also reflected the prioritization of intentions by young people that tended to take place when they experienced crises or instability.

Learning environments and experiences are powerfully involved in the shaping of habitual patterns of personal agency, as well as in its immediate exercise. The influences of learning organizations are perceived through a primarily relational lens, and are again mediated through discursive interactions and agentic modelling, with the attendant motivational effects. NEET young people may often perceive learning provision as being aloof from their real needs, particularly where they are experiencing crises and instability, indicating again the inseparability of EET from their wider lives.

Mentors and youth workers

Mentors were found to have a distinct and powerful role in influencing the exercise of personal agency. Effective mentors were highly skilled in the use of discursive interactions and agentic modelling to achieve their goals. Anthony spoke of a mentor he had in school who would challenge him discursively when he was acting up. He was not used to the challenge. He explained:

> The first time I met Mr Wright … I thought I'm going to have a fight with him because I knew for a fact that I can't [get away with anything] … He wouldn't let me go … I used to get mad on him … and I fought back.

The challenge caused Anthony to reflect. He recounted:

> I said to myself, is he trying to keep me [from failure or trouble], or does he want me to get excluded? I thought … 'hang on what's he trying to do'? Does he want me to actually learn or something like that?

He concluded Mr Wright was guiding him as a father would, making sure he would not fail. Anthony began to place an extremely high value on his discursive interactions with him. He explained:

> He always wanted to see me do good, and others do good. That's the major thing he always spoke to us about … Money and all them things don't mean nothing, but when someone is there for you to actually talk to, to help you understand what life is really about …

At this point Anthony became very quiet and contemplative as he reflected on his feelings.

Anthony continued by explaining that after his father's death, he had found similar help in another mentor, Chris. 'Chris is the same', he said. 'I didn't even know where to start or where to go [but] I had someone to guide me and help me.' Chris would guide him on how to think about his past, the death of his dad and on not losing vision for his life. He believed Chris had prevented him from slipping into depression or nihilism, saying, 'He never let me go.' Anthony also discussed how for a time after his bereavement, he had identified with local NEETs hanging out on the streets. He said:

> Seeing people outside on the road, I wanted to get myself involved with a lot of people that are not even into college. So I thought to myself 'let me join you', I'm a part of you, I don't even want to go to college.

Chris was a preserving influence however, and Anthony claimed some of his peers changed too as he cascaded his mentor's ideas to them. Anthony later spoke of agentic modelling by his mentors. He said:

> Mr Wright would always make us look at it like we could be someone like him. When we came into school, all Mr Wright used to hear us talk about was cars, girls, clothes, everything, but he would come into school suited up, looking healthy, and you would be like 'yeah, that's someone you want to be like as well'. But it took me a while to realize that I want to be like him.

Anthony suggested that this realization came as he increasingly identified culturally and emotionally with Mr Wright. Several other interviewees discussed the discursive influences of mentors. Brian said:

> Everything I do, they'll tell me I've done well … I don't know what it is … but I trust them. When they say to me I can do it, I believe I can do it.

He claimed this had made him more confident and less lazy, and that he had noticed similar results with other young people, an observation corroborated by the data. He contrasted this with experiences in schools, college and the Job Centre. He said: 'Before … I was told I was just bad … They were trying to push me … telling me you have to do this, you have to get this job.' He likened this to being bullied at school, and acted out his corresponding habitual response. He said, 'I was … being put down, so I just hid', indicating deliberate absence. Caroline said she had been made more confident by mentors in a similar way. 'Instead of telling me I can't do something, they've told me if I want something go and do it.' Other participants also related impacts on their exercise of agency. Elaine spoke of her mentoring experience, saying, 'I think, since coming here they've changed the way I think about things. Like they've made me think better of myself, like I can do it instead of I can't.' Orlando gave mentors and youth workers an 8 for importance on the survey tool and commented, 'They … talk to you on a personal level and they can … sway your opinion on stuff. And it's kind of … intense.' Pam explained that mentors had helped her to develop her aims, forethought and planning. Gina had found similar support at Connexions in a 'little office' at her school.

Some participants linked discursive interactions with mentors to the development of particular features of agency. These could help young people to consider new intentions or refine existing ones, structure and enhance their forethought, consider alternative ways to react to situations and draw meaning out of self-reflection. Jeanne also spoke positively of mentors, but introduced the possibility that other elements in the NEET topography could mitigate their effects. She spoke of a mentor she had been given when her family had run into trouble with the social services. She recognized the value of her mentor's advice and support, but had shut her out. She explained that her family

> didn't want her to have nothing to do with me … My family didn't really like people … getting into our business … That's why I had that brick wall … I used to make her life a misery whenever I had to go and see her.

Jeanne felt she would have done better if she'd been more open to her mentor's influence.

Some young people delineated the role of mentors within NEET very clearly. Gina felt they were very important but marked their importance as only 'a 5 out of 10' on the survey, after differentiating between the power to influence a young person, and the power to place them into EET. She explained, 'They haven't really got the opportunity to give you a job, but they can advise you on how to go about it.' Kevin corroborated, saying they 'can help you … but they won't necessarily put you there'. For other young people however, mentors had indeed been a source of work opportunities. Brian's current job had come through a relationship one of his mentors had with a local business, as had an interview for a new position. He was also relying on his mentors to negotiate a full-time post for him with his present employer. Similarly, Darren had just had a work trial with a local business that was set up by his mentor. He went as far as to say:

> I actually think jobs these days are pretty much about people you know and not about your grades or your applications … If you know someone … you have a pretty good chance of getting a job.

He supported this claim with several examples from his own life.

Mentors received a much better and more extensive commentary than youth workers. The image of the youth worker was comparatively lacklustre and surprisingly they were hardly discussed. Hannah was unimpressed with the youth workers she had come across in her local community hall. Kevin said disparagingly, 'I always thought these … youth workers are a waste of time. You know I always had a youth worker approaching me back in the days when I was in school. Yeah come to the youth club, we got these things going on and all that stuff.' Many participants indicated that they had no meaningful experience of youth workers. It was not clear from the data whether this was simply a matter of terminology, or genuine unfamiliarity.

Skilled mentors can exercise powerful and sometimes crucial influences on the exercise of personal agency through discursive interactions and agentic modelling. These influences can stimulate and develop the particular features of personal agency. The role of mentors in NEET was seen by some as distinct; they could influence young people but not personally determine their outcomes. Several other young people did however find EET through opportunities created by their mentors.

Friends and peers

Similar themes emerged in the findings on friends and peers. Discursive interactions were again centrepiece. Neil's experience was that 'friends … motivate you … speak to you and encourage you'. Pam had a crowd of older friends that she suggested were 'like a little instruction book'. Their conversations helped her to find her way in new scenarios, manage her expectations and handle challenges. She even explained how a conversation with one friend had crucially edged her into going to college when she had been on the verge of disengagement.

These interactions were not always helpful. When Elaine was employed her unemployed friends would attempt to have her call in sick so they could go out together. She had to be careful and sometimes quite forceful with them. She said if she wasn't careful, their words could have had a serious impact on her perceptions, since 'they just influence the way you think about work'. She elaborated:

> Say I did have work on the weekend and it was a Friday night, I did get every one of my friends bang off my phone, like 'are you coming out tonight' and I'm like 'no just leave me alone!' I've nearly smashed my phone up.

She explained it was better not to be able to go out because she had to go to work, than not to be able to go out because she was unemployed and had no money.

Friends and peers were also important agentic models. Caroline had considered going into hair and beauty, but the experiences of friends persuaded her otherwise. She said:

> What they're doing is … too complex. So it gets a lot of them in tears, because if they do it wrong they get shouted at, proper beaten on. It's horrible … and it's like they're trying their utmost best. They're left in pieces then. It shouldn't be like that.

She continued:

> I would rather see how everyone else is coping … than go into it and find out that it's not all that it's made out to be.

Caroline was one of several who had taken cues from friends in this way. Similarly, Elaine's brothers and friends were a key factor in her choice of college, and Pam said her friend had edged her into going to college:

> To be honest, I wasn't going to college. It's just my friend was 'oh you have to go college, what you going to do?' I was like okay, I signed up for college. She did it actually. She signed [me] up for one college and I got in.

She explained, 'At that stage I was not bothered. I didn't know what I was doing. It was a confusing time.' This clearly showed that the influences of friends could be critical to determining a young person's EET status at pivotal moments.

Anthony again suggested that a model's influence was associated with perceived similarities between the model and young person. Particularly, he felt if a young person related to a model's thought processes, experiences and social position, the effects could be profound. On this basis, NEET young people should be exposed to slightly older peers who had once thought the same way as them, and gone on to do well:

> They need more students that had these types of thoughts … If you think about a student talking with another student, they're on the same level … When you have someone inspirational, who actually explains themselves to you, and you can see his feelings … there's a possibility.

Caroline's friends were a more powerful influence than family, also on the basis of affinity. She said, 'They know how to relate to me. It's easier … when someone is going through the same thing as you, you don't feel so alone'. Without them:

> It'd be quite bad … it would get to the point where people were feeling so stressed and so alone they wouldn't turn up and their life would go to shit then.

She agreed that having friends in the EET environment was an important motivator to stay engaged.

Once again a distinction was made between the ability to influence the exercise of agency, and the ability to change a young person's EET status. Caroline said, 'You need your friends. Obviously they're not going to help you get a job … but they can support you.' Interestingly, the modelling of friends and peers could trigger rather particular reinterpretations of personal circumstance. Elaine felt she could not get a job because there were none to be had, but after seeing friends get jobs she reassessed the problem as her being too lazy. Fiona reflected similarly after seeing friends get work. 'I was a bit shocked and a bit sad … because you see everyone getting a job and you just think what am I doing wrong?' She indicated that she became increasingly self-conscious as a result.

Young people differed widely on the level of influence they felt friends had on their exercise of agency, and not all felt compelled to have close friends. This was a distinctive feature of their role in NEET, as unlike relatives, young people could choose who they were and were not. Local violence had made Anthony wary of friendship: 'There's nothing called a friend … Today I could be a friend, tomorrow I'm going to stab you.' He had resolved friends and peers would have no influence on him. Brian had dropped a number of friends he felt were taking advantage of him. They would invite him out only once a fortnight, suspiciously close to the arrival of his Jobseeker's Allowance. He would buy rounds for them at the pub and, once his money was gone, not hear from them until the next time. He explained:

> I don't really have any close friends anymore … it's like they just want my money. They'd invite me out on weekends when I had money, and get me to buy drinks and stuff, but when I had no money I wasn't invited out.

Caroline had helped him to gain the confidence to detach himself from those friends. He had put a block on them on Facebook and stopped talking to them. Megan, however, allowed herself to be motivated considerably by her friendships. She spoke of a time when she had enrolled on a college course she had not enjoyed. She completed it nonetheless. She argued, 'Why give up? Why give people the satisfaction that you dropped out?' She explained she had a point to prove to friends that had predicted she would fail. She continued:

> Friends think … 'oh Megan, you're a pike, blah, blah, blah. How can you afford a pikey lifestyle? If you can't afford it why go out and drink? Oh … you're too lazy.' I'm not lazy.

Her current motives continued to be shaped by this kind of intent.

Relationships with friends were again avenues to opportunities. Two of Brian's three jobs since leaving school had come through friends. Caroline had found her current training opportunity through boyfriend Brian. This opportunism through relationship overcame an absence of effective agency. Caroline said:

> It was like I had no plans whatsoever, my life's going nowhere, to [suddenly] I've actually got something to do. … If that hadn't happened, I'd probably be stuck at home still not knowing what I'm doing.

This would have meant at least six further months in NEET. The two were now planning an EET future together. He claimed '[We] have a plan for the future … to own our own pub.' This indicated that the category of friends and peers might be usefully extended to include romantic interests. These interests could produce relational stabilities and instabilities in the young person's life similar to those considered earlier. Lisa found herself NEET for several months at one point, partially preoccupied with such an issue. She said:

> I was … in a relationship with some Essex girl. Then … the girl wouldn't leave me alone. It took 3 months for her to actually piss off and leave me alone. I was going through other stuff as well. It was a difficult time.

Lisa's new partner was having a more positive influence, and had encouraged her to start job searching. At the time of interview Lisa had just arranged to start a new job found for her by her partner, who had signed up for some work at a temping agency 'and … asked the person if I can start the same job, and she's said "yes"'. It turned out that Lisa had quit work at a Greggs factory the day before the interview to take this new job, because 'who wants to work in Greggs?' When asked how that might affect her relationship with the temping agency that had found her the work, it transpired she had not formally quit but rather had told them she was sick. It seemed she preferred the prospect of working with her partner.

Tensions between different elements of the topography appeared, as they had before in Jeanne's mentoring relationship. These tensions could have the effect of exerting pressure on the agent, and like a crisis, force a prioritization of intensions. Caroline, for example, ended up 'kicked out … at the age of 17' of home after conflict erupted between her family and boyfriend. Discussing why she left home she said, 'Well my parents don't like Brian, so I chose him over them.' She explained further that this was not the first time that she was faced with the choice. It had negatively impacted her EET status the first time around as it had prevented her from visiting the agency where she had found her current training:

> The first time I chose them. That's the worst decision I ever did. I was stuck at home. That was when I was supposed to be here. I missed two months of coming here, because they didn't want me to be anywhere near Brian, and they weren't helping me get a job or anything. Basically I was stuck at home all day every day for 2 months straight. I didn't go out once. It was bad. It was like I was digging myself a hole. They thought I was depressed, and I was put on antidepressants. But I'm not taking them, because I'm not depressed. I was just bored …

She felt that this time she had made the right choice.

Friends and peers are meaningfully represented within the influences of the discursive environment and agentic modelling. The affinity young people are apt to feel with friends and peers may heighten the strengths of these influences, and stimulate particular reflections on their personal efforts and efficacies. Friends (as opposed to peers) were positioned distinctively within the NEET topography, as unlike relatives (and to an extent educators and work colleagues) young people could choose who they were and whether to have them at all. Like other relationships, friendships could open up EET opportunities. The category of friends and peers can be usefully extended to include romantic interests, which were found to be a locus of relational stabilities (and hence instabilities) akin in effect to those associated with parents and families.

Employers

Like parents and families, employers were associated with both 'hard' and 'softer' influences. The 'hard' influences related to the job opportunities made available to young people, and their associated contract types, wage levels and shift structures. Brian had become a 'churner' by walking repeatedly into commission-only and temporary jobs. After enduring a commission-only job for just two days, he 'waited a couple of weeks … and … applied for the Royal Mail Christmas jobs'. He 'did that for December and then went back onto Jobseeker's in January'. He indicated lots of young people were passing through the same commission-only job:

> Now, everyone is saying if you want a job just go to Zenith. And I'm saying I've already worked there. It's like everyone I know now has gone there for a couple of days and just left.

In another case, Darren found his ideal job working for Sega, testing the latest computer games before release. He was on a zero-hour contract however, and after about three months of regular work the calls stopped coming in. Almost ten months later, he was still on the contract but had done no further work. He had also 'churned' over the previous Christmas period with Royal Mail. Although he was still not certain about what he wanted to do with his life, he had come to think that 'it wouldn't be so bad if I got a permanent job that I could just stick with and get paid' and was looking for a means to that end.

Elaine found that the £100 per week full-time wage she was earning in a local pub was not stretching far. It quickly dissipated through a combination of emergency tax, travel costs and a £20 levy raised by her mum. The remaining money went on her phone bill and cigarettes. She decided the meagre pay and difficult hours were too much for her. She claimed to have worked often from '10 in the morning to 10 at night' on consecutive days and had become 'knackered'. She left the job, saying, 'I just didn't want to get up and go back for £3.65 an hour … I was in depression.' She reckoned she could 'go into a pub and get a job the same day' but would rather have nothing. The critical factor was a lack of long-term prospects. She explained, 'I can't see myself getting any better staying in that job.' In a similar case, Fiona had found a job waitressing. She found the low pay, low prospects and awkward hours unsustainable. She left the job, saying:

> You get so much shifts and hours and you don't get that much pay … I want to get a proper job so I can provide for myself and my mum and for my little sisters.

Shift structures caused her to give up another waitressing job, this time for personal safety reasons. She explained:

> Sometimes they would finish at three o'clock in the morning and I would get a bus or get a taxi and you know … I was kind of worried for my safety. You know, I don't live in a bad area but anything could happen.

She became NEET for several months each time. In Gina's case, sheer convenience prevailed where safety had for Fiona. She had a work trial arranged for her by her mentor, but didn't like it however because of the hours and length of travel.

> I didn't want to do it because I had to get up at like three o'clock in the morning, walk to the bus stop at like five o'clock in the morning and then walk like 20 minutes, and it was just so long, so I didn't really like it. That was the only thing that was bad about it.

She decided not to go for the full job.

Employers were seen by young people to be an important, if often dysfunctional part of the discursive environment. The dysfunction related to a common practice of not providing young people with feedback on unsuccessful job applications. Fiona discussed this in detail. Among many comments, she said:

> When you go to an interview and they don't call you back to even say you did ... or didn't get the job, or to know what ... [to] improve on ... I just feel like ... I'm doing something wrong, [but] I just don't know what it is because they're not telling me ... yeah that's one thing that really gets on my nerves. No feedback.

Not receiving feedback lessened her sense of value, making her feel 'like I'm not worth it' and stopped her from improving although she was 'willing to learn'. Neil articulated similar views. Feedback was not only valuable for failed applicants, but also for those in post. Gina claimed to have been quite shy when she first found work in a hair salon, but to have grown quickly in confidence when she received positive feedback from colleagues and satisfied customers. Pam aspired to a job in the City of London and commented:

> If it's your first job, everything you learn from them is how you're going to be in the workplace. If they are not correcting you, when you go into the City ... you're going to be failing. So it is important.

Another key finding was that many participants felt they were more likely to find employment through relationships than through the conventional approaches of completing applications and distributing CVs. As has been indicated throughout, many of the participants had found jobs through family members, mentors and friends. Many had come to the conclusion that seeking employment conventionally was a dead-end, particularly if the young person had no experience, or low qualifications. It was argued that for these young people, a CV was not a good representation of their abilities, and that employers could redress this by offering work trials. Lisa agreed with Gina on this point, and contrasted the 'typical' employer with one who had recently allowed her to take on a temporary catering job despite not having the experience and qualifications for it. She claimed she had both enjoyed and performed well in the job. She said:

> [They] gave me that opportunity to prove myself. So … I think employers need to give people chances … instead of taking one look at their CV [and saying] … 'they're going to be shit'.

Kevin argued:

> Grades is only paper … what [people] can do physically is a different thing. I mean, I know more than enough people that are actually shit at doing the test bullshit … but give them something to do and they will do it better than anyone. That's how it is … don't use grades as an excuse not to give people an opportunity … An eight-hour trial's not going to kill you, in fact don't even pay me, let me just do it for free, for fuck's sake, and see how I do.

He spoke positively of his current apprenticeship provider saying:

> They understand that people have got to start somewhere … No one is fucking Hercules out here. You know what I mean, born with all beards and shit.

Neil put it far more gently, suggesting the role of employers was to give young people 'their first opportunity to work, whether in retail or in a bank perhaps, or mostly in supermarkets' indicating this could be beneficial for both parties.

Volunteering was a related way to break through the experience barrier. Some participants had volunteered their way into jobs or apprenticeships. Kevin unexpectedly gained a chance to do voluntary work after giving a dance performance for the opening of a local café. He was desperate for paid work, but went with it. He said:

> I know what volunteering means, which means no money. What am I doing? But … I thought, you know what, I've tried all these things and they didn't work. It ain't going to kill me if I try this.

He was asked to run a dance project in the centre where the café was based. He taught his skills to other young people, while also doing a qualification in project management. He was out of NEET for the first time in over three years. He became a full-time volunteer and had his expenses covered. He explained:

> I wasn't getting no £100 a week … but it was more than enough for … travel and food … and that's all I wanted, because I knew once I had this, I'd be making friends here.

He deliberately built relationships in the centre with the hope of generating opportunities. The strategy was successful. After three months of full-time volunteering, an opportunity came up within the café itself. He was offered an apprenticeship in customer service, and had been in the role for about four weeks at the time of interview.

Employers are associated with both 'hard' and 'softer' structural influences. The 'hard' influences relate to employment opportunities and their associated contract types, wage levels and shift structures. Temporary, commission-only and zero-hour contracting appear to be a driver of NEET churn, and minimum wage jobs with difficult hours and low prospects were found to be untenable for some young people. Employer feedback is an important component of the discursive environment and has meaningful motivational, developmental and orienting effects. Conventional approaches to job searching were often perceived to be ineffective relative to seeking jobs through relationships, particularly for those with limited experience and qualifications. Work trials, including voluntary work opportunities, may be an important route into employment for young people with these barriers.

Government

Government was typically viewed in cynical terms, and was the part of the topography most likely to be dismissed by participants as irrelevant. Brian stated, 'They're useless. They don't really do anything ... other than making me struggle to get a job.' Caroline was even more harsh. She proclaimed, 'The government is fucked ... load of pigs. They can't help us whatsoever. They don't know what they're doing. They're all just snobby idiots.' These views seemed to be rooted largely in negative press coverage, related, for example, to unemployment levels, school failures and the 'Baby P' incident. In Caroline's case this was aggravated by difficulties she had experienced in accessing social housing after leaving home.

Some participants felt the government had let them down with the rise of university fees. Hannah's view was that the government 'make[s] it so difficult, so difficult ... to go to university'. She indicated that because of the financial implications she was 'avoiding' university: 'the best thing for me is to just stay away from it, because I'm not looking to be in any debt'. She explained that accumulating a high level of debt would be psychologically and emotionally troubling for her, particularly given her current housing and family circumstances, which meant she had little support to help her carry the pressures; it would 'be playing on my mind'. She felt that the government should make it easier for her go to university, given that it was 'for education … something for me to be a better person', implying that where good choices were made more difficult, bad ones became more likely. Lisa expressed some similar views, saying, 'Your education is basically fucked … unless you go and get yourself a 50 grand debt … who wants to do that nowadays? Nobody's got any money.' She then explored a tricky and interesting scenario rooted in a perceived flaw in government policy. She intimated she had covertly enrolled on her current course. This was because it was 'the only one worth … doing' but her Job Centre had refused to pay her benefits if she enrolled. She said:

> I've been … crying because of it. I've had to lie to the Job Centre that … I'm volunteering. But I'm not. I'm on a course trying to get a qualification.

She was officially NEET, but was really in training and part-time work. She explained the Job Centre's view was 'if you go to college, you're technically not looking for a job' and argued that this view was flawed because it assumed college was full-time and precluded her from finding part-time work. She felt she could both study and have a part-time job as 'college isn't a full-time thing … you can do three days there and three days working'. She suggested a better policy would allow unemployed young adults to better themselves without the potential financial repercussions.

Anthony captured a general sentiment of the government being distant when he declared 'the government doesn't fit in anywhere for me … nowhere at all … MMG, double M fits in for me', referring to his favourite music label. Anthony entirely denied a role for government in his decision-making, saying:

> No government can tell me they took me … this way. I took myself … I had a choice … I could have gone to the wrong side. I could have gone to the right side. It was my choice. It's up to me to decide.

For Darren, the sense of distance was due to a lack of direct discursive interactions, observing that in all likelihood 'I wouldn't get David Cameron coming up and talking to me in the Job Centre'. He opined further that the government were 'not really helping … it's all really down to the people who work in the Job Centre, the personal advisers and that'. These ideas suggested the relational views of institutions that were evident in regards to other elements of NEET's structural topology were also relevant here.

The sentiment of distance was not all-prevailing, however. Some young people associated local youth provision with government funding, and a variety of agencies were seen as proxies for government including the police, social services, schools and colleges and most often the Job Centre. Interactions with these agencies was seen by these young people as interaction with the government. In these instances, a relational view again prevailed. Lisa, for example, blamed a period of her churning in and out of EET on the government broadly, but in elaborating on this, claimed it was actually the fault of a single social worker who, she reckoned, had a habit of enrolling her on various 'crap' courses. Also, where these agencies were felt by young people to have failed in their duties, this was interpreted as failure of government. Lisa, again, laid at least partial responsibility at the government's feet for her experience of being bullied. She felt they were not responding well enough to bullying in schools, saying, 'Oh yeah, we'll do something, we'll crack down on bullying. The next week you're still feeling the same.' Other than funding youth provision, the singular positive act attributed to government was the funding of apprenticeships. Neil remarked, 'That's them trying to help us to get … like a job.' Gina and Orlando also spoke positively about government provision of apprenticeships, with Gina going as far as to suggest that they should be made mandatory for young people. She claimed to have benefited tremendously from them, but may never have taken one up if her parents had not pushed her.

Government was typically characterized as unhelpful or distant to young people. These views were associated with negative press coverage, negative personal experiences of government services, perceived EET barriers linked to specific policies (e.g. high university fees, and welfare payment rules) and a lack of discursive interactions with notable government figures. The funding of apprenticeships and local youth provision stood out from this general backdrop as positive acts of government.

Young people

Many young people's perceptions of their own roles within NEET were profound. Darren summarized the position of most participants when he suggested the young person's role was 'the biggest one … it's all on them'. Sometimes this view was communicated in almost absolute terms. Anthony said, '100 per cent. There's no doubt about it … It's down to them.' Likewise, Pam said:

> Everything is down to them. Everything … Things can be given, like information and stuff, but it will stop there if they're not willing to do anything with that … So everything is down to the individual person, if they really want to do it.

When asked how much her outcomes were down to her own agency, Megan declared emphatically, 'All of it! Every single bit of it. It's me, my effort.' She implicated her own poor self-management as the central factor in her becoming NEET. Numerous comments of this nature were made, and were underlined in the survey, where half the young people scored their importance in determining their own outcomes as '10 out of 10'; this was more than for any other element. Sometimes this position was held in almost absolute terms. Caroline asserted:

> You've got to do it yourself, because no one else will help you … Whatever happens [to young people is] their own fault, because they decided for it to happen that way. It's not anyone else's doing.

When asked how this applies to young people who find themselves in adverse circumstances she maintained her position. 'They've got to get on with it. They've got to choose' she opined quite bluntly. Her underlying position was that although it was not easy for young people to determine their outcomes, they were ultimately capable of doing so.

Other participants expressed fundamentally similar views, although with some reservations. Brian believed that young people were most important in determining their outcomes, but confidence levels had to be taken into consideration. Confident people who were not job searching were 'lazy', but the unconfident needed support to do well:

> If people are not confident, do they need someone to come to them … Can they be the ones to go out and get help? I think it depends on the situation. Some people can do it themselves, but like with me it's much easier just having the help there.

According to Hannah, young people 'have the control' but might have difficulties in acting independently 'because they may not have a backbone'. Without this 'backbone', control was yielded to friends or others. Pam posited 'everything is down to the individual person', but then spoke of intelligent people she had met in school who were now NEET. She laid blame for this at their own feet but cautioned that 'it could also be because their parents have babied them', again indicating her views on the importance of personal independence.

Elaine emphasized the heightened difficulties facing those with no work experience: 'once you've had a first job it's easy getting a second … But it's hard getting the first … because of the experience needed'. The support of employers was needed in such cases. Elaine identified both personal agency and structures as issues in her own NEET experiences, ultimately fixing the blame on herself:

> It is me. It is my fault. That's what I'm saying … because it's always been my choices. But it's been other people as well, instigating them choices, and the way I feel … I felt like I didn't get enough help, but then again I didn't help myself to do my best.

She identified the psychology of the young person as important in such circumstances: 'young people are their own worst enemy … it's the mindset of the person'. Gina corroborated, expressing how important she felt the thinking processes of young people were:

> I think they've got to be in the right mindset. They've got to think, this is what I want to do … if they have the mindset of I'm going to sit here and not do anything then they're not going to do anything.

Kevin also considered both personal agency and structures to be implicated jointly in NEET, since although it was ultimately up to the young person to have the determination to succeed, government and employers had to create the right labour market conditions for it to amount to something.

Orlando was more cautious than most. Alluding to the influence of the discursive environment, he felt young people were primarily responsible for their outcomes, but 'their views can be distorted through people telling them things … everything that was on this [survey], and even like the media'. Hannah rounded up the softer edge of opinion by qualifying her perspective with a quintessentially dialectical caveat. Posing and responding to her own question, she said, 'But it depends on the situation don't it? Yeah. It depends on the situation of the person. What's going on in their life.' Somewhat surprisingly, despite clear opportunities to do so, none of the young people argued for the dominance of structural forces over agency in the determination of EET outcomes.

Participants generally viewed themselves as the primary determinants of their EET outcomes, and as ultimately capable of trumping structural forces. The strengths of these views varied considerably, from being almost absolute at one extreme to a near balanced dialectical view at the other. The ability to act confidently and independently was identified as a key factor in whether young people exercised agency effectively to access and sustain EET.

Other influences

Two further distinct sets of influences appeared in the data. The first of these related to celebrities and popular media. Once again, these exercised their influence through discursive interactions and agentic modelling. The distinctive difference in this case was that the relevant discourses were one-way rather than two-way, being instantiated, for example, in song lyrics and online artist interviews. Anthony talked extensively about a particular music label, MMG, and two of its artists, Rick Ross and Meek Mill. He explained that they would constantly convey messages about how a person could make it through difficult circumstances to become successful, as they themselves had. He identified with them, and said he had learnt from them that hardship produces the character needed to fulfil personal dreams. He believed they wanted him to achieve the same success as they had. He said:

> When I see Meek Mill lifting up his hands to the crowd … you're telling me to join you, you want me to be who you are … MMG made me who I am. Focus in life, don't ever stop. Whatever you're good at, don't ever stop.

This translated into a strong coping mechanism for Anthony, by which he could accept the immediate difficulty of his life and circumstances, while also considering those difficulties to be temporary, and conquerable by his efforts. He said:

> MMG … makes me feel that … one day you're going to get somewhere … Everything has a time, there's no rushing things. I have to go through that … I have to see the hard life.

He felt that by facing up to the 'hard life' he was actually carving out his success story.

Other young people also used music to help them to cope, think and receive inspiration. Kevin used music and dancing to help him deal with the stress of job hunting. Jeanne's main influences were 'the close ones in my family, and my music'. Orlando detailed his beliefs that popular musicians, and celebrities more generally, have a huge impact as agentic models. He said:

> I think it affects [young people] a lot, because it's … people they look up to. It sounds … like everyone says that, but it is true … If you look up to someone then you're going to try and do what they're doing, especially if it looks like they're been successful.

In his opinion this impact was typically negative. Young people's views were being 'distorted' by materialistic messages, and the advocacy of drugs use in many songs.

Celebrities and popular media were found to influence young people primarily through one-way discursive interactions and agentic modelling. These influences were implicated positively in young people's coping mechanisms, and constructed negatively by one young person as drivers of materialistic views and substance misuse.

The second distinct set of influences was related to young people's faiths or religions. These were found to be a source of hope, positivity or direction. Anthony said his belief in God as a Muslim helped him to believe things could get better for his family. He also believed that faith could turn people's lives around. He spoke of a Christian friend he had recently seen on the street, whom he indicated might once have been involved in local violence. He said:

> Today, you can stab someone, anyone could do it. You go and repent [because] you're hurting inside that you actually did it. Them are the type of people that bring goodness, tell people to change their life around. Like one of my boys was out here the other day and he started preaching to me.

In this way faith and religion were seen to feature in the discursive environment. This could be through words spoken by believers and in those offered by the young person in prayer. Jeanne had a habitual pattern of turning to prayer when she was dealing with difficult circumstances. She said of the time when she was dealing simultaneously with her mum's sickness and EET worries:

> I was just praying, God please make her live. If she lives I'll be happy. But then again, I'll be coming back to England not knowing what to do … if any colleges will let me in … I was just praying, praying a lot.

Jeanne felt that ultimately God could bring good out of any situation, no matter how difficult.

In a couple of instances young people communicated concerns that their expression of religion would or had impacted on their EET. Fiona, who attended the interview in hijab, said:

> There was one point where I actually thought that the reason I wasn't getting any jobs was because I was Muslim … But you know, that wasn't the case and I did get a job doing waitressing, so …

Ishmael had a successful interview for some voluntary work that could have led to paid work, but he did not bother to turn up. He explained this was in part because he had been 'stupid' and 'lazy', and partly because the work would have begun during Ramadan, when he would have been fasting and too tired to work.

The influences of faith and religion were seen to feature in the discursive environment of some young people, whether through the words of others, or through their own acts of prayer. These influences could translate into more positive intentions, or into coping resources associated with pursuing and sustaining EET. Young people could also experience concerns about discrimination because of religious expression, and about the impact of religious fasting on their ability to carry out work tasks.

Conclusion

The findings of the study as reported in this and the following chapter describe in detail the function of the personal agency of NEET young people, and the nature of its interactions with social, political and economic structures in the determination of EET outcomes. This chapter discusses young people's perceptions of the roles of each element of the NEET topography in determining their outcomes. The findings show that 'the function' is highly complex; it varies by young person, and each element of NEET's topography makes a distinctive contribution to it. Crucially, however, a number of clear and powerful ideas convincingly explain its broad operation in the lives of a diverse range of young people, and across a range of highly varied circumstances. These can be used together to develop a cohesive and comprehensive understanding of the function, at least as it pertains to the sample of the study.

EET is perceptually and mechanistically inseparable from the wider life of the young person. The exercise of personal agency towards EET is typically subsumed within the exercise of agency towards the young person's wider life, and factors related to the wider life of the young person continuously and meaningfully impact upon their EET. The possible influences of structures on the function may be classed into 'hard' and 'softer' types. 'Hard' influences are associated with structural conditions which are intractable, or otherwise largely not amenable to a young person's direct influence, that is, they set the conditions in which agency must be exercised. Some of these are directly related to EET, others to the young person's wider life.

In wider life, 'hard' influences relate primarily to relational, domestic and financial stabilities associated with parental, familial and other close relationships (e.g. romantic interests). Crisis or instability in any of these, as may be instantiated, for example, in bereavement, illness in the family, parental divorce, financial crises, relational fallouts or the unavailability of safe accommodation, can trigger disengagement from EET. Although such circumstances may be considered to be somewhat coercive, disengagement is not automatic; they do not negate a young person's agency but rather force upon them a prioritization of intentions. Typically, familial concerns are prioritized by young people, and their intentions directed towards resolving crisis or instability. Disengagement from EET may often be undesired by the young person in such circumstances. A limited capacity for effective agency is indicated within this.

Within EET, 'hard' influences relate to the stabilities and structures of EET opportunities, that is, the types of opportunities available, and their attributes, for example, entry requirements, success criteria, contract types, wage levels and shift structures. Instabilities which may proceed from them include provider closures, the reduction of working hours on flexible contracts and redundancies. Temporary, commission-only, zero-hour and minimum wage contracts, and unsociable working hours are found to be important drivers of disengagement and NEET 'churn'. A lack of experience and low qualifications are particular barriers to employment, but young people can circumvent these through opportunities derived from personal relationships, or by volunteering.

The 'softer' influences of structure are not necessarily less powerful, but are different in kind to the 'hard' influences. Rather than setting the conditions in which agency must be exercised, they influence the manner in which it is exercised. They are mediated through two key mechanisms: discursive interactions and agentic modelling. Discursive interactions are the instances of conversational and communicative relations that young people have or experience within their environment. These interactions are predominantly personal in nature and may be with parents and other relatives, teachers and other learning professionals, mentors, employers, friends and peers, civil servants and persons within the community, and even be directed towards Deity. They can also include less personal communications such as are delivered through popular media. The totality of the discursive interactions taking place within the life of the young person is termed the 'discursive environment'. Discursive interactions are closely associated with motivational states and dispositions, and the refinement of agentic activity at a feature-specific level.

Agentic modelling denotes the influence on young people's agency that comes through observing the interactions of others with their environments, and the resulting outcomes. Young people may adopt and adapt thoughts and behaviours from agentic models for their own use. Models were generally found to be more influential where there was positive emotional regard between the young person and model, proximity in terms of age and culture, an affinity to the (past or present) circumstances of the model and aspiration to achieve similar outcomes to the model.

The influences of agentic modelling and the discursive environment are catalytic to one another, as young people were more likely to respond to the discursive influences of effective models, and discursive interactions could lead towards a particular individual becoming an effective model. These 'softer' influences can be deliberately harnessed, for example, by skilled mentors, to steer and shape the development and exercise of personal agency. Some elements of the NEET topography (e.g. parents and families, and employers) definitively have both 'hard' and 'softer' influences on the function of personal agency, whereas others are predominantly associated with one or the other (e.g. mentors are predominantly associated with softer influences and government with hard influences).

Despite circumstances that could provide powerful excuses to the contrary, the young people interviewed overwhelmingly tended to regard the EET/NEET outcomes of both themselves and other young people as one ultimately determined by their own agency. Whether young people meaningfully realized this agentic potential was associated with a number of factors including their ability to act confidently and independently, and as is developed in the next chapter, the perceived prospects associated with their actions, and their positioning within perceptual zones of optimal pressure.

6

Secret Agency: The Four Core Features of Personal Agency within the NEET 'Black Box'

This chapter builds on the findings offered in Chapter 5 relating to young people's perceptions of the various elements of the NEET topography in determining their outcomes. It develops the findings on the exercise of each of the four 'core features' of agency (intentionality, forethought, self-reactiveness and self-reflectiveness) by young people in their pursuit or otherwise of EET outcomes. Young people's exercise of each of the four 'core features' of personal agency in the pursuit or otherwise of EET outcomes was found to be complex. For each feature a number of key variables are found useful for describing the way in which it was differently exercised by individual participants, and each has a number of interesting associations to the structural environment, to other features and to the determination of EET outcomes. There is a clear continuation of the themes developed in the previous chapter. Particularly prominent themes in this regard include the evidence of persistent and habitual patterns of agency, the shaping of these patterns throughout the life course and the role of the discursive environment in producing them. Further themes are developed including: the eminence of intentionality, the importance of perceived prospects, and zones of optimal pressure. The idea that features of agency are meaningfully influenced by others is termed intra-agency. This is developed along with the sub-concepts of intra-agentic facilitation, compensation, suppression and undermining, and the related idea of intra-agentic quorums.

Intentionality

Intentionality was found to be powerfully involved in the determination of EET outcomes. There were three key variables in the way it was exercised. These were its level of definition, level of strength (ability to effect change) and level of persistence. Intentionality did not have to be well defined to be strong. It could be as vaguely defined as the intent to 'do something' as one interviewee put it, without losing its power to determine the young person's EET status. In one instance Anthony attributed his breaking away from groups of local disengaged young people, some of whom were criminal, as being simply to do with 'having a goal'. He referred often to this ultimate but rather vague 'goal' of becoming a rich and successful businessman, and how important it was. He was forthright in his view that the detail of the goal did not matter for now as long as it inspired the right action in the present. Right now, it meant returning to college. Several young people had arrived at such undefined yet efficacious EET intentions at one point or another. This was sometimes already the case at the point of leaving school, and at other times the product of initial plans not working out. The former was true for Darren who ended up enrolling on a college engineering course after school because his 'next step was – if I wasn't interested in anything else – was that'. The latter was true for Brian who enrolled on a hospitality course after 'churning' for over two years and finding himself with nothing to do. By then 'it was just basically anything that comes'.

Intentionality could however be very clearly defined, and survive disengagement. Fiona was clearly intent on a career in Heathrow airport, and could demonstrate how this had driven her EET decisions over several years, and past a number of challenges and periods of being NEET. Neil felt all young people should set themselves a 'five-year plan' as he had. Intentionality could become defined at any point. For some it had developed throughout the life course as a result of experiences within the family and school environments. For others it was during a period of being NEET or when they were going through 'churn'. Caroline had clear intentions to study childcare on leaving school, which she did. These were linked to a personal assessment of the qualities and skills she felt she had developed at home. She explained:

> I'm one of eight. Where I'm second oldest I've been around kids since I was born, and I do find it quite easy to handle kids.

Jeanne offered a very similar story. Darren found that a lack of clear intentions became more problematic over time and said:

> I guess it's nice having choice, but when you don't know what you want to do with the rest of your life, it's pretty bad ... do I want to play video games until I'm 80? Do I want to skate until I'm 80?

This showed that for Darren, like many of the interviewees, a sense of discomfort and pressure came with an absence of clear intentions.

Negative experiences could disrupt intentions. Where Caroline's intentions ultimately changed after a negative experience with a childcare employer, Jeanne's survived. It appeared that it could take some time for intentions to be reoriented after such experiences, and whether the original intentions persisted was dependent on how young people evaluated alternatives. After leaving her childcare placement, Caroline became NEET for two months and 'was feeling quite lost'. She eventually settled on different intentions. Jeanne briefly tried studying hair and beauty before bouncing back to her original intentions. In another case Gina, who had always wanted to work in hair and beauty, found herself employed with a professional salon soon after leaving school. This was an ideal position for her. As she explained:

> I was just so happy ... that I was working, and I could be in a salon, and [had the hope that] one day I could be a successful stylist there and earn loads of money.

However, a negative experience put her off it for some time. Her managers found fault with her work, and she was eventually fired. She became angry and apathetic. She recounted how

> I got really offended, because [of] all the time I worked there by myself. The December I had to work by myself ... cleaning up by myself ... I had to ... lock up that week, cashing up ... carrying about ten grand's worth of cash to Earl's Court. Yeah I just had to do stupid stuff, and then ... if they want to sack me, then sack me ... I don't really ... I don't really give a fuck.

She developed a negative view of her once ideal profession:

> That made me ... think I don't want ... a job doing hairdressing anymore ... I thought all hairdressers are going to be like that.

She became NEET and turned her intentions towards the hospitality and catering industry. However, after a stint there, she went full circle, and on the week of interview had just returned to working as a hairdresser. In the long run her original intentions prevailed. Interestingly, positive experiences could also help produce new intentions. Brian unexpectedly found himself enjoying a catering course, and had since taken several steps to pursue a living in that field.

Where even undefined intentionality could be efficacious, a loss of intentionality appeared to inhibit the exercise of agency towards EET altogether, and was disastrous for EET prospects. When Elaine was refused entrance to the second year of college due to poor attendance, she unsuccessfully canvassed other colleges. Her hopes of getting to university ground to a halt, and after failing to get a job or apprenticeship, she practically forsook her intentions and became long-term NEET. She said, 'I just gave up … I literally did nothing for a year … literally nothing.' Her thinking became utterly despondent. 'I ain't going to get nothing. Do nothing. That basically is what it was.' This case was one of many that illustrated that intentionality is mediated by perceived prospects. Jeanne indicated this in her discussion of NEET males selling drugs in Hackney, attributing their behaviour to not having any greater vision for their lives. She said:

> I feel like they're only doing it because they feel like they can't do nothing else. They [feel they] can't get any jobs … because they haven't been in school.

The ability to perceive meaningful prospects in given circumstances varied by young person. Kevin, who considered himself 'lucky', was inclined to perceive prospects more easily than others, and needed minimal persuasion to pursue them. Discussing EET opportunities, he said, 'Even if I had a one per cent chance I still counted it as a possibility.' This translated into his making persistent efforts to enter EET despite not finding success for over two years.

Many interviewees evidenced underlying patterns or 'principles' of intentionality that ordered their EET decisions, and often their wider lives. These had typically developed throughout the life course and their shaping often had little direct relation to EET. For Brian the principle was to do whatever seemed easiest, or otherwise follow the path of least resistance. He enrolled onto an IT college course 'because it was … easy looking'. He said he would even have quit the hospitality and catering course that had led to his current job if he felt he had the choice. He said however that the Job Centre had threatened to 'stop my money' if he did not attend.

Caroline, when asked about her future intentions, said, 'Probably to prove a lot of people wrong and … do what I want to do.' This was consistent with the pattern of asserting independence and disabusing expectations that underpinned not only her EET decisions, but those relating to her personal and family life. Like Brian's pattern, hers was rooted in experiences of being bullied. The core intention of proving others wrong was also a key theme for Megan, and it seemed her EET choices were sometimes more a tool to this end than anything else. Hannah reckoned negative discursive interactions in her home had hindered her development of clear intentions. Lisa felt similarly about discursive interactions in the school environment, and at the same time invoked the idea of the prioritization of intentions. She recalled how she had not wanted to achieve anything at school. All she had wanted was relational support to cope with her emotional difficulties. She said:

> I needed the support more than the qualifications. And nobody was there to support me. I just needed someone to speak to really, and it took them [until] I was in Year 11 to realize that.

She left school without any plans. She eventually developed her intentions while 'churning' in and out of NEET at least ten times, and five years after leaving school had three defined career objectives that she was consciously working towards.

Intentions unrelated to EET could nonetheless have impacts on EET, as indicated by Bandura's (2001: 6) discussion of the 'unintended consequences' of intentionality and the perceived inseparability of EET from the young person's wider life. The most common examples of this involved intentionality in the use of drugs and alcohol. Lisa was committed to a college hospitality and catering course, but on a drunken night out met with an accident falling 'off a podium'. She turned up to the course kitchen on crutches, and because she could not stand was 'kicked … off'. This began her eighteen-month absence from EET of which time she said, 'I just sat on my arse and did fuck all.' Megan attributed being fired on one occasion to a late-night drinking session the day before. After two months of being NEET, she had got her first job in a shoe shop. Her drinking habits, however, got her into trouble when she had been doing

> a three-day bender with my friends … I got in at half four in the morning … 6 in the morning I had to get up for work, have a shower, all that bullshit and [I] … went to work … I walked in staggering.

She recalled laughing at the manager questioning her about her apparent condition, and then getting into an argument with a customer. She was fired the same morning. This incident had future repercussions. Although was good at getting interviews, explaining 'I have the grades to back myself up … I don't get nervous', the next three jobs she was considered for all went back to the shoe shop for a reference and refused to offer her a post. She reflected on those days, exclaiming, 'Before I wasn't ready for jobs. I'm not going to lie to you, I wasn't ready. But now I'm ready.' Not being ready meant a habit of staying up late and drinking with friends. Several other young people reported usage of drugs and alcohol which impacted in generally less dramatic, if still notable ways on their EET.

The exercise of intentionality was found to be powerfully involved in the determination of EET outcomes. It was found to vary in its levels of definition, strength and persistence. Relatively undefined intentionality could still be highly efficacious, whereas a loss of intentionality altogether could inhibit the overall exercise of agency, and was highly detrimental to EET prospects. Intentions could be disrupted by negative experiences, and young people may take some time to reorient in such situations. Whether intentions persisted after such experiences depended on how young people evaluated alternatives. It has already been seen that unexpected positive experiences can stimulate new intentions. The exercise of intentionality towards EET may be moderated by perceived prospects, and a perceived lack of prospects may be associated with apathy and perhaps even antisocial or criminal behaviours. Patterns of intentionality which underlay EET decisions were often found to have been shaped throughout the life course, and discursive interactions in the home and school environment were strongly implicated in their development. Intentions unrelated to EET could nonetheless have serious and unexpected impacts on EET outcomes.

Forethought

The key variables in the exercise of forethought included to what extent it was engaged, how effectively it was pursued and the length of time over which it was projected. The extent to which forethought was engaged by interviewees had interesting associations with intentionality variables, most particularly the level of definition. Fiona and Neil demonstrated the most defined intentionality of all interviewees, and also the most extensive uses of forethought. Fiona had been specifically set on working in Heathrow for several years, and articulated in quite some detail what this involved, and how she had and would work towards it. This included a relatively detailed understanding of her intended future job, what her prospective employer was looking for, how she was preparing to meet the standards and how she expected to feel on achieving her goal. Her present plans revolved around building a five-year employment history in order to pass the necessary security checks.

Neil not only had clear plans, but often referred to his 'backup plan' and at one point his 'second backup plan'. He had intended to study business upon leaving school and had done so, but had also been ready to take up English if he did not get the grades for business. Even his choice of business course was steeped in forethought. He reasoned:

> If I did my diploma that's worth three A-Levels, I had more chance of going to university then people that had the National Certificate, even if they get a double Distinction, which is like two As. I'd have an extra one.

This calculated, contingency-driven approach was characteristic of Neil's overall exercise of agency. In contrast, Brian's EET intentions at one point were to find 'anything', and he took a chance at a job when 'a mate put it on Facebook'. He applied and was successful. He said, however, 'I didn't know what it was for until I started … then they took me out and told me to go knock on the doors.' When asked why he accepted it without first knowing what it was, he replied, 'I didn't ask. I was just going with it because it's a job.' He had been told that 'you get a lot of money for it, and its £50 for everything you sell'. He found out he was a door-to-door salesman selling home improvements on a commission-only basis. After a day's induction, and a single day of trying to make his first sale he 'just never turned up again'. After being asked whether he had a plan after quitting the job, he responded, 'No, I didn't know what I was doing.' His undefined intentions were accompanied by almost negligible forethought.

Sometimes forethought was ineffectively pursued. Brian, in another case, chose an IT course immediately after leaving school, conceiving of it as involving tasks not unlike his everyday use of computers, such as surfing the Internet. He found within 'a couple of weeks' that it was too difficult and went in search of an easier course. Darren chose an electrical engineering course after leaving Year 11, based on a positive work experience placement in a train depot. He had not evaluated the level of maths required to do well on the course, however. Having only achieved an F in his GCSE maths, he dropped out after four months and became NEET. Sometimes forethought was pursued more earnestly, but still yielded problematically inaccurate expectations. Caroline found through her placement in a school nursery that childcare was 'not how I thought it was going to be. I thought it was going to be easy. I genuinely thought'. She had little difficulty in engaging with the children, as per her assumed strength, but found the administrative side of the job overwhelming. She had not expected to encounter such onerous paperwork and decried the profession for focusing on monitoring regimes more than the child's enjoyment and nurture. She eventually dropped out due to severe stress and became NEET.

Whereas Neil advocated long-term forethought, other young people advocated a much more limited projection, and others, like Ishmael (whose account is discussed further on), preferred to defer it indefinitely. Caroline discussed this in detail, feeling that applying forethought to the day ahead was progressive, but projecting too much farther was potentially destructive. She said:

> Basically I'm taking every day at a time. I don't want to think ahead too far so I don't start stressing about things that are not even there. I've got my birthday to look forward to [on Saturday], and past that I'm going to the Job Centre to say to them 'look I'm 18 now' [on] Monday. I'm on the ball, planning it out every day what I'm doing.

She found thinking through potential future scenarios largely pointless. She would think up to the point to which she had total control, and stop once it involved what others might do. She felt, at that point, reacting to situations as they happened was a better approach. This could be

> very difficult, because you don't know what the cards are going to be … But it can be quite easy at times, because if you know how you want your day to go, just [decide] how you want it to go.

Caroline was thus found to be exercising a form of intra-agency in which she intentionally limited her forethought, and used self-reactiveness and intentionality to compensate for it. These behaviours might be termed intra-agentic suppression and compensation respectively.

Kevin was another who deliberately used intentionality to compensate for forethought. Opportunism and strength of determination were his tools of choice for finding success in EET. He explained:

> I don't really like to plan for the future … When I get [a chance at] something I just want to stick to it no matter what. Even the devil himself, let him come out, chat shit. Fuck him, I'm going to … work hard. I'm not going to put it to waste.

He preferred to pursue opportunities without too much deliberation, and see where they led. He had always done things this way, and recounted how he had got his first job. He would hang around in his local games store, and claimed:

> One day I thought I'm just going to say … for the fun of it, give me a job, so I did … and the guy said okay, go home get your coat, you're starting today. And I was like 'what?' Yeah I was a lucky fuck, I'm telling you man.

He considered his current apprenticeship to have come through much the same use of agency.

Patterns in the exercise of forethought were often found to be associated with dynamics in the home environment. High levels of parental dependency and low levels of parental pressure typically corresponded to a lesser exercise of forethought. Darren enjoyed such an arrangement, and would go in and out of EET without too much forethought, knowing he had his parents to fall back on. He once joined a course on the basis of their encouragement, without thinking much about what it entailed, saying to them, 'Sure, I'll give it a go and if I don't like it I'll drop out.' He dropped out after a few months without any particular plan in mind. Ishmael exhibited a high level of parental dependency in a partly collective agency, partly proxy agency arrangement with his mother; Ishmael's first college was picked jointly with his mum, and his second had been her choice alone. He had turned up at his first college without having given any thought to what subjects he would do. He was advised by a college adviser and took the advice he was given. He had done similarly with his current training provider. He explained he did not like to think too far ahead. His next step after finishing his current course was 'something I don't think about'. He continued:

> It's just that . . . if I think about going ahead . . . about the future, what if I don't get there? If I plan it now and don't end up there, then obviously there was no point planning it. So whatever happens, I'll plan it after that.

He concluded about planning, 'It doesn't really matter to me, I'm not into it'. This was consistent with the rest of his account.

Instead of benefiting from low pressure home environments however, many young people found themselves under unprecedented levels of personal pressure upon leaving school, not only within the home but within EET also, when parental and broader societal expectations of them flexed suddenly. This higher pressure could have motivational effects that stimulated the exercise of forethought, but excessive pressure could cripple it. Some young people even disengaged from EET in order to alleviate sufficient pressure for them to exercise it. Caroline remarked about leaving her childcare course:

> I was basically just trying to get myself away from it [so] I can get a clear head and think 'right what am I doing next?'

Certain features of agency, therefore, may be in their most engaged state in a zone of optimal pressure, where the sense of pressure perceived by the young person is neither too low, nor excessive.

A number of further thematic ideas might be developed from Caroline's case and the others discussed. Caroline's choice to leave her course was an intentional act to avail herself of her capacity for forethought. This was not only consistent with the earlier observation that young people have a limited capacity for agency at any given time, but also further evidence of how one feature of agency might be used to facilitate another. This type of intra-agentic activity might be termed 'facilitation'. Also, the observation that young people may, whether intentionally or ignorantly, not exercise forethought indicates that agency may be exercised without all four of its features necessarily being evident. It may be exercised with only a subset of features active, these constituting an intra-agentic quorum. All four features being exercised together is thus an ideal, not always reflected in reality, assumed in and from Bandura's (2001) model of agency. In the example above, Caroline's quorum consisted of intentionality and self-reactiveness, seen in the data to be the minimal quorum.

It is also observed throughout the findings that intentionality typically directs intra-agency, making the other features its subject. This, together with the earlier-developed idea that intentionality regulates the overall exercise of agency towards EET, may be captured in a suggestion that intentionality is eminent among the features. Finally, it is evident from the cases above that the exercise of forethought is often associated with the coping mechanisms of the young person. This has mostly been associated with the extent of use; some had learnt to cope better by limiting forethought, others by increasing it. There was evidence that it ought to also be associated with the manner of use; some young people deliberately manipulated their forethought as a way to cope with the potential for disappointment. Fiona said:

> I … don't get my hopes up. If I'm going to an interview, I just think I might not get the job, so if I don't … I won't be sad about it, I'll just move on.

Fiona's 'might' indicates that forethought had to be carefully balanced with optimism if it were not to become depressive.

Key variables in the exercise of forethought included to what extent it was engaged, how effectively it was pursued and the length of time over which it was projected. The extent of its use was associated with levels of definition of intentionality, where higher definition corresponded to higher use. Where forethought was ineffectively pursued young people could develop inaccurate expectations of their EET choices, and this could be a contributing factor to disengagement. Forethought could be projected over the long-term, restrictively over the short-term or indefinitely deferred. The fact that forethought was ignored by some young people indicates that subsets of the features of agency, or intra-agentic quorums, are sufficient to enable agentic expression. Patterns of forethought were linked to patterns of dependency and pressure in the home and other environments, and high parental dependency was associated with lesser use of forethought. Whereas high pressure circumstances could stimulate forethought, excessive pressure or stress could disable it, and so it appears to be in its most engaged state in a zone of optimal pressure. Intentionality was exercised in various ways to affect forethought, including disengaging from EET to facilitate it, manipulating it to moderate expectations and suppressing and compensating for it through other features of agency. This is associated with an idea that intentionality is eminent among the features.

Self-reactiveness

Participants displayed unique patterns of self-reactiveness to a number of key types of events including crisis, ejection from EET, risk of failure, stress and opportunity. Key variables included the cues that would trigger self-reactive behaviours, tendencies towards the use of 'fight' or 'fold' reactions and the underlying tensions and specific coping behaviours they were associated with. Elaine's account of her EET history is useful for examining several of these ideas.

Elaine had a recurring pattern of poorly managing her EET, which would eventually give way to crisis moments. This pattern was already evident in her later school years, and immediately impacted on her post-school EET when low attendance figures resulted in her being refused entrance to her school's sixth form. She had to react quickly to find a college place, and managed to do so. She provided a contradictory account of the experience, expressing both surprise and a lack of surprise at not being allowed entrance. She first indicated surprise, saying:

> Shit. Literally, that was my reaction, like what am I doing to do? It was late by the time they told me … nearly September … I was like 'oh my god'.

She then went on to say that 'it was more of an expectation. My attendance was low … and I could have improved it but I didn't. I chose not to'. As her account progressed this apparent contradiction unfolded. Elaine would be somewhat conscious of the risks she was incurring in a given situation, but would not self-react until prompted by a cue in the discursive environment, typically an ultimatum of some kind. Her self-reactive tendency was then to 'fight' the risks through improved effort and self-management.

This was true for the example above, and others. She fell into low attendance again in her new college, saying:

> I'd just bunk off a lesson. Stay at home ... do nothing ... as soon as they'd tell me it's your last warning, I'd go back in, do what I had to do, finish all the coursework. I caught it all up!

Despite this, and achieving good grades, she was refused entrance to the second year of college, again for poor attendance. She attempted once again to cast around quickly for a new college, but this time was unsuccessful. Four months later she realized her tried and trusted pattern of self-reactiveness had not worked for her, and she finally 'folded'. Despondent, she ended up NEET for nearly fourteen months.

When Elaine eventually obtained a full-time job in a pub, she demonstrated considerable self-management to adapt quickly to its demands, as was typical for her when under pressure in EET. She explained, 'Obviously you have to get out of habits of staying up late ... You have to get into a routine and realize that shit is real.' After a few months, however, due to the low hourly pay rates, difficult shifts and a sense of low prospects, she became highly stressed. She called in sick for several weeks due to depression. When asked about what was depressing her, she said:

> Reality, completely and utterly ... It just felt like I weren't going to get nowhere through what I was doing. I want to ... make myself better, not stay in a dead end job.

Elaine's comments demonstrate that the exercise of self-reactiveness, like forethought, is associated with a zone of optimal pressure, and perceived prospects. When Elaine experienced her environment as one of low pressure, as in her days of low attendance, she would become lax. When the pressure became too high she disengaged, as Caroline was seen to have done earlier. In between the two she demonstrated responsibility, determination and heightened self-management.

Elaine's extended absence from work eventually resulted in her 'forfeiting' the job as she described it; although there was no formal interaction with her employer to this effect, they no longer made contact. Sometime later, she felt better and thought she had found work at another pub after doing a work trial and completing a P46. To her surprise, however, a few days later she 'literally woke up to a voicemail' from her new supposed employer saying, 'We're not employing you anymore ... we don't want you back.' Her self-reaction was to look quickly for an alternative, just as she had twice done with college. She called her previous employer again. It did not go well. Elaine explained, 'I tried being clever and he basically just told me to fuck off.' Elaine was still NEET three months later.

Like Elaine, Caroline reacted to excessive stress with disengagement. A couple of months into a work experience placement at a school, linked to her course in childcare, she developed symptoms of chest infections. It is unclear whether these were related directly to the stress, but she felt this may have been the case. She was certainly under intense mental pressure, and this was bringing out aspects of her character that she didn't like. She explained:

> I was thinking I ain't going to be able to handle a whole year of this … I did try and stick it out, but I couldn't. I was basically digging myself a hole … the stress … was bringing me down. I didn't want to be around anyone … I weren't myself. I was a completely different person … I didn't want it turning me into anyone vicious, because that's how it was seen.

Caroline attended her GP and was prescribed anti-depressants. Eventually she decided to cut her ties with the childcare course and the school. She said:

> I went straight to college and said look 'I ain't coming back tomorrow, I've only come to get my folder and stuff, and I'm off.' [My tutor] said, 'You're going to tell the school', and I said, 'no it's your job to tell them that, I've left college now, it's not my business', and walked off.

She didn't go back to the course, and gave up on professional childcare altogether.

Hannah's account underlined the patterned nature of self-reactiveness. Her pattern included panicking – or 'freaking out' as she described it – and then 'folding', typically at the last hurdle of an EET endeavour. After her GCSEs she had gone to live with her friend and enrolled on an entry level childcare course. She attended all her lessons but fell behind on her work. She said, 'When it came to the end of the year, to hand in all my units, I just freaked out and just avoided it basically.' She failed to complete and the next year went on to do a beauty therapy course. She did fine in the classroom, but when the doors opened for real-life clients towards the end of the year, she became very nervous and once again 'freaked out'. She decided to drop out and look for work.

Like Elaine, Orlando was refused entrance to his sixth form, but on the basis of poor grades. He had also had a sense that things might not go well, but still felt surprised when he saw his GCSE results were worse than anticipated. The results came with a letter saying he had not got into the sixth form. His surprise was like Elaine's, but not his self-reaction. He 'folded' straight away. Sixth form had been his only plan. He sat at home 'doing nothing' for the better part of a year.

He said, 'I was just waiting for something to happen. But I wasn't doing anything … I didn't realize how hard it was to get a job.' The tendency to fight or fold reactively in roughly similar circumstances was therein seen to vary by young person, and appeared to be mediated by their perceived prospects of resolving the issue at hand. In another comparison – of which many could be made from the data – when Brian noticed he was getting behind on a course, he stayed late after college for a number of weeks to catch up before eventually moving to 'an easier course' when his efforts did not pay off. Darren folded ahead of the effort in similar circumstances, explaining simply, 'I thought I was going to fail the course so I dropped out.' He went to look for work instead.

Patterns of self-reactive behaviours were shown often to be the result of underlying personal tensions, and when a young person was able to go through catharsis, these patterns could change noticeably. Jeanne had recurrent anger issues. After going through two secondary schools she was sent to a boxing academy to deal with her temperament. It helped. She explained, 'I went … for a year. And that actually made me better … it just made all my anger go.' She was far more capable of handling stressful situations without becoming angry. She considered this a change for the better, but not a panacea. She was still experiencing ongoing stress, and was using a combination of prayer, tears and drugs and alcohol to manage it. Her drug use resulted in her been thrown out of college after it had been spotted by tutors. Her improved anger management showed when she was told she could not come back; she reacted calmly, but was nonetheless emotionally distressed. She explained:

> Physically, you can't see my emotions … it's all inside … I … look like I don't care … But inside it burns. When I got kicked out I was like 'oh my God, why do I keep on messing my life up?' Why do I keep on going the wrong way and not making my life better – just for me and my family, for them to be proud?

Grief, rather than anger, was characteristic of her new temperament.

Kevin used dancing as a method of ongoing catharsis in his pursuit of EET. After returning from Poland he had initially thought job searching would be easy, but after one, and then two years without success, frustration had set in. He became more and more obsessed with little details he thought might be costing him his breakthrough. He started practicing for interviews in the mirror, using YouTube videos to get tips. He explained what was going through his mind, saying:

> When you sit in an interview, your hands got to be on your lap because you're going to be shaking your hands. You don't want your hands to get sweaty, you

> don't want to be getting the shakes. You know, you don't want to give a guy a handshake with your sweaty hands. It is these little things ... these little bits just add up on top ... until it gets to the part where you blow, you're like ... fuck this.

Dance helped him to cope. He explained:

> It ... gave me a chance to ... get rid of that ... stress, that anger that was making me think differently. And when I was ... rid of that anger ... that's when I was able to think ... okay, I can try again.

Kevin kept trying and eventually entered training after forty months of being NEET.

Hannah's catharsis came when she finally had her own accommodation. While she had been living with others she felt she had little control over her life. Moving in on her own had helped her to feel more in control. It took a while however for her to adjust to self-responsibility. She recalled, 'When I first moved into my hostel I was really wild ... I was forever out on the weekends.' This time of 'wild' living was her cathartic period. She explained:

> I think it was good that I had that ... because now I'm focused. I got everything out my system ... now I'm in control, because I've got my limits and my boundaries.

For the first time since leaving school, she felt settled and able to give herself fully to EET. She had recently returned to study and said, 'So now I'm in this place ... and I'm focused now.' She had been back in EET for just three weeks at the time of interview.

Similar ideas were present throughout the rest of the data. As in Elaine's account, self-reactive patterns were often associated with self-management behaviours, and the ability to sustain EET. Self-reactive 'folding' behaviours, driven by stress (as in Elaine's case), an inclination to panic or become angry (like Hannah or Jeanne respectively) or otherwise by shyness, laziness, irresponsibility, low self-efficacy or peer pressure (as per other cases in the data) were often implicated in disengagement. As with Hannah, the gaining and exercising of effective self-management skills through the change of self-reactive behaviours was often a key turning point towards EET stability.

Participants displayed unique patterns of self-reactiveness towards events involving crisis, ejection from EET, risk of failure, stress and opportunity. These patterns varied in respect to the cues that would trigger self-reactive behaviours, tendencies towards the use of 'fight' or 'fold' reactions, and the underlying tensions and coping mechanisms associated with them. The exercise of self-reactiveness, as with forethought, appeared to be associated with a zone of optimal pressure, and perceived prospects. Self-reactive behaviours were seen to be an important component of self-management and the ability to sustain NEET, and self-reactive 'folding' behaviours were often implicated in disengagement. Self-reactive behaviours associated with underlying personal tensions could be modified by cathartic experiences.

Self-reflectiveness

The key variable in the exercise of self-reflectiveness was the extent to which it was engaged. Self-reflectiveness, like forethought, was a feature of agency that young people could intentionally opt out of. When this occurred, it was again typically reflective of a coping mechanism. There were several instances of such intra-agentic suppression. While Kevin was in Poland, he focused on 'having fun' with his cousins, and avoided reflecting on his circumstances, wanting to avoid depression. He explained, 'I knew that if I was going to think about shit too much then I would end up fucked up in the head, depressed.' Gina conveyed similar ideas, saying, 'If I spend a lot of time thinking of what went wrong, then obviously it's going to get me down.' Avoiding depression or the like however was not the only reason for opting out of self-reflection. Pam, in another case of conscious intra-agentic compensation, saw self-reflection as somewhat redundant given the amount of forethought she exercised. She explained, 'I don't spend a lot of time [reflecting], because … I've already thought about it before[hand].' This was somewhat justified; Pam evidenced more use of forethought than the vast majority of participants.

Self-reflection could indeed cross into depression. Elaine described how she became depressed as a pub assistant. The more she thought about her role, the more she perceived she was stuck at a dead end. She explained:

> I wanted a job … but not that job … In a pub you can climb ladders to get to management … but it's not even worth it because pay is shit. I don't want to be stuck in Brentford, in a flat, with a baby, like most of my friends will be. I want to be rich, and do something with my life. But that weren't happening.

This fed a growing sense of stress which ended with her quitting. Another bout of self-reflection came soon after, and was perhaps her biggest turning point. She said it came 'when I was signing on. That really got to me. [Having] to stand outside the Job Centre … it's like "shit, where am I now?"' She went into a deep and quite regretful reflection that caused her to look differently at her past behaviour, and resolve to make more of her opportunities. However, self-reflection was not always depressive. The fact that Caroline felt she had made some good decisions helped her to cope with difficult repercussions that had come her way. She said, 'I don't feel down about it … I've done a good thing … so I'm not bothered by it whatsoever.' A shrug of the shoulders emphasized her point.

As suggested by Elaine's story, periods of disengagement could be key times of self-reflective activity. These were often associated with the chance to make significant changes in intentions and freely exercise forethought. Anthony spoke about his year of disengagement in such terms saying, 'During that time I had a lot of thinking in my head.' He assessed his sense of identity, the dependencies in his life and how comfortable he was with them. He determined he was to become a successful person despite his setbacks and that this required independence, particularly from NEET peers. This was an important turning point for him. Sometimes young people even valued disengagement for these reasons. Lisa talked about her time as a 'long-term' NEET saying:

> I just wanted some space … to gather my thoughts, and actually think about what I wanted to do in life. I took a year and a half out and thought … then I went back to college to get the stuff that I needed to do it.

Many of the interviewees indicated similarly how time spent in NEET while 'churning' had helped them to know what they really wanted to do with their lives, as they reflected on their latest and previous experiences.

Just as young people could opt out of self-reflection, they could opt in again. Kevin opted back in when he felt it would lead to progress instead of depression. He recalled that when his family returned to the UK, he had reflected on his past experiences to identify strengths that could help him into EET. He said:

> When we got back here, that's when I really started thinking 'I've got the experience … I got my prior knowledge … Let's see what I can do with it.'

He also identified his ability to build positive relationships as a strength. He went about building relationships and evaluating (i.e. reflecting on) the opportunities they afforded him. He explained:

> I started getting back in contact with people. That's when things became easier … clearer. Okay I can do this. Okay I can't really do that. So it became easier for me to make decisions.

Self-reflection had also enabled him to consider the way in which he exercised agency, and the outcomes it had wrought for him. He reflected particularly on the strength of his intentionality, saying:

> You know, going back all those five years … I can … see that I've actually … made nothing into something … There were a few moments where I was like fuck everything, but grabbing a reason that's just big enough for you, some sort of reason that God Himself can't fucking move you from … get that reason and just stick to that.

He felt his eventual outcomes had justified his approach.

It was interesting that Kevin did not consider himself to spend a lot of time in self-reflection, despite clear evidence of periods where he did. This perception appeared to come from his intentional habit of drawing a line on self-reflection when it risked crossing into depressive thinking. He remarked during his completion of the survey:

> The key word there is a lot of time. I won't spend a lot of time thinking about why things happen. They happen, you got to move on, fuck it. That's the way I think.

As well as catalysing major change in the exercise of personal agency, self-reflectiveness could also be used to enable incremental improvements. Patterns of self-reflectiveness developed in other areas of life could also be transferred and applied to EET. Kevin likened job searching to body-popping, a dance discipline he practiced regularly. He explained that as a dancer, he had become better over the years through a process of improving one day at a time, to the point that he was now a confident and popular performer. He would tell himself job searching was the same; if he could make improvements each time he attended an interview, eventually he would get a job:

> It might sound dodgy, but what I was doing with body-popping, it actually influenced … the way I was thinking. It changed me … I learnt that I can do what I want to do, as long as I put my head into it.

Neil also used self-reflectiveness this way. He spoke of a time where after a few months of diligently applying for jobs at the rate of four applications a day, he had got himself ten interviews but without yet obtaining a job. He would reflect on his interviews however and try to improve himself for the next. He eventually secured a job.

However, self-reflectiveness did not always lead to behaviours that might normatively be considered improvements. In a rather dramatic episode that led to a change in Hannah's accommodation circumstances, some questionable lessons she had learnt through self-reflectiveness surfaced in a moment of desperation. After her initial violent experience of living with her sister, she had found it very difficult to obtain a place to live from the local authority, and had eventually moved back again to her sister's home. She had a similar second experience. However, physical signs of the violence changed the way that her case was handled by the local authority:

> Every day I had to go into the housing [office] and talk to someone, but I felt like I wasn't getting anywhere, until they saw the bruises on me that my sister did to me. [Then] they got me a social worker.

This didn't get Hannah a home, but she had learnt to use crisis as a trigger point for support from government services. This led her to what was ostensibly an act of petty crime, but was in fact a somewhat sophisticated, if desperate, attempt to circumvent the constraints she felt she was up against. She explained:

> In order to get my own place, I had to, to be honest with you … [steal] something from Primark … I got halfway up Mare Street … The security [guard] was trying to stop me from going, and I could have went, but because I knew I was homeless, I [said] no, call the police … I don't care … It's this serious. So they called the police.

Hannah claimed to have come up with the plan while standing in Primark shortly after having another fight with her sister. She had no intentions of returning to her sister's home:

> It was more or less in the moment, when I was in Primark. I was thinking, after I come from Primark, where am I going to go? I'm literally homeless, and it was raining as well, pouring rain, and me and my sister had our little fight, argument, what not.

After explaining her predicament to the police, they arranged for her to have temporary accommodation in a bed and breakfast for a few days, and she was then fast-tracked into a hostel. Her plan had, for all her intents and purposes, been successful. This was despite its ostensible criminality, and despite the fact that Hannah seemed not to think of herself, or the incident, on authentically criminal terms. This reflects some of what are perhaps the more controversial ways in which young people's agency may be shaped by their environments, and lessons that they may learn as they attempt to navigate through difficult situations.

Orlando presented a somewhat different and very interesting case. He saw himself as a habitually reflective person. He explained:

> I think about a lot of things in life. I have since I was little. When I was in bed, or in the bath … That's what I do when I'm at home … I don't really watch TV. I spend a lot of time … just thinking about past, future and present.

What was particularly interesting was the outcome of his reflection. Orlando had come to disagree in principle with a labour market system where people worked for their whole lives 'complaining about their jobs', and then died. He had in effect, reflected his way out of any strong intentions towards EET. This was an intra-agentic undermining of intentionality through self-reflectiveness. He instead dreamt of an agrarian life where commodities could be bartered. He said:

> If I could, I would … want to move … somewhere like some nice island in the Caribbean. Like build a house, have like a little farm … fruits, vegetables … yeah, chickens, goats … And I'd learn fishing … I'd just live there with my future wife and all that.

He chided the education system for taking children away from their parents for too much time, and waxed melancholy about the gapless procession from primary school to 'secondary school … then college … university … then … working' suggesting it denied people time to 'just live'. He felt other young people needed to reflect more on their intentions:

> I think … they need to really look from a clear point of view … I know a lot of people don't really think deeply like about their life … but … they need to ask themselves … do I want to do this for the right reasons? What are the effects of me actually doing that? Will I be happy?

This modification of intentions through self-reflection was also indicated in Elaine's account of losing her intentionality towards EET, and her later recovery of it. Several further such cases could be highlighted. Although intentionality may be eminent among the features, self-reflectiveness then is the key feature that enables for its development and reconstruction.

Like forethought, self-reflectiveness could intentionally be opted in and out of. It appeared particularly susceptible to intra-agentic suppression and compensation. Its suppression was associated with young people's coping mechanisms. Self-reflectiveness during times of disengagement was associated with the development and exercise of intentionality and forethought, and was a catalyst to major changes in the exercise of agency. It could also be used in the pursuit of more incremental changes. Not all such changes might be considered improvements in a normative sense, even where they are shown to be effective for the young person. Patterns of self-reflectiveness from the young person's wider life could be transferred and applied to EET. Self-reflectiveness was found to be powerfully involved in the modification of intentionality.

Conclusion

The findings of the study as reported in this and the previous chapter describe in detail the function of personal agency of NEET young people and the nature of its interactions with social, political and economic structures in the determination of EET outcomes. This chapter explores the ways in which the exercise of the four core features of agency by young people helps to shape the extent to, and manner in, which they pursue or do not pursue EET outcomes. It is clear that young people exhibit heterogeneous habitual patterns of agentic thought and behaviour that are not only influenced in the immediate, but are also shaped throughout the life course, by structures and self. The home and school environments are particularly implicated in the shaping of these patterns, and the patterns in turn are often implicated in engagement and disengagement from EET. These patterns not only relate to interactions between the agent and the environment, but also between the features of agency. This sophistication of the function of personal agency is termed 'intra-agency'. Four types of intra-agentic interaction are identified. The first of these is termed 'facilitation', where one feature of agency enables another to be carried out more effectively. The second is termed 'suppression', where intentionality is used to suppress or limit the role of forethought or self-reflectiveness. The third is termed 'compensation', where one component is used more intensively as a compensation for the underuse or suppression of another. The fourth is termed 'undermining' and relates to instances where self-reflectiveness largely undermines a young person's intentionality towards EET. The connotations of intra-agency include the idea that agency may be exercised with only a subset of features active, with these features constituting an intra-agentic quorum, and the idea that the role of intentionality in directing and enabling intra-agentic activity gives it eminence among the features.

7

Inside the 'Black Box': An Empirical Model and the Implications for Policy, Praxis and Research

The function of the personal agency of NEET young people ('the function'), and the nature of its interactions with NEET's structures, is detailed empirically in the previous two chapters. This chapter develops and discusses the relevance and application of the findings in respect to the study's three aims. The first section presents a model of the function of personal agency within NEET based on the findings. The second section discusses the findings in the context of the NEET literature reviewed earlier in the book. The third section develops the relevance of the findings to NEET policy and praxis. The fourth section discusses the influence of the theoretical approach on the findings. Further support is given to the argument that theoretical approaches sensitize investigations to particular dynamics within dialectically complex phenomena. The approach developed in this study is useful because it is possible to distinguish between agency and structure roles in relatively precise terms.

The function of personal agency within NEET: A model

The findings of this study can be taken as a whole to develop an empirical model of the function. The core features of this model are the perceptual and mechanistic inseparability of EET from the wider life of the young person, the distinction between 'hard' and 'softer' structural influences, the influencing mechanisms represented in the ideas of the discursive environment and agentic modelling, and personal agency itself, with recognition of intra-agency. The model is presented diagrammatically as Figure 7.1.

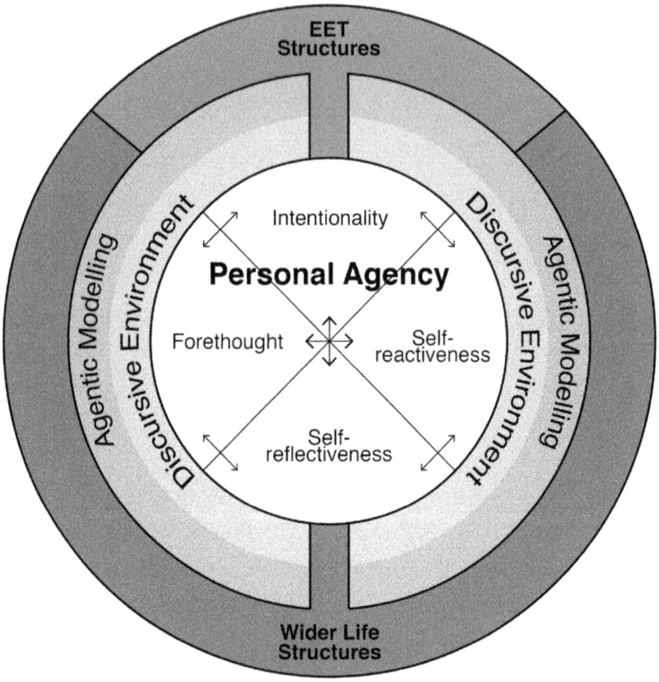

Figure 7.1 The empirical model of the function of the personal agency of young people within NEET ('the function')

The underlying form of the model consists of three concentric circles, with the personal agency of the young person represented by the innermost circle. This denotes two things: first, the focus of this study on the function of the young person's agency; and second, the perception of the young people that their own agency was the most important determinant of their EET outcomes. The circle is divided into four, representing the four features of agency in Bandura's (2001) conceptualization. Intentionality is represented in the uppermost quarter, in the direction of the EET structures represented in the outermost circle. This represents the eminence of intentionality, both in its role of enabling or inhibiting the overall exercise of agency towards EET, and in its capacity to manipulate the exercise of the other features of agency directly. Although this capacity was not unique to intentionality, it was by far the one for which it was most pronounced. The arrows between each of the four features represent the function of intra-agency. As discussed earlier, the interactions between features can include facilitation, suppression, compensation and undermining. An 'anchoring' bar is extended from the lower part of the innermost circle to the outermost circle, representing the young person's dependency on a number of 'hard' structural stabilities in their wider life if they are to exercise a stable agentic expression. Another bar is extended from the upper part of the innermost circle to the outermost circle, representing the influence over the young person's agency that comes directly from their experiences of EET.

The second circle represents the 'softer' structural influences over the young person's agency, and the two key mechanisms of this influence, namely, the discursive environment and agentic modelling. The discursive environment is the totality of the discursive interactions that young people have and experience within their environment. These are instances of conversational and communicative relations with parents and others relatives, teachers and other learning professionals, mentors, employers, friends and peers, civil servants, persons within the community, celebrities and even Deity. These interactions were found to have direct effects on the exercise of features of agency by, for example, helping young people to consider new intentions or refine existing ones, structure and enhance forethought, consider alternative ways of reacting to situations, and prompting or drawing meaning out of self-reflection. The direct nature of the discursive environment's influence on agency is represented by its inner positioning relative to agentic modelling. Agentic modelling denotes the influence on young people's agency that comes through observing the interactions of others with their environments, and the resulting outcomes. Agentic modelling can inspire new intentions, provide 'blueprints' for action that are incorporated into forethought, present alternative ways to react to common situations and provide a resource for reflection. The observation that much of this modelling occurs in the model's interactions with EET and wider life structures is represented by its outer positioning relative to the discursive environment.

The outermost circle represents what are termed the 'hard' influences of structure. The circle is divided into two parts. The upper part represents structures pertaining directly to EET, and relates to the stabilities and structures of EET opportunities, that is, the types of opportunities available, and their attributes, for example, entry requirements, success criteria, contract types, wage levels and shift structures. The lower part represents structures in the young person's wider life, and particularly relates to relational, domestic and financial stabilities. The lower part has been depicted as larger than the upper. This represents the finding that decisions made by young people in regard to EET are typically subsumed into decisions being made about their wider life. It also represents the related finding that a young person's limited capacity for agency is typically directed to address issues relating to their wider life rather than to EET, where crisis or instability forces such a prioritization of intentions on them.

The diagrammatic model has several strengths. It is derived directly from empirical data. It rationalizes a complex range of influences on the function, making the types and means of these influences comprehensible in relatively straightforward terms. The major thematic findings are cohesively contextualized with respect to one another, enabling the function to be usefully visualized as an empirical whole. Yet it retains enough sophistication to explain the complex dynamics represented in the individual exercising of agency by a heterogeneous group of young people. The model can be related back to the literature from which the research problem was developed, and applied usefully to refine and build upon existing knowledge, and address policy and praxis concerns, as is pursued further on.

There are also a number of weaknesses in the model. This includes the loss in detail associated with describing the complex social and psychological phenomena present in the findings in such a simple model. This detail relates to the unique and distinctive contributions made by each of the various elements of the NEET topography, and features of agency, that are presented in the findings but cannot be captured in the diagram. It is suggested, therefore, that the model is not a replacement for the findings, but a useful representation of them, and the two ought to be used side by side. Consequently, throughout the following discussions there is reference to 'the model' and to 'the findings' as appropriate. The distinction between 'hard' and 'softer' structural influences also needs to be qualified. Although it is argued that the data justifies a distinction, it is misleading to conceive of it as absolute. For example, discursive interactions are implicated in the breakdown of relational stabilities in the young person's wider life. This might not be immediately apparent from the model, and so again the need to keep 'the findings' in view might be emphasized. It is also possible that other oversimplifications might be inaccurately assumed from an isolated consideration of the model.

Revisiting the NEET policy literature

The first two objectives of this study have been met through the presentation of the findings and model. These were first to examine the nature, extent and efficacy of the exercise of personal agency by NEET young people to determine their education, employment and training outcomes, and second to examine perceptual factors that mediate the exercise of personal agency by NEET young people. Discussion will now return to the literature from which the research problem was developed, to examine the relevance and application of the model and findings in the study's originating contexts. Through this and a pursuant discussion of policy and praxis implications, the third objective is addressed. This is specifically to identify how policy and praxis for NEET might be improved by accounting for the function of the personal agency of young people, and thereby providing greater clarity on NEET's 'vexed question'. The discussion also indicates how the model and findings may be utilized to examine a spectrum of ideas and claims across NEET literature more broadly. Four key items of literature were reviewed: Colley (2006), Wolf (2008), the LGA and Centre for Social Justice (2009a) and Sodha and Margo (2010). The relevance of the model and findings for each of these is now discussed in turn.

Colley (2006) critiques the EU policy documents and actions that induced the social exclusion and NEET discourses, and the use of Engagement Mentoring (EM) as a tool to reduce NEET. She presents two case studies of NEET young people participating in an EM programme, to illustrate that EM does not work as envisaged by policymakers. The findings of this study comment on Colley's discussions in several ways. She argues that the EU policy narratives characterize young people as passive recipients of interventions but this is an inaccurate representation of their role within NEET; she presents evidence from her case studies that young people actively exercise agency in their own interests to subvert the agendas of EM. The findings largely support Colley's arguments in this respect; a passive model of young people is largely incongruous with the data. Young people were apt to assess the agendas being worked out in various situations and interactions with others, and consciously to steer, subvert or reject these.

It should be noted however that one particular sample contradicted this overall pattern. Ishmael demonstrated a high degree of passivity in his decision-making that might be considered congruous with the EU characterization, often allowing himself to be the subject of proxy agency. Ishmael's counterexample signals an important caveat to the findings by raising a question of whether patterns of personal agency may vary with culture. Ishmael was the only participant from his ethnic group, and studies in related fields indicate that tendencies towards passivity in young people can have cultural dimensions. For example, Chuah (2010) agrees with an observation that East-Asian learners are more passive than Western learners. Toivonen, Norasakkunkit and Uchida (2011: 1) make related observations of Japanese young people, noting 'how complex and painful the psychological and sociological effects' of modern sociostructural changes can be for 'young people in conformist societies'. They find unique patterns of culture-specific adaptation in which the young people are 'unable to conform … yet also unwilling to rebel', and thus 'deviate from typical Japanese motivational patterns but have not necessarily become more Western'.

The question of culture also raises questions of ethnicity. There are reasons to think that a young person's ethnicity may well be associated with differences in the likelihood of them becoming NEET. As indicated in the opening chapter, young people from Black, Asian and Minority Ethnicity (BAME) backgrounds have been disproportionately represented within the UK NEET figures (HM Government 2012a; Pickard 2014; Taylor 2015). The House of Commons (2012: 15) youth unemployment report noted that 'disproportionate rises' in unemployment among some groups were 'particularly true of young black men', citing evidence suggesting that '55.5% of economically active black men aged 16–24 were unemployed and that this figure had almost doubled since 2008'. Such observations are not limited to the UK. The OECD (2010: 41) reports, for example, that in New Zealand 'NEET youth are mainly of Maori/Pacific Islander origin … so the phenomenon has an ethnic dimension'. Other similar instances might be pointed to elsewhere, and Eurofound (2012: 53) recognizes a general association between 'membership of an ethnic minority group' and a higher risk of becoming NEET, possibly due to higher likelihoods of accumulating educational disadvantages and developing disaffection. Although the study presented in this book did not aim directly to investigate issues of culture and ethnicity, its findings do open up avenues for exploring how agency and structure interact to produce the higher likelihoods of becoming NEET that are associated with them. This might be related to trends towards domestic and economic instabilities in some cases, perhaps particularly where ethnic minority membership is linked to migration. Dalakoglou (2013), for example, comments extensively on the accumulation of disadvantage among migrant groups in the build-up to the Greece youth riots. Tamesberger and Bacher (2014) note specifically the prevalence of young people from migrant families in Austria's NEET population, and Eurofound (2012: 2) observes that in the EU broadly 'young people with an immigration background are 70% more likely to become NEET than nationals'. The issues may well be very different among non-migrant ethnic minority communities, however, and this might somehow be reflected, for example, in the patterns of discursive interaction that develop between those communities and the wider society. Such possibilities could be explored in future research. In any case, Ishmael's example helps to highlight the strength of the model, as it nonetheless holds valid for the way in which personal agency functioned in Ishmael's life, despite clear differences in his patterns of agency relative to other young people. The model is thus useful for handling heterogeneity in NEET cases. It also affirms Colley's (2006) observation that the characterizations of young people in some NEET policy narratives can be shown to be inaccurate through empirical evidence.

The model and findings also provide additional explanation for the subversion of EM agendas observed by Colley (2006). They indicate that the agency of young people that might be exercised towards EET is subsumed into a limited capacity for agency in their lives as a whole, and that where particular personal or circumstantial issues are present, a prioritization of intentions takes place, typically towards resolving those issues rather than towards pursuing or sustaining EET. This not only explains why Colley observed mentees subverting EM agendas to procure support for personal issues, but also indicates that such behaviours might be predictable given an improved model of the function of personal agency. They also offer a possible explanation for why the EM approach may often appear to be 'hit and miss'. Mentoring is likely to produce impacts on the young person's wider life before impacting on their EET. If programme evaluations focus on measuring the latter at the expense of the former, the primary effects of programmes might well remain invisible, and findings across programmes may thus appear inconsistent. This all suggests that the agendas for EM, and the processes for evaluating its impacts, may be too narrow, as Colley also argues (3). Further, the underlying assumption that EET is a part of the young person's life that can be treated discretely is wrong. It is argued then that the model developed in this study offers explanatory (and perhaps even predictive) power for observations made in other empirical studies, and may be useful for addressing deficiencies in the tacit models underlying existing NEET policy and praxis.

The work of Colley (2006) raises questions as to how and to what extent young people in possibly coercive circumstances were genuinely exercising agency. Even in the most coercive of circumstances, the behaviours of young people can be explained wholly in terms of genuine agency. However, a number of key ideas must be taken into account to understand properly the specific ways in which personal agency functions under such conditions. This again includes the idea of the prioritization of intentions, which indicates that where young people are subject to circumstances involving personal or family crises or instabilities, they may disengage from EET to address these. The coerciveness of such circumstances was evident where disengagement from EET was clearly and strongly against the young person's underlying desires, as evident with Jeanne who cried as she flew to visit her ill mother during her GCSEs, or Kevin who angrily confronted his parents when he realized their divorce would result in him missing his exams. Even then, disengagement was not automatic and typically involved the young person going through a process of deliberation involving some or all of the four features of agency, and strengthening their personal resolve, before it took place. There is also the associated idea of zones of optimal pressure, in which a sense of excessive pressure can be disabling to the exercise of certain features of agency. Young people experiencing extreme stress were seen at times to disengage intentionally from EET, often in order to recover their capacity to exercise these features of agency properly. This idea of stress-induced disengagement appears particularly to fit the case in Colley's work from which the questions were raised.

An important note might be made here. In arguing that such an intentional disengagement reflects the genuine exercise of agency, a position is taken that the genuine exercise of agency need not require the exercise of all four features. The support for this position is taken from the findings on intra-agentic quorums, wherein the exercise of as little as two features of agency (i.e. intentionality and self-reactiveness) could constitute a conscious and perhaps even efficacious strategy for pursuing EET. That the limitation of the use of forethought and self-reflectiveness is done consciously and intentionally suggests that it is genuinely agentic. Rather than questioning the genuineness of agency in such circumstances then, it appears it is more useful to focus on the limited capacity young people have for effective agency. The prioritization of intentions, zones of optimal pressure and intra-agentic quorums all invoke considerations of limitations on agentic capacity; the first two due to mechanisms seemingly inherent to agentic function, and the last due to practices in how it is exercised that may have developed throughout the life course. This might be important in terms of Colley's (2006) contentions with EU policy characterizations. A young person thought to be exercising a 'fully-featured' expression of agency without crisis or stress-induced limitations might be more justifiably vilified than one exercising a partially incapacitated agency due to circumstantial or developmental limitations. It is argued therefore that behaviours associated with disengagement under potentially coercive conditions are best explained in terms of limitations on agentic capacity, rather than in terms of agency being overridden by structure in some unknown way. Such an account defends the autonomy of agency from structure, as is vital for the integrity of a dialectical model. In this, it is argued that this study has enabled the empirical elucidation and detailing of some of the more problematic areas of dialectical interaction in NEET.

Colley (2006: 12) proposed that 'close relationships … cannot sweep away the institutional and structural forces that hold sway over young people's lives'. The findings from the current research, however, indicate this is not entirely true. In numerous cases, young people expressed how conventional approaches to job searching had been fruitless for them. What had proven successful instead was accessing opportunities through relationships with mentors, family members and friends. Relationships had therefore provided access to valuable experience and income that institutional forces would have otherwise denied the young people. Some young people even explicitly expressed opinions that relationships were *the* way into EET, including Kevin whose modus operandi was to develop relationships that might lead to work, as per his last two jobs, and Darren who said:

> I actually think jobs these days are pretty much about people you know and not about your grades or your applications … If you know someone … you have a pretty good chance of getting a job.

Such views may be quite widespread among young people. Agnew (2014), for example, finds similar opinions among 16- to 24-year-olds in Suffolk, particularly those in more rural locations.

Colley's (2006) conclusions, therefore, probably apply only to a proportion of NEET cases. There is considerable heterogeneity among NEET cases (e.g. Furlong 2006), and her presentation of only two case studies in support of her position clearly risks missing some of this; although she claims to have observed other cases which involved similar dynamics. Alternatively, her conclusions may apply more broadly, but have their proper effect at a macro-level scale, rather than the micro-level scale considered here. Russell, Simmons and Thompson (2011: 103), for example, argue that informal networks may enable young people to find employment, but the quality of this employment may be poor and still reflect 'broader constraints imposed by macro-level social systems'. The findings in the study would support this idea, as the employment found by the young people often involved unfavourable contract types, low wage levels, awkward shift structures and limited opportunities for progression. These conditions however could equally apply to the employment they found through conventional means, suggesting the quality of employment obtained by young people is not necessarily related to the means by which it is accessed. In any case, it may be argued that the model and findings in this study are useful for accounting for heterogeneity among NEET cases, relative to literature using less diverse sampling. This points towards what may be another of the most important aspects of the findings. The heterogeneity of the NEET population is such that the classification has been described as a 'flawed concept' (Furlong 2006: 553, cited in Cuzzocrea 2013) on account of its inclusion of young people with ostensibly very different life circumstances (see also Yates and Payne 2006). The ability to encompass this diversity within a single empirical model may help researchers, policymakers and practitioners to work with the classification despite its flaws.

Whereas Colley (2006) argues that the capacity of NEET young people to exercise agency is limited, Wolf (2008) contends that young people were very much in control of the determination of their EET outcomes. The participants in the study largely concurred, and were overwhelmingly assertive about the centrality of their own roles. However, Wolf developed this to argue that if young people were not in EET it was because they 'really and definitely do not want to enter any of the programmes on offer' (12). There was no support for such a conclusion in the findings of this study. None of the young people reported that they had not taken up further education or training because there was nothing they wanted to do. Instead, a simple intention to just do 'something' or even 'anything' often resulted in young people enrolling for courses. The actual reasons for young people not taking up FE or training tended to be family crises, failure to meet the requirements to enter or continue in college (i.e. grades or attendance) and difficulty in coping with educational or personal pressures. Other reasons included the preference or need to find employment instead for financial reasons, and a lack of clarity about what the right choices in life and learning might be. Although young people may indeed be the ultimate determinants of their outcomes, disengagement is therefore not nearly as whimsical as Wolf makes it appear. Young peoples' role in determining their outcomes is not a simple choice to 'opt-in' or 'opt-out' but rather a prerogative to define, redefine and ultimately fulfil personal intentions in the face of sometimes adverse conditions; the general consensus of interviewees was that if they displayed enough will, confidence and persistence in pursuing EET, they would eventually triumph over whichever structural obstacles they faced.

Wolf (2008), however, also argued that the quality and attractiveness of the education and training options available to young people was an issue. There was some limited support for this in the findings. If new options were to be useful, it would not be because they would inspire engagement where there was otherwise no desire for it, but because they might better accommodate the challenges and difficulties young people face. On this basis, the young people indicated that an increase in the number and types of apprenticeships available could be useful. This was because apprenticeships resolved some of the life challenges faced by young people by bridging the divide between learning and earning. Wolf provides little empirical evidence to support her points as developed above, and so it is argued that although she is correct to characterize the NEET young person as meaningfully volitional, she problematically obscures the complexity of the circumstances and psychological processes that underlie disengagement, and possibly misdiagnoses the benefits of adjusting education and training frameworks.

The LGA and Centre for Social Justice (2009a) emphasized the importance of close relationships in determining EET outcomes. Although they offered little evidence to support this, the findings of this study indicate that their claims actually have some merits, although with caveats. Familial and other relationships (including mentors, friends and peers, and others) were found to exercise very powerful influences over young people's agency. These were particularly represented in the concepts of the discursive environment and agentic modelling, and in the relational, domestic and financial stabilities associated with the family (and sometimes romantic interests). These relationships could also often become avenues to circumventing structural obstacles to EET. Relationships are nonetheless not a panacea and there often remains a distinction between the power of relationships to influence agency and create opportunities, and the power of employers and institutions to provide actual EET placements. It is argued from this observation, as it might have been in the discussion of Wolf (2008) above, that the model and findings are useful for assessing and critiquing, on empirical grounds, unsubstantiated claims made in the NEET policy literature.

Sodha and Margo (2010) advocate an early intervention approach to addressing NEET, delivered through the network of local statutory organizations interacting with the young person and family. The findings of this study give some support to this argument, again with caveats. Particularly it must be pointed out that the 'passive recipient of interventions' model of young people implied, although not explicitly posited, by Sodha and Margo is rejected. While the findings support the idea of early intervention, this is not so much in terms of what might be done 'to' a young person to prevent them becoming NEET, but rather how they might be worked with as a 'highly agentic agent' to develop an effective use of personal agency. This is argued for on the basis that the patterns of agency expressed by NEET young people proceed from patterns developed earlier in life, typically through experiences in the home or school environments. These patterns are often problematically implicated in disengagement, for example, through the underuse or poor execution of agentic thought (e.g. poor planning), and counterproductive self-reactive behaviours. Early intervention, as delivered through Sodha and Margo's organizational networks, might support young people to develop effective patterns of agentic thought and action throughout the life course, and to address 'risky' patterns before they become problematic. It is argued from this that the model and findings are useful for developing policy ideas in the literature, and outlining, from a different perspective, how and why they may be of utility. Altogether, it is suggested that the model and findings have a diverse applicability for the examination and critique of ideas and claims across the NEET literature, as has been represented here, and also more broadly as is developed in the following section.

Policy and praxis implications

The model and findings clearly have implications for policy and praxis. These are developed here with the caveat that they appear to exceed this study's capacity to treat them; there are numerous details within the findings which might singularly be examined to this end (including those specific to individual features of agency and elements of the topography), and numerous dimensions of NEET policy and praxis to which they might individually or collectively be applied. The following discussion is therefore restricted to a number of broader 'in-principle' implications relevant to the study's context and objectives, with some limited development of more specific applications, and some cues for future research. The overarching implication, already evident in many ways and further developed in the immediate discussion, is that NEET, and all its related policy and praxis, is inescapably situated in a multi-element dialectical arrangement. The findings make it clear that agency and structure in their various forms both have crucial and dynamically interactive roles in the production and transformation of EET outcomes. NEET is therefore empirically a dialectical problem, and requires dialectical solutions. The following discussion develops some of the aspects of what these solutions might include. This overarching implication is associated with some interesting observations about the nature of the relationship between agency and structure, which are discussed in the concluding chapter. A second overarching implication, developed in the preceding discussion, is that 'the function' is often handled or represented problematically in NEET policy discourses. NEET discourses, and the policy and praxis ideas developed from them, should therefore seek to be grounded in an empirically sound underpinning model of the function, as presented in this study.

The major ideas within the findings each have particular implications consistent with these overarching ones. First, the underpinning models of the function used in discourses, and the development of policy and praxis, should account for the inseparability of EET from the rest of the young person's life. It was consistently evident that the characterization of EET as a discrete component of the young person's life was true neither perceptually to the young person, nor mechanistically in how their outcomes were determined. As suggested earlier, recognizing this may enable improved predictions of the impacts of interventions, and therefore lead to improved praxis. Specifically, the agendas and evaluatory processes for some mentoring programmes may be too narrow, and could benefit from being widened to address the young person's life as a whole rather than simply their EET status. On this basis, revised mentoring praxis might involve routinely assessing young people's wider life circumstances, their capacity for agency and how this agency is habitually patterned. This may yield information on how individual mentees may respond to difficult impending situations, how they might subvert or manipulate mentoring agendas and how they might thus be supported better. Future research could consider in detail the implications of the findings for mentoring interventions, and perhaps include some action research to this end.

Policymakers and practitioners might also consider how 'hard' structural influences in the young person's wider life, particularly the relational, domestic and financial stabilities associated with the family and home, can be better protected and supported. The findings suggest any actions that achieve this may contribute to reducing NEET. Positively, the UK coalition government's Social Justice Strategy (HM Government 2012b; 2013b) pursued policy developments in this very direction, stating the family is 'the most important building block in a child's life' (HM Government 2012b: 1), and focused on promoting 'family stability' as a key objective. 'The Strategy' (HM Government 2012b; 2013b) justified its approach on the basis of other studies including Mooney, Oliver and Smith (2009) and Moore, Kinghorn and Bandy (2011). Mooney, Oliver and Smith (2009) associate negative familial experiences (e.g. low quality parent-child relationships, repeated changes in living arrangements and financial hardship i.e. 'relational, domestic and financial stabilities') with mental health and well-being issues, alcohol use and lower educational attainment in young people. Moore, Kinghorn and Bandy (2011: 1) also find the quality of relationships between parents is 'very consistently and positively associated' with better outcomes for children.

This study's findings thus appear to agree with a wider body of literature on the importance of familial stabilities in determining outcomes. This indicates positively that the findings may hold true at scale. However, where this literature draws conclusions from large-scale survey data (e.g. Moore, Kinghorn and Bandy 2011), or otherwise seeks to establish broad associations between conditions and outcomes (e.g. Mooney, Oliver and Smith 2009), there is little development within it of the young person's role and capacity as an agent. It is argued therefore that this study builds usefully upon the existing knowledge by elucidating behavioural, perceptual and dialectical mechanisms that mediate between the conditions and outcomes. This study therefore not just accounts for whether these conditions are meaningfully implicated in determining outcomes, but also provides specific insights into how this is so. Future research could explore the relations of the findings to this literature in more detail, and how knowledge of the function of personal agency could be usefully integrated into it.

The Strategy (HM Government 2012b) also aligns with other findings of this study, for example, it advocates an early intervention approach (see Field 2010; Allen 2011). However, the role of young people's agency is again hardly developed within it, perhaps with the exception of brief references to the impacts of adverse conditions on their coping mechanisms. This kind of omission is problematic. It was strongly asserted and often evidenced by young people that they would eventually find their way into EET when they were intentional, persistent and had sufficient agentic capacity to do so. Supporting young people to develop an effective and resilient exercise of agency ought therefore to be a priority of policy and praxis. Several of the major ideas within the findings might be referred to here. Among the most important is the observation that patterns of agentic expression can be and are shaped throughout the life course. Teachers, social workers and practitioners might thus be encouraged to incorporate strategies into their praxis to help young people define and strengthen intentionality, cultivate positive self-management behaviours and develop effective planning, coping and problem-solving skills related to practical and emotionally meaningful situations. This may be particularly important where the home and family environment is not facilitating this kind of development effectively.

This praxis ought to account for the key means by which influences over young people's agency are mediated, including the discursive environment and agentic modelling. Here the old adage might be adjusted on the basis of empirical evidence to read 'sticks and stones may break my bones, but words may make me NEET'. It was repeated many times and in different ways by participants how discursive interactions with others, including teachers, could make or break their confidence and motivation, and with it the ability or inclination to exercise intentionality and self-reactiveness in productive ways. All practitioners interacting with young people, therefore, ought to reflect meaningfully upon, and possibly be made to account for the influence of their words, interactions and modelling behaviours on the development of young people's agency. Young peoples' family members might also be brought into scope here, and supported to improve their influence on the development of young people's agency, potentially through parenting programmes or whole-family therapies. Praxis relating to the leadership and management of the young person's environment and experiences are also highly important. Negative experiences such as school bullying that were not addressed effectively could continue to have impacts on agentic function long beyond their duration.

Support for these ideas is found in other recent research. For example, a Prince's Trust report (2013) concluded that one in ten young people feel unable to cope with day-to-day life, and NEET young people are twice as likely to fall into this group as their EET peers. It found that over one in five young people (22%) did not have someone to talk to about their problems while growing up, and NEET young people were again more likely to fall into this group. A YoungMinds survey suggests there is a risk of these issues becoming generationally endemic (Leaman 2014). It found that of two thousand children and young people surveyed, half claimed to have been bullied, and a third claimed to not know where to turn to get help when they felt depressed or anxious.

To enable consistent praxis in respect of all this, leaders and managers might use the model and findings to develop frameworks for cultivating and enabling the effective use of personal agency by young people. The frameworks might be usefully applied to casework (e.g. within social services settings), within classrooms and across organizations, or even networks of organizations, such as those discussed by Sodha and Margo (2010), or more recently by Simmons et al. (2014), who envisage a 'Youth Resolution' in which employers, education and training providers, voluntary organizations and local authorities work together to provide a cohesive sociostructural environment in which the EET provision offered to young people ultimately leads to sustainable local employment. Simmons et al.'s designs for the local environment might be fitted together with such a framework to enable a genuinely dialectical approach to NEET's dialectical problem.

Whether this can be achieved will depend in part on the development of the relevant policy, systems and legislative structures. Newton et al.'s (2014: 135) evaluation of the Youth Contract echoes the 'need for a coordinated response to identify, support and meet the needs of young people who are NEET or who are "at risk" of disengagement'. Their commentary suggests, however, that the required cooperation between public, private and voluntary sector organizations at the local level depends on aligning priorities among those organizations. Eurofound (2015: 37) observe similarly at a national level that, to make initiatives like the Youth Guarantee effective, EU member states 'need to ensure that their legal, political and financial frameworks, and their institutional capacities, are equipped to do so'. The findings of this study might also be used to support such larger-scale efforts.

This includes paying attention to the availabilities and structures of the EET opportunities created as policy, systems and legislation develops. Employment practices, particularly including the use of temporary, zero-hour and commissioning-only contracts were found to have mixed impacts on NEET. Such opportunities enabled young people to gain valuable experience but were also prominent drivers of 'churning'. Future research might specifically investigate the net effects of such contracting practices and what ought to be done about them. Minimum-wage jobs with limited career prospects and demanding shift structures were found to be the bane of some young people, and could trigger depression or nihilism. Apprenticeships, however, which may pay lower than the minimum wage but offer a greater sense of progression, were popular and several participants called for increases in their availability. The prospect of progression, therefore, may be more vital for continued engagement than a particular basic level of income. This observation might be used to restructure opportunities and pathways for young people to attract and retain their talent. The positive view of apprenticeships was also linked to their usefulness for resolving dilemmas in the context of the young person's wider life, particularly by bridging the gap between learning and earning. Taken with the numerous statements made by participants about their perceived failure of EET to help them deal with 'life' challenges, future revisions of education and training frameworks should consider how such challenges might be usefully addressed.

Further studies to develop the application of specific findings might also support improved praxis. Action research projects might investigate whether interventions focused on young people's coping behaviours are able to increase their resilience and positively shift zones of optimal pressure, so that 'folding' behaviours are delayed and capacities to handle crisis and stress are increased. Other studies might investigate whether or how interventions might address habitual and ineffective patterns of agency. It appears from the findings that the strongest shaping effects on agentic patterns are associated with emotional closeness or intensity, such that family members and romantic interests, emotionally intense experiences in formative years (e.g. bullying) and emotionally skilled mentors have some of the most profound effects. Studies might seek to validate this observation, and consider how it might be made of practical use.

The major ideas represented in the findings may be presented coherently in relation to each other as a diagrammatic model of the function of personal agency. The model and findings are useful in numerous ways. They have a diverse applicability for the development of ideas and arguments in the NEET literature. This includes identifying deficiencies in the models of 'the function' underlying NEET discourses, providing enhanced explanation for observations made in other studies, handling unsubstantiated claims and accounting for heterogeneity in NEET cases. They are also useful for elucidating previously difficult areas of the dialectical interactions within NEET, identifying the mechanisms that mediate between conditions and outcomes and assessing and developing potential policy and praxis solutions. It is ultimately established that NEET, and all its related policy and praxis is inescapably situated in a complex multi-element dialectical arrangement, and requires a genuinely dialectical solution.

The influences of the theoretical approach on the findings

It was argued in the literature review that the approach taken to the conceptualization of agency and structure could sensitize a study to particular findings. This discussion provides further evidence of this, while also accounting for how this study's findings may be reflective of its approach. This may be useful for comparative examinations of related studies. It is also useful for developing a key argument underlying the study, specifically that an original theoretical approach to the investigation of agency and structure might be conducive to producing original knowledge relevant to the research problem.

Bandura's (2001) agentic perspective on social cognitive theory was used to conceptualize agency, and to inform data collection and analysis on its exercise. It was argued that this avoided issues of abstraction, politicization and polarization that problematized the use of alternative conceptualizations. The use of the conceptualization is reflected in the findings in several important ways. Most importantly, the approach successfully enabled the study to empirically demarcate the exercise of personal agency within dialectically complex situations. This has enabled a usefully precise observation of the interactions within NEET's dialectical 'black box', and allowed the study to coherently describe, for example, how agency functions even in seemingly coercive circumstances, as was problematized in the literature review. In this way the conceptualization has enabled the study to achieve its aims in a way that, it is argued, the alternatives could not.

Most visibly, Bandura's (2001) four 'core features' of agency are used to structure an entire section of the findings, and are explicitly featured in the diagrammatic model. Some important and original observations are specifically associated with their use. This includes the elucidation of functional activity within agency, that is, the ability of agentic features to act upon one another. This has been termed intra-agency, and its numerous connotations are an important part of the findings. Intra-agency adds sophistication to the dialectical interactions that take place in NEET by, for example, indicating that the agency of a young person might be compromised in certain instances, but not necessarily by structures. This enables the rationalization of some empirically observed behaviours that would be otherwise problematic. It is unlikely that intra-agency would have been observed with any of the other conceptualizations of agency considered.

Lopez and Scott's (2000) institutional and relational structure types were used to conceptualize structure. This sensitized the study in a number of ways, including a sensitivity to how NEET's structures tend to be perceived by young people. It became apparent that participants were predisposed to view their interactions with NEET's structures in relational (i.e. dyadic) terms, even where they were discussing the influences of organizations. This is useful for understanding how the influences of those structures are mediated to young people.

The conceptualizations were overlain with the topography of NEET to operationalize them for data collection and analysis. This is also reflected in the findings in several ways. Most visibly, an entire chapter of the findings is structured according to the topography. This has enabled the operation and relationship of the function of personal agency to be articulated specifically in respect to individual elements of NEET's structures, as may be useful to policymakers and practitioners working in particular fields. Perhaps more importantly, by examining the relationship of the function to diverse structural elements, the approach has enabled the study to identify and classify common principles and mechanisms that appear to underlie the influences of all the structures within NEET. This is seen in the distinctions between, and constitutions of the 'hard' and 'softer' influences of structure in the model. This in turn provides a basis for identifying the salient interactions and conditions that may affect a young person's agency within any given environment, whether addressed directly by the study or not. It also signifies the potential for introducing commonalities of practice for working with NEET young people that can be applied in any, or across all environments. The approach was also useful for handling unanticipated data. Celebrity and media influences, and faith and religion, both emerged unexpectedly within the data as meaningful influences on the agency of young people. The topographical approach to structuring data analysis however provided a convenient means for classifying them, and allowing their relevance to be coherently developed and presented in the findings.

The study's theoretical approach is reflected in the findings in important ways, supporting an argument that different approaches to conceptualizing agency and structure sensitize studies to particular dynamics within phenomena. This study's approach is seen to have supported the resolution of difficult empirical questions about dialectical interactions within NEET, sensitized the study to original findings about personal agency (e.g. the concept of intra-agency), enabled the handling of potentially problematic data (including some unanticipated data) and supported the development of the study's relevance to particular policy and praxis concerns. Insofar as these achievements would not have been possible with other conceptualizations of agency and structure considered, it is suggested that this study's approach has proven to be a useful one. It is also argued on this basis that this study offers a response to Coffey and Farrugia's (2014: 473) call for a 'more useful account of agency which is better able to respond to the complex challenges of theorising and researching youth'. This is developed further in the concluding chapter.

Conclusion

The major ideas within the findings may be coherently presented in relation to one another as a diagrammatic model of the function of personal agency. Together, the model and findings empirically elucidate NEET's dialectical 'black box', and account for a number of complex and problematic dynamics within NEET. The model and findings have a broad and diverse applicability to the concerns of the NEET literature. Their usefulness includes identifying deficiencies in the models of 'the function' underlying NEET discourses, offering enhanced explanation for observations made in other studies, and handling unsubstantiated claims in the literature. They are also useful for accounting for heterogeneity in NEET cases, identifying the mechanisms that mediate between conditions and outcomes, and assessing and developing potential approaches to policy and praxis. Several potential avenues for future research stem from their consideration. It is established from them that NEET, and all its related policy and praxis, is inescapably situated in a complex multi-element dialectical arrangement. NEET is empirically a dialectical problem, and genuinely dialectical solutions to it are to be pursued.

The findings of the study support an argument that different theoretical approaches may sensitize investigations to particular dynamics within the relationship between agency and structure. The particular theoretical approach of the study is reflected in its findings in important ways, and is clearly associated with some of its original contributions to knowledge. The approach developed in this study is shown to be particularly useful as one that can empirically demarcate the function of personal agency in dialectically complex situations, and thereby enable its operation to be detailed in usefully precise terms.

8

The 'Black Box' and Beyond: Conclusions and a Way Forward

This chapter explores the content of the NEET 'black box' by summarizing the findings of this study and the insights that it has established. This is done in five sections, tracing a path from the specific aims of the study to its broad relevance for policy and praxis. The first section reviews the three aims of the study. The second reviews the efficacy of the approach adopted for this study and develops some particular implications of the approach. It is argued that the study has delivered strongly on its three aims although a number of weaknesses are noted. The third section indicates the relationship of the study to wider educational and sociological literature. The fourth develops some of the broadest and most important implications of the study, including its potential for responding to some of the larger current issues in youth transitions theory, and for supporting the resolution of NEET. Within this, the current inability of the study to account fully for the effects of structural inequalities in the production of NEET is discussed, and a further study to redress this is proposed. The fifth section explores the nature of the relationship between agency and structure. The chapter conclusion brings this all together and reviews the directions for future research indicated throughout the study.

Approaching the 'black box'

This research study set out to address NEET's *vexata quaestio*, the question of the extent to which young people are responsible for determining their own EET outcomes (Cuzzocrea 2013: 7). It was shown from Colley (2006), Wolf (2008), the LGA and Centre for Social Justice (2009a) and Sodha and Margo (2010) that the determination of these outcomes can be variously attributed to young people themselves and to structures within NEET, and that this broadly problematizes the development of policy and praxis. A response to the question was to be pursued by examining the function of personal agency ('the function') in determining outcomes. The function was developed to denote both the exercise of personal agency by NEET young people, and the way in which this exercise is itself influenced by individual perceptions. The investigation was to be empirical, and grounded in the dialectically complex cases of individual disengagement that characterize NEET. By examining the function of personal agency, and its interactions with NEET's structures, it was intended that NEET's dialectical 'black box' (Coffey and Farrugia 2014: 461), within which the roles of agency and structure in determining EET outcomes were seen to be problematically indistinct, would be elucidated.

Three aims were associated with this. The first and primary aim was to contribute to NEET policy and praxis discussions by developing the empirical understanding of the function of the personal agency of NEET young people, as above. The second aim was to contribute to the theoretical treatment of NEET by positioning it within a conceptual framework that enabled the roles of agency and structure within it to be discerned in dialectically complex situations. The third aim was to contribute to methodological thought and practice by developing an approach to operationalizing the concepts of agency and structure in such a way as to provide consistency across the theoretical and methodological aspects of the study, and to enable the genuine use of personal agency to be empirically identified and examined. Thus, the second and third aims had to be achieved ahead of the first.

The theoretical, and by extension methodological, aims were pursued by positioning NEET within the structure-agency debate (Archer 1995). This was supported by an argument that the NEET policy literature would often invoke the concepts of the debate, but not necessarily identify them as such (Akram 2010). It was observed that this study is not the first to take such an overarching approach. It was argued however that the particular theoretical approaches developed in other studies were not suitable for addressing this study's research problem. The study was seen to require the coherent operationalization of a clear conceptualization of agency, and a complementary conceptualization of structure, if NEET's dialectical 'black box' was to be explored. It was argued from Coffey and Farrugia (2014) that the conceptualizations of agency and structure typically used in the 'youth transitions' literature were problematized for such use by abstraction and politicization. It was argued from Parker (2000), Akram (2010) and Porpora (2013) that similar issues problematized the use of the prominent conceptualizations of agency and structure in the broader sociological literature. Issues relating to polarized academic positions on the nature of agency and structure were also identified, as represented in the debates on duality and dualism (Parker 2000), and the debates on institutional and relational views of structure (Lopez and Scott 2000). Akram (2010) identified a fundamental problem in operationalizing the concepts so as to allow for a consistency between the theoretical and methodological levels of studies.

The study therefore sought to develop a particular approach to conceptualizing agency and structure, which would resolve the issues of abstraction, politicization and polarization, and enable the conceptualizations to be operationalized usefully and consistently. It was also sought that the conceptualizations would be broadly compatible with their key counterparts in the historical sociological literature, and would exhibit sensitivity to the underlying concerns of the NEET policy literature. The approach would necessarily be original, and it was intended it would therefore be useful for stimulating new thought and practice in research. Bandura's (2001) agentic perspective on social cognitive theory was used to develop and operationalize a suitable conceptualization of agency. The conceptualization was seen to meet the normative criteria for contemporary concepts of agency, while avoiding the politicization, polarization and abstraction that can typically be associated with them. It was proposed that the four 'core features' of agency detailed within it – intentionality, forethought, self-reactiveness and self-reflectiveness – might be empirically known, and used as indicators of the genuine exercise of agency. It was argued that this offered the potential for consistency between the theoretical and methodological representations of the concept, as the same definitions for each feature appear applicable at both levels. Lopez and Scott's (2000) typology was used to classify and handle two dominant concepts of structure identified in the NEET policy literature, by means of the institutional structure and relational structure types. The two types together provided a suitable conceptualization of structure for the study. The conceptualizations of agency and structure were used together with a topography of the actors and structures within NEET, developed from the NEET policy literature. The topography circumscribed the empirical context within which NEET's dialectical interactions were thought to take place, and included government, education and training organizations, employers, mentors and youth workers, parents and families, friends and peers, and young people themselves. The topography was used to facilitate the operationalization of key concepts and to co-ordinate data collection and analysis.

This approach provided a conceptual framework that offered the sought after consistency between the theoretical and methodological aims of the study. The framework then needed to be embedded within an appropriate research design. Several risks were associated with the design and method including gaining access to NEET young people (who it was argued are by definition more conspicuous by their absence than presence in settings where they might be readily accessed), eliciting relevant data from them and procuring its authenticity. A research design centred on semi-structured interviews and a short survey was argued to be the most suitable means of mitigating these. The benefits of the design included a relatively small time commitment for prospective participants over a limited number of instances (reducing access risks), and the opportunity to prompt directly for data (optimizing the chances of securing relevant and authentic data). It was identified that the method was susceptible to further risks associated with incommunicative or deceptive behaviours, and several provisions were made to encourage participant openness and honesty. These included locating interviews within comfortable settings, offering confidentiality, the use of casual dress by the researcher and an informal and conversational interview style.

A probability sampling approach was ruled out as impossible on the basis of unknowns in the most comprehensive local data on the NEET population, and a purposive sample of fifteen young people within the seventeen to twenty-one age group was sought instead. It was argued that this was conducive to generalizability, and to the study's longer-term relevance to NEET discussions as legislative changes shift the age brackets with which they are concerned. Sampling at the local authority area level was preferred on the basis of providing analytical recourse to official datasets if desired, and was carried out in three areas, through a single training and mentoring agency in each.

An original approach to addressing NEET 'churn' (e.g. Maguire and Thompson 2007) was proposed, involving the sequential exploration of participants' EET history since leaving school. This was preferred to approaches that sought to distinguish between NEET 'types' by the length of their disengagement, on the basis that these could overlook potentially useful information, further problematize access to samples and that the means for implementing them were effectively arbitrary. The preferred approach possibly had a reverse effect, enabling not only present NEETs to be in the scope of the sample, but also those in 'churn', increasing the pool of potential participants, and opening the study to valuable data related to repeating cycles of disengagement. Seven of Creswell's (2003) eight strategies for establishing qualitative data validity were incorporated into the method, and were shown to overlap with suitable methods for establishing reliability. The method was piloted with a single participant and a number of relatively small changes were made. Interview data was to be transcribed in full, supported by ongoing use of the audio recordings, coded and analysed together with the survey data. The research aims, the concretized conceptual framework and the research design and methodology together constituted this study's approach to elucidating NEET's dialectical 'black box'.

Inside the 'black box'

The function of personal agency has been elucidated through a set of empirical findings that account coherently for a number of complex, heterogeneous and problematic dynamics within NEET. The findings detail the function's relationship to ten discrete elements of the NEET topography, and its outworking through the four 'core features' of agency. These are each and collectively useful since they can be used to isolate and examine individual components or sets of components within the function. From, and in addition to these, a number of cross-cutting principles and mechanisms describing the function are developed. In regard to the interactions between the function and the structures of NEET these include the inseparability of EET from the total life of the young person, the idea that instability and crisis often precede and compound disengagement and a distinction between the hard and softer influences of structure. They also include the shaping of patterns of agentic behaviours throughout the life course, the mediation of structural influences to young people through the discursive environment and agentic modelling, and the perceived primacy of agency in determining EET outcomes. With reference to the function itself they include observations of the young person's limited capacity for agency, the prioritization of intentions, the importance of perceived prospects, zones of optimal pressure and the eminence of intentionality. The concept of intra-agency was developed, along with its sub-concepts of intra-agentic facilitation, compensation, suppression and undermining, and the related idea of intra-agentic quorums. Each principle or mechanism has its own particular relevance and application to empirical processes of engagement and disengagement.

Together the findings account for observations of agentic function, and the production of outcomes, in over ninety highly varied EET/NEET transitions. The findings interlink coherently with one another to provide an overall account of the function. This is developed and presented in the form of a diagrammatic model which describes the relations of the major thematic findings to one another, providing a useful panoramic overview of the function as an empirical whole. The model and findings are demonstrably relevant to the research contexts from which the study derives, and can be applied usefully to refine and build upon existing knowledge. Their uses are shown to include identifying deficiencies in the models of 'the function' underlying NEET discourses, offering further explanation for observations made in other studies, handling unsubstantiated claims in the literature and accounting for heterogeneity in NEET cases. They are also useful for elucidating previously difficult areas of the dialectical interactions within NEET, identifying the mechanisms that mediate between conditions and outcomes and assessing and developing potential approaches to policy and praxis.

It may also be argued from this that the overarching strategy of situating NEET within the structure-agency debate has proven successful. It has enabled the study to articulate and frame meaningful problems in the broad NEET policy literature, and has ultimately led to findings that account coherently for the determination of EET outcomes in terms of agency and structure concepts. The particularities of the approach have also been useful in several ways. The adaptation of Bandura's (2001) conceptualization of agency appears to be justified by the findings, as through it, it was possible to empirically demarcate the exercise of personal agency within dialectically complex cases of disengagement. This has enabled a precise detailing of the interactions within NEET's dialectical 'black box, and allowed the study to describe how personal agency functions in a highly diverse set of circumstances. It was also seen to enable original findings including those related to intra-agency, wherein features of agency act upon one another with meaningful effects. As indicated earlier, intra-agency enables the explanation of some empirically observed behaviour that would otherwise be problematic, and highlights an otherwise unobservable sophistication of the dialectical relationship, that is, by indicating a NEET young person's agency might be compromised in certain instances, but not necessarily by structure.

The use of Bandura's (2001) conceptualization indicates an interesting observation, not yet discussed, that challenges notions of disengagement. By associating agency with perceptual activity, it presents somewhat of a conundrum; if, as seen in some cases within this study, a young person disengages from EET deliberately to give themselves more space to think, and engages in intentional thinking, forethought and self-reflection during this time, it may not be entirely true to say they are disengaged. Although they are formally disengaged, they are not disengaged in agentic terms. This challenges the sometimes implied association of a young person's formal NEET status with a disengaged state of mind and affect. Such associations are implicit in some policy narratives, and, as Colley (2006) argues, may be unhelpful. The findings in this study may help to redress this, and cultivate awareness that although some NEET young people may indeed be psychologically disengaged at times, many others may not.

The adaptation of the conceptualization of structure developed from Lopez and Scott (2000) has also been useful. This sensitized the study in important ways, including to an observation that young people are perceptually inclined to view structural influences, wherever feasible, in personal and relational (i.e. dyadic) terms. The influences of schools, for example, were consistently located in relationships with individual teachers, and the influence of government policies were often pinned on individual civil servants and even 'David Cameron'. For NEET young people then, structures appear to be located in, and produced and transformed by individuals, and structural influences most meaningfully effected through personal relationships. The conceptualization also enabled the handling of key narratives in the data, and allowed for meaningful links back to the literature from which the research problem was developed. This was instantiated, for example, in the earlier contestation of Colley's (2006) suggestions about the potential of relationships to transform outcomes.

The use of the topography to concretize and operationalize the concepts was productive. It enabled the study to develop the findings on the ten discrete elements of NEET. This enhances the utility of the findings to academics, policymakers and practitioners seeking to understand particular areas of NEET relevant to their fields. It also sensitized the study to differences in the kinds and classes of structural influences in NEET as are reflected in the diagrammatic model. Crucially, it enabled the study to identify a number of common mechanisms underlying the influences of all structures within NEET. This provides a basis for identifying and handling salient interactions and conditions that may affect young people, and for introducing commonalities of praxis for working with them, that are applicable within any given environment, whether addressed directly by the study or not. It also enabled the coherent handling of unanticipated data, such as surfaced in the form of two additions to the topography: media influences and religion.

A particular weakness in the approach might be associated with this last observation. It is clear that the topography of NEET developed from the literature was incomplete. Celebrity and media influences, and faith and religion, both appeared unexpectedly as influences on the agentic expression of young people towards EET. This occurred in a sample of sixteen, compared to a total population of 1.04 million NEET young people (aged sixteen to twenty-four) around the time of the sample (ONS 2014a). It can be reasonably argued that further sampling might uncover more influences, and so the topography of NEET presented in the study may be an incomplete one. This potential criticism is accepted, although it is somewhat mitigated on the basis of the intentionally formative nature of the approach. Future research may seek to address this.

As sought, the theoretical approach facilitated the exploration of otherwise unexaminable areas of dialectical interaction in NEET. It was also seen to be useful for addressing a range of conceptual and empirical challenges that have historically been problematic for researchers. It provides an example of how original conceptualizations of structure and agency might be effectively operationalized through careful theorizing, and lead to findings which address difficult empirical problems. On this basis it can be seen that the approach provides a response to the specific concerns underlying Coffey and Farrugia's (2014) call for new approaches to the treatment of agency and structure in youth transitions, as will be developed below.

Several aspects of the approach might be particularly interesting to other researchers. This includes examining discourses of interest for the underlying concepts of structure and agency present within them, and developing theoretical frameworks that allow them to be treated integrally (as was done in the association of the institutional and relational structure types to the dominant forms of structure in the NEET policy literature). It also includes developing topographies of phenomena as a means to approaching the examination of the dialectical interactions within them. The concept of the function of personal agency might be used directly. It is intended that the consideration, critique and adaptation of the approach by other researchers will yield further benefits.

A methodological consistency with the theoretical approach of the study was also achieved, and the overall results of this are indicated above. The major risks to data collection were effectively mitigated, and several positive indicators about the quality of data were observed. A demographically diverse sample of sixteen young people (including the pilot) was obtained, containing a relatively balanced representation of genders, a mixture of ages within the target age bracket and a spectrum of NEET types (i.e. short-term, 'churners' and long-term NEETs). White British, White Irish (Traveller), Eastern European, Black Caribbean, Black African, Bangladeshi and Mixed White/Asian ethnicities were represented. The diversity was not only demographic, but also qualitative in terms of personality and character types, personal backgrounds and life stories. The data obtained from participants was voluminous and rich in relevant content, even from those expected to be shy or otherwise problematic. The decision to address NEET 'churn' as proposed was a boon; the ninety instances of EET/NEET transitions were observed in the data on its account, and this was very useful for identifying and verifying key findings.

Indicators suggested the data was strongly valid and reliable. In terms of the planned indicators, these particularly included the triangulation of data, which was linked both to validity and reliability. A high level of integrity across all three proposed sources was found once interpretive factors in the completion of the survey were accounted for. Two unintended indicators also supported this. First, in exploring their EET histories, and then their perceptions of the NEET topography, it was found that interviewees criss-crossed over the same stories and perceptions from multiple angles. It was possible therefore to assess the data for consistency within interviews, and this was found to be very high. Second, some participants intimated that the data might have an unusual level of authenticity. This was linked to perceptions of the interviewing researcher as a peer, and it was indicated by them that this allowed greater openness and frankness than might otherwise be expected. This was immediately useful for this study, but does problematize its replicability for other researchers if they are unable to be perceived similarly.

A limited case may be made for the generalizability of the findings, as was expected. This is primarily supported by the heterogeneity of the sample and the NEET cases within the data, and the capability of the findings to account for this heterogeneity. It is also supported by indicative evidence in the wider literature that some of the key findings hold true at larger scales. The limitations are associated with the small sample size, and the observation that the small number and type of sampling sources may have introduced unknowable biases. Ultimately, generalizability cannot be properly determined without further investigation.

An original methodology consistent with the theoretical approach was successfully developed, and enabled the elucidation of NEET's dialectical 'black box'. The major risks associated with the population under study were mitigated. The findings benefit from high levels of validity and reliability. This was largely by design, but a number of unintentional factors also contributed to this, and leave some small concerns about replicability. A limited argument for the generalizability of the findings can be made, but cannot be ultimately determined without further investigation. The study has also gone beyond its aims in some ways, as is developed in the following discussions.

Thinking outside 'the box'

As indicated, the achievement of these aims has culminated in a set of useful and original findings. That the findings are original is in some instances a claim at the conceptual level (e.g. intra-agency and its sub-concepts) and in other instances a claim related to the means by which they were arrived at, that is, through data collected from a unique population by means of an original method. The claim that a particular finding is original does not however necessarily mean it is without precedent or relation in the existing literature. For example, the idea that instability and crisis are associated with disengagement is not new (e.g. MacDonald and Marsh 2001), but the findings may nonetheless provide new insights into the ways in which this might be true. Ultimately this links the study to a broader literature than it was originally concerned with. The links between the study and this literature might be useful to both; the findings of this study might be further developed by their use, and their utility might be extended into the domain of NEET.

For example, the original concept of the discursive environment might be related to and developed in the context of the literature on the dialogic, which includes Bakhtin (1981), Habermas (1984), Wells (1999) and Freire (2005). Bakhtin's (1981) concept of dialogism states a relation among language, interaction and social transformation, wherein the individual does not exist outside of dialogue, and wherein present dialogues stem from historical chains of dialogue. Habermas (1984) develops a theory of communicative action, according to which the notions of objectivity driving social action are produced and reproduced through dialogue, and particular social institutions may emerge through the control of communicative platforms. Wells (1999) discusses 'dialogic inquiry', which involves a language-based theorizing of human development and posits the centrality of linguistic discourse in learning and socialization. Freire (2005) considers human nature to be fundamentally dialogic; education and social change largely involves the use of dialogue to create the capacity for discovery and awareness. These discussions clearly relate to the idea that agentic patterns develop over the life course through discursive interactions, and impact upon educational and social outcomes. An examination of the findings in relation to these texts might develop their ideas specifically in relation to NEET, and inform the pathways of future studies that seek to further explicate the importance of the discursive environment.

Developing the findings' relations to broader areas of sociological, psychological and educational thought might therefore comprise the focus of much future research. This could be done in relation to specific individual findings as just discussed, and also to wider considerations that might be made. For example, a future study could examine notions of social capital (Bourdieu 1980) present in the findings. It is clear that families and other relationships exude significant influence over the agency of NEET young people, and as was found earlier, a number of young people circumvented structural barriers through advantages derived from relationships. These ideas suggest that social capital may be a key factor in the production and transformation of NEET. It is not apparent whether the observations made in this study similarly apply to young people who do not become NEET. It may be that a focus on social capital is an intentional strategy used by NEETs to compensate for poor grade performance or lack of employment experience. As Bassani (2007) indicates, despite a number of existing studies on social capital in youth transitions, there is much that remains unexplored. Numerous other avenues by which the study could be linked to theory in the broader literature could be similarly developed.

The catharsis of the *vexata quaestio*?

Cuzzocrea (2013: 7) posited that the question of the extent to which young people are determining their own outcomes is NEET's *vexata quaestio*, or 'vexed question'. The question is both a theoretical and an empirical one. The findings of this study open more clearly for examination the nature of the problem underlying the question. The three circles in the model (Figure 7.1) indicate three extents to which young people are implicated in their own (dis)engagement. The outer circle is associated with intractable circumstances which force disengagement on young people (e.g. through redundancy or provider closure) or otherwise force on them a prioritization of intentions that may well result in their disengagement. The middle circle is associated with the subtler or 'softer' influences of structure on the young person, which interact with young people's existing intentions, motivational dispositions and processes of choice and self-reactiveness. It is in this middle circle that the influences of agency and structure are at their most fluid and overlapping. The inner circle is associated with the volitional activity of the young person in its least restricted and even whimsical forms.

The primary driving factors within each of the more than ninety EET transitions observed in the data can be located more or less strongly within or across these circles. The vexed nature of the question is brought to the fore when it is realized that even within the life of a single young person, the circle with which one instance of disengagement might be most closely associated differs from the circle with which their next instance of disengagement might be most closely associated. Darren enrolled onto an FE course at the encouragement of his parents (middle circle) and then dropped out at his own volition (inner circle). The next two instances of disengagement in his 'churning' process, however, resulted from his employment on zero-hour and then temporary contract types (outer circle). Attempting to reduce the causation of NEET to primarily agentic or structural forces is therefore sometimes not sufficient to explain the events in the life of a single individual, let alone anything broader. The extent to which a young person is determining their own outcomes changes with every transition. Even the association of particular transitions with one or more of the circles, although useful, might be too tidy; none of the circles are able to retain their capacity for influence if decontextualized from the others. Although then, this study's findings therefore refute the simplification, or reduction, of the problem in this way, they do not leave the addressing of the 'vexed question' without hope of resolution.

Rather, the empirical detailing of the function of personal agency signals a powerful opportunity to move productively beyond the contestation between relatively intentionalist and structuralist positions on the determination of EET outcomes, as is present in the current discourses of the sociological youth transitions literature (Heinz 2009; Thompson 2011; Coffey and Farrugia 2014) and in the NEET policy literature more broadly. This is because the model and findings contain and then transcend the dominant intentionalist position, associated (although not necessarily fairly) with Beck's (1992) individualization thesis (Woodman 2009). Individual biographies and the outworking of personal choices are the key units of the individualization thesis (Woodman 2009). These are subsumed within the model and findings, and positioned coherently in respect to the complex empirical settings and structures of NEET, in a way that accounts for a multiplicity of transitions. The result is a cohesive set of principles and mechanisms that describe the joint production of outcomes by agentic and structural influences, for a heterogeneous group of young people in a highly varied range of conditions. In this way the model and findings reach from the 'bottom-up' towards the sought after 'middle ground' of youth transitions theory, while ostensibly avoiding the particular issues of abstraction and politicization that have problematized previous attempts (Coffey and Farrugia 2014). They are not simply an affirmation that NEET is produced through dialectical interactions, but offer particular empirical detail of what these interactions consist of, how they are important and which aspects of them can be said to belong to agency and which to structure. Coffey and Farrugia seem to suggest this may not yet have been attained elsewhere.

At this point, a further opportunity to progress the study's contribution to transitions theory coincides with what is perhaps its most important weakness. In taking a 'bottom-up' approach, that is, one in which the life and circumstances of the individual young person are the focal point, the study may partially overlook 'broader constraints imposed by macro-level social systems' (Russell, Simmons and Thompson 2011: 103) that are thought to be crucially implicated in the production of NEET. These broader constraints are typically associated with gender, ethnicity and class status (e.g. Aaltonen 2013; Simmons, Russell and Thompson 2014). Where the sample is sufficiently diverse to support a very limited argument for the generalizability of the findings across the first two of these, the issue of class status has been little attended to; class data is not recorded in the CCIS data from which this study developed its demographic concerns (DfE 2013b). Class status, insofar as it may be reduced to notions of socioeconomic status, may be meaningfully associated with NEET status. Yates et al. (2011) who largely define class status in such terms, find that young males from lower socio-economic statuses are up to 300 per cent more likely to become NEET, after controlling for certain aspirational and educational factors. This study provides evidence that arguments overemphasizing structural inequalities are essentially incapable of accounting for NEET in any comprehensive sense; the diversity of cases in the life of a single 'churner' imposes an acute and quite indispensable sense of individualization, and by no means do all young people of lower class groups become NEET. Such relatively structuralist findings as those of Yates et al. must nonetheless be accounted for. More work must be done for the 'middle ground' to be fully explored.

A future study might comparatively examine the function of personal agency in determining outcomes for groups of young people from different class backgrounds, using the model, and perhaps the topography developed in this study. By deliberately revisiting the investigation of the function in this way, findings may be produced that account for the effects of macro-level structural inequalities (i.e. top-down influences) in producing EET outcomes. This would help to reconcile the findings of this study with the literature that observes the influences of these inequalities on outcomes, securing the grasp of the findings on the 'middle ground'. It may also provide revealing information on how the influences of inequalities such as class status are mediated to individual young people and their outcomes. Breen and Rottman (1995) discuss the difficulty of determining how class status influences the determination of outcomes across generations.

Cultural factors in the home and school environments, personal and familial social capital and access to differentiated resources and opportunities may all play a part. The model and topography might well be used to understand the interactions of these, and their relative contributions to outcomes for different class groups. This might then be used to reduce the impacts of inequalities. 'Hard' economic inequalities may be difficult to redress, but if young people in higher class statuses are found to benefit from cultural factors in the home or school environment associated with the quality of discursive interactions and the more effective shaping of habitual patterns of agentic behaviour, these may be transferable.

The approach of utilizing a conceptual framework that afforded consistency across the theoretical and empirical levels of the study now offers its greater good; the theoretical potential of the study is matched by a practical potential. Pushing into the 'middle ground' with the level of empirical specificity provided in the findings is not only a progressive act within itself, but also offers a platform for the development of a genuinely dialectical approach to resolving NEET. It has been established that the model and findings have a diverse applicability to issues of policy and praxis, and open up avenues to a broad range of future studies and action research projects. They thus engage the 'triangle' of policymaker, researcher and practitioner (Cuzzocrea 2013) in the consideration of NEET's multi-element dialectical arrangement, and indicate an opportunity to pursue a coherent and coordinated approach to the treatment of the arrangement as a whole. Within this, the fuller explication of each principle or mechanism within the 'black box', and the development of its applications for policy and praxis in respect to NEET's topography, may represent a step towards the catharsis of the issues underlying the *vexata quaestio*, and towards the reduction of NEET.

The nature of the policy and praxis that emerges from the catharsis might be unconventional. For example, earlier discussions indicated that the output of a good education ought not to be only thought of as the acquisition of literacy and numeracy skills and a set of basic qualifications. Rather it ought to include a healthy motivational disposition, effective coping mechanisms and perhaps a keen metacognitive awareness. Perhaps the discursive practices of teachers by which they shape the motivations and patterns of agentic behaviour in learners may eventually come to be seen as no less important than the more conventional purposes and practices of pedagogy. This is not yet clear. The challenge now lies with policymakers, researchers and practitioners to consider how the function of personal agency might be harnessed to produce better outcomes for those in their charge.

What is clearer is that the various elements of the NEET topography ought to be looked at as comprising a whole, or parts of a whole. On this basis, the findings of this study support in principle the arguments of Simmons et al. (2014) for a 'Youth Resolution' in which employers, training providers, voluntary organizations and local authorities work together to provide a cohesive EET environment. This kind of approach might be complemented by frameworks for cultivating the effective use of personal agency by young people, developed from this study and embedded across such environments. If policy elements such as those represented within the government's Social Justice Strategy (HM Government 2012b; 2013b) are also considered, particularly those relating to supporting familial stability, then many of the major components of a complete dialectical approach could be said to be emerging. The influences of organizations, relationships and the function of personal agency itself (i.e. the main building blocks of the NEET topography) are all represented. The scene is thus set for a fresh consideration of NEET, and a new attempt at solving it. It is hoped that the 'triangle' of professionals will respond to this call based on a deeper understanding of the nature of the relationship between agency and structure as it has been articulated by the hidden voices of the NEET young people in this study.

The nature of the dialectic

The overarching implication of the model and findings is that NEET, and all its related policy and praxis, is inescapably situated in a multi-element dialectical arrangement. It was indicated earlier that this is associated with some interesting abstractions about the nature of the dialectical relationship between agency and structure, or in Akram's (2010) shorthand, 'the dialectic'. These proceed from the observation that the model of the function of personal agency developed in the study is essentially a model of 'the dialectic' as it is represented within the minds of young people. This is consistent with the use of Bandura's (2001) agentic perspective on social cognitive theory, which conceptualized agency as an essentially psychological phenomenon, and with the observation that the findings are developed from young people's subjective accounts. Although the findings definitely appear to have meaning and application beyond simply understanding the subjective views of young people, the model is rooted and grounded within that subjectivity. The function of personal agency is given effect through young people's mentally held perceptions of how structure and agency interact to determine outcomes at a given point in time. Structure is therefore perceptually internalized within agentic function, which is then not only a reflection of intentions, plans and self-managing and self-reflective behaviours, but also of the words and actions of others, and the acceptance of particular conditions as intractable.

A more sophisticated picture of agency develops when consideration is also given to the evidence in the study's findings that habitual agentic behaviours are shaped throughout the life course. This evidence suggests that the entire representation of the dialectic (i.e. not only the representation of the sociostructural environment, but also of the agentic responses to it, as represented together in the three concentric circles of the model) becomes subsumed within the agentic function (i.e. the inner circle alone), so that as time progresses and new circumstances and environmental conditions surround the young person, this entire representation is carried forward into them. The mentally held dialectic is then played out in the context of the new 'real' dialectic, shaping its representation and the interactions that occur within it, as it itself also becomes subsumed into the agentic function. This may explain, for example, Brian's association of his experiences in the Job Centre with playground bullying, and his common responses to both.

The picture of agentic function emerging from this consideration of the model is analogous to the development of tree rings. Each subsumed representation of the present dialectic becomes another ring, this ring being shaped partly by those that went before and partly by the present environment. Particularly potent interactions (e.g. those that are emotionally charged, or otherwise occur within key formative moments) thus shape the entire subsequent development of the agentic function until such a time as a process of catharsis, for example, mitigates their effects. The ultimate picture of personal agentic function then is one within which a concatenation of sociohistorical dialectics are perceptually represented and superimposed upon one another, and invoked to interpret and respond to present conditions. Within this, countless historical and present discursive interactions mediate motivational states and intentions, a library of agentic models offers choices for courses of action and new 'hard' environmental conditions whimsically summon old senses of fear or opportunity. Sociohistorical structural influences become so intrinsic to the function of personal agency that, viewed over sufficient time, the notion of agency and structure being truly independent within it appears irretrievable.

These abstractions find strong parallels in the work of Norbert Elias, who develops the view that not only can the individual not be taken out of society, but society cannot be taken out of the individual. Elias (1991: viii) suggests that the 'patterns of self-regulation which the individual has to develop within himself or herself' are sociohistorically constructed through a 'civilising process'. It is 'only in relation to other human beings' that the individual becomes a 'psychologically developed person with the character of an individual' (21). This is akin to the ideas that unique patterns of agentic function are shaped throughout the life course, and through relational influences as are severally represented in the model. In Elias (2000), behaviours that begin as responses to the social environment, which he labels sociogenic behaviours, eventually continue without the social conditions or prompts that first caused them. Instead, having been internalized and personally validated, they are reproduced on the agent's own terms, as seems fit to them. The behaviours have become psychogenic. The transition between the sociogenic and psychogenic appears in essence to be the subsuming of the dialectic into the agentic function through a process of mental representation as has just been developed.

Although this study supports Archer's (1995) view that maintaining the independence between agency and structure is analytically useful, as it was by such means that the study arrived at its findings, it seems therefore the two cannot ultimately be separated in the long-term production of empirical agentic behaviours. At this level at least it might be concluded, as conveyed by Elias (1991), that agency and structure are a false dichotomy (Little 2010). The concluding implications of this are meaningful. Even in circumstances where personal agency may be held to be the most important singular influence in the determination of EET outcomes, the young person appears not be singularly responsible for how their agency is exercised. Rather responsibility for the exercise of individual personal agency appears to be shared with those with whom the young person has interacted and observed over the life course, and with those near and far who have influenced the conditions in which their agency must be exercised. The catharsis of NEET's *vexata quaestio* might eventually show that we are all somehow implicated in its production. Standish's (2007: iv) discussion of NEET indicated that it is 'incumbent on us … to take seriously the ways in which our social world and our place within it are reconstructed'. This study confirms that it also incumbent on us to do our part in finding NEET's solution.

Conclusion

This study set out to address NEET's *vexata quaestio*, and identify the extent to which young people are determining their own EET outcomes. An original theoretical and methodological approach was developed and carried out to obtain empirical findings on the function of personal agency in the lives of NEET young people. The investigation coincided with Coffey and Farrugia's (2014) call to researchers to develop a better defined and less politicized account of the 'middle ground' of youth transitions theory. This study's bold approach to elucidating NEET's dialectical 'black box' has provided a formative response to this call, and met its own aims in the process. The findings of the study subsume and transcend an individualization thesis, to present a cohesive set of principles and mechanisms that empirically describe the joint production of outcomes by agentic and structural influences, for a heterogeneous group of young people in a highly varied range of circumstances. The findings stand to be useful for researchers, policymakers and practitioners from the diverse fields of expertise represented in NEET's topography.

A number of cues for possible future research pursuits are indicated throughout the study, and are summarized here. First, it is noted that the data obtained by the study has not been exhausted. Future research could return to it with different questions, or narrow in on particular content within it. The study might be replicated in whole or part with different samples. These might be drawn from relatively similar populations (e.g. young people with similar demographics from other UK cities), or quite different populations (e.g. young people from ethnic minorities, or those in international cultures where it is accepted that there are common differences in assertiveness levels or psychological responses to sociostructural changes; Chuah 2010; Toivonen, Norasakkunkit and Uchida 2011). Comparative studies might be carried out with young people of different class backgrounds, to reconcile the findings with observations of the effects of structural inequalities on NEET, and thereby better secure the position of the findings in the 'middle ground'. Such research will enable further consideration of the generalizability of the model and findings, and develop the base of empirical evidence on the function of personal agency.

Future studies might also seek to examine specific aspects of the model and findings in more detail. This might pertain to observations extrapolated directly from the data, for example, the potential relationship between habitual patterns of agency and emotionally intense events in the life course. It might otherwise be done by first developing the findings in the context of other educational, sociological and psychological literature. For example, the concept of the discursive environment might be developed with respect to the literature on the dialogic (e.g. Bakhtin 1981; Habermas 1984; Wells 1999; Freire 2005). The role of discursive environments in NEET could then be revisited with attention paid to their particular theoretical concerns. It might also take place through action research projects focused on the application of findings to praxis. This indicatively includes applying considerations about the inseparability of EET from the wider life of the young person to the design and evaluation of mentoring programmes, and investigating how interventions to address young people's coping behaviours might positively shift zones of optimal pressure. It might also involve the extension of the model and findings to the critique of literature, policy and praxis in other fields, perhaps far beyond NEET.

In all of this, the study offers a platform for a catharsis of NEET's *vexata quaestio*, and the development of a genuinely dialectical solution to what is, ultimately, a dialectical problem.

References

Aaltonen, S. (2013) '"Trying to push things through": forms and bounds of agency in transitions of school-age young people', *Journal of Youth Studies*, 16 (3), 375–90.

ACEVO (2012) *Youth unemployment: the crisis we cannot afford*. [online] Available at: http://www.learningandwork.org.uk/sites/niace_en/files/event_downloads/ACEVO_report.pdf?redirectedfrom=cesi [accessed 29 March 2016].

Agnew, S. (2014) *Youth unemployment: what makes a difference?* [online] Available at: http://societycentral.ac.uk/2014/03/11/youth-unemployment-what-makes-a-difference [accessed 30 April 2014].

Akram, S. (2010) *Re-conceptualising the concept of agency in the structure and agency dialectic: habitus and the unconscious*. Unpublished PhD thesis. Birmingham: University of Birmingham. [online] Available at: http://www.scribd.com/doc/60179160/Habitus-and-Unconscious [accessed 26 April 2014].

Alexander, J. C. and Colomy, P. (1985) 'Toward neo-functionalism', *Sociological Theory*, 3 (2), 11–23.

Allen, G. (2011) *Early Intervention: The Next Steps. An Independent Report to Her Majesty's Government*. HM Government.

Archer, M. S. (1995) *Realist Social Theory: A Morphogenetic Approach*. Cambridge: Cambridge University Press.

Arnett, J. J. (2000) 'Emerging adulthood: a theory of development from the late teens through the twenties', *American Psychologist*, 55, 469–80.

Ashton, D. and Maguire, M. (1988) 'Re-structuring the labour market: the implications for education and training', Labour Market Studies Working Paper 14. Leicester: University of Leicester.

Ashton, D., Maguire, M. and Garland, V. (1982) *Youth in the Labour Market*. Research Report 34. London: Department for Employment.

Bakhtin, M. (1981) *The Dialogic Imagination: Four Essays*. Austin: University of Texas Press.

Bandura, A. (2001) 'Social cognitive theory: an agentic perspective', *Annual Review of Psychology*, (52), 1–26.

Barabási, A. (2003) *Linked*. New York: Plume.

Barker, C. (2003) *Cultural Studies: Theory and Practice*. 2nd edn. London: Sage.

Bassani, C. (2007) 'Five dimensions of social capital theory as they pertain to youth studies', *Journal of Youth Studies*, 10 (1), 17–34.

BBC (2011) 'England rioters "poorer, younger, less educated"'. 24 October. [online] Available at: http://www.bbc.co.uk/news/uk-15426720 [accessed 29 March 2016].

Beale, I., Bloss, C. and Thomas, A. (2008) 'The longer-term impact of the New Deal for Young People', Working Paper 23. DWP. [online] Available at: core.kmi.open.ac.uk/download/pdf/4157044.pdf [accessed 22 May 2014].

Beck, U. (1992) *Risk Society: Towards a New Modernity*. Sage: London.

BERA [British Educational Research Association] (2011) *Ethical Guidelines for Educational Research*. [online] Available at: http://www.bera.ac.uk/wp-content/uploads/2014/02/BERA-Ethical-Guidelines-2011.pdf [accessed 22 May 2014].

Berry, R. S. Y. (1999) 'Collecting data by in-depth interviewing', paper presented at *The British Educational Research Association Annual Conference*, University of Sussex, Brighton: 2–5 September 1999. [online] Available at: www.leeds.ac.uk/educol/documents/000001172.htm [accessed 4 May 2014].

Boffey, D. (2015). 'Youth unemployment rate is worst for 20 years, compared with overall figure'. *The Guardian*, 22 February 2015. Available at: https://www.theguardian.com/society/2015/feb/22/youth-unemployment-jobless-figure.

Bogdan, R. G. and Biklen, S. K. (1992) *Qualitative Research for Education: An introduction to theory and methods*. 2nd edn. Boston, MA: Allyn and Bacon.

Bourdieu, P. (1979) *Distinction: A Social Critique of the Judgement of Taste*. London: Routledge, 1984.

Bourdieu, P. (1980) *The Logic of Practice*. Cambridge: Polity Press, 1990.

Bourdieu, P. (1999) *The Weight of the World: Social Suffering in Contemporary Society*. Polity Press: Cambridge.

Bourdieu, P. and Wacquant, L. J. D. (1992) *An Invitation to Reflexive Sociology*. Cambridge: Polity Press.

Boydston, J., Cullather, N., Lewis, J. M., McGerr, M. and Oakes, J. (2001) *Making a Nation: The United States and Its People, Combined Edition*. New York: Prentice Hall.

Bradshaw, J. and Mayhew, E. (2011) *The Measurement of Extreme Poverty in the European Union*. Brussels: European Commission, Directorate-General for Employment, Social Affairs and Inclusion.

Breen, R. and Rottman, D. (1995) 'Class Analysis and Class Theory', *Sociology*, 29 (3), 453–73.

Bruno, G. S. F., Marelli, E. and Signorelli, M. (2013) 'People in crisis: NEETs and unemployed in EU regions', paper presented at *The 53rd ERSA Congress*, Palermo, Italy: 27–31 August 2013. [online] Available at: http://www-sre.wu.ac.at/ersa/ersaconfs/ersa13/ERSA2013_paper_00895.pdf [accessed 29 March 2016].

Bynner, J. (1991) 'Transitions to work: results from a longitudinal study of young people in four British labour markets', in D. N. Ashton and G. S. Lowe (eds), *Making Their Way: Education, Training and the Labour Market in Canada and Britain*. Milton Keynes: Open University Press, 171–95.

Bynner, J. (2005) 'Rethinking the youth phase of the life course: the case for emerging adulthood?', *Journal of Youth Studies*, 8, 367–84.

CAB [Citizens Advice Bureau] (2013) 'Access to education'. [online] Available at: http://www.adviceguide.org.uk/england/education_e/education_school_education_ew/access_to_education.htm [accessed 1 May 2014].

Carcillo, S., Fernández, R., Königs, S. and Minea, A. (2015) 'NEET youth in the aftermath of the crisis: challenges and policies', OECD Social, Employment and Migration Working Papers, No. 164. Paris: OECD Publishing. [online] Available at: http://dx.doi.org/10.1787/5js6363503f6-en [accessed 29 March 2016].

Charles, C. M. and Mertler, C. A. (2002) *Introduction to Educational Research*. 4th edn. Boston, MA: Allyn and Bacon.

Chen, Y. (2011) 'Once "NEET", always "NEET"? Experiences of employment and unemployment of youth participating in a job training program in Taiwan', *International Journal of Social Welfare*, 20 (1), 33–42.

China Today (2005) 'NEET generation refuses to grow up', *China Today*, 54 (6), 9.

Chuah, S. (2010) 'Teaching East-Asian students: some observations'. [online] Available at: http://www.economicsnetwork.ac.uk/showcase/chuah_international [accessed 1 May 2014].

Churchland, P. M. and Churchland, P. S. (1998) *On the Contrary: Critical Essays, 1987–1997*. Cambridge: The MIT Press.

Coenen, G., Straub, R. and Trabandt, M. (2012) 'Fiscal policy and the great recession in the Euro area', European Central Bank Working Paper Series No. 1429. [online] Available at: https://www.ecb.europa.eu/pub/pdf/scpwps/ecbwp1429.pdf?b430b9518b0feb0e2fe8195f65a7b465 [accessed 29 March 2016].

Coffey, J. and Farrugia, D. (2014) 'Unpacking the black box: the problem of agency in the sociology of youth', *Journal of Youth Studies*, 17 (4), 461–74.

Cohen, L., Lawrence, M. and Morrison, K. (2011) *Research Methods in Education*. 7th edn. Hampshire: Routledge.

Coleman, J. C. and Hendry, L. B. (1999) *The Nature of Adolescence*. 3rd edn. London: Routledge.

Colley, H. (2003) 'Engagement mentoring for socially excluded youth: problematising an "holistic" approach to creating employability through the transformation of habitus', *Journal of Guidance and Counselling*, 31 (1), 77–100.

Colley, H. (2006) 'Mentoring for young people not in education, employment or training: a "NEET" solution, but to whose problems?', paper commissioned by the *Nuffield Review of 14–19 Education and Training*. [online] Available at: http://www.e-space.mmu.ac.uk/e-space/handle/2173/14199 [accessed 3 May 2014].

Cooper, C. (2012) 'Understanding the English "riots" of 2011: "mindless criminality" or youth "Mekin Histri" in austerity Britain?', *Youth & Policy*, 109, 6–26. [online] Available at: http://www.youthandpolicy.org/wp-content/uploads/2013/04/cooper_riots_2011.pdf [accessed 29 March 2016].

Creswell, J. W. (2003) *Research Design: Qualitative, Quantitative and Mixed Methods Approaches*. Thousand Oaks, CA: Sage.

Creswell, J. W. (2012) *Educational Research: Planning, Conducting, and Evaluating Quantitative and Qualitative Research*. 4th edn. Boston, MA: Pearson.

Cuzzocrea, V. (2013) *Projecting the Category of NEET into the Future*. Strasbourg, France: Youth Partnership, European Union and Council of Europe. [online] Available at: http://hdl.voced.edu.au/10707/285216 [accessed 3 June 2014].

Dalakoglou, D. (2013) 'The crisis before "the crisis": violence and urban neoliberalization in Athens', *Social Justice*, 39 (1), 24–42.

Davidson, M. (2009) 'Neets: the forgotten underclass', *The Telegraph*, 17 July. [online] Available at: http://www.telegraph.co.uk/lifestyle/5844568/Neets-the-forgotten-underclass.html [accessed 29 March 2016].

de Vaus, D. A. (2003) *Surveys in Social Research*. 5th edn. London: Routledge.

DfE (2010) 'NEET statistics – quarterly brief: November 2010'. London: DfE. [online] Available at: http:tinyurl.com/DfE-NEET-Statistics [accessed 3 May 2014].

DfE (2011) 'Youth cohort study and longitudinal study of young people in England: the activities and experiences of 18 year olds: England 2010'. [online] Available at: https://www.gov.uk/government/uploads/system/uploads/attachment_data/file/219058/b01-2011v2.pdf [accessed 29 March 2016].

DfE (2013a) '2012 local authority NEET figures'. [online] Available at: https://www.gov.uk/government/publications/neet-data-by-local-authority-2012-16-to-18-year-olds-not-in-education-employment-or-training [accessed 3 May 2014].

DfE (2013b) 'Management information requirement from the Client Caseload Information System: 2013–2014'. [online] Available at: https://www.gov.uk/government/uploads/system/uploads/attachment_data/file/294915/nccis_mi_requirement_2013_to_2014.pdf [accessed 24 May 2014].

DfE (2014) 'NEET statistics – quarterly brief – October to December 2013'. London: DfE. [online] Available at: http:tinyurl.com/DfE-NEET-Statistics [accessed 3 May 2014].

DfE (2015a) 'NEET statistics – quarterly brief – July to September 2015, England'. London: DfE. [online] Available at: https://www.gov.uk/government/uploads/system/uploads/attachment_data/file/478391/NEET_Brief_Q3-2015.pdf [accessed 29 March 2016].

DfE (2015b) 'Statistical first release: NEET quarterly brief – April to June 2015'. London: DfE. [online] Available at: https://www.gov.uk/government/uploads/system/uploads/attachment_data/file/454401/Quarterly_Brief_NEET_Q2_2015.pdf [accessed 29 March 2016].

DfE (2016) 'NEET statistics – quarterly brief – October to December 2015, England'. London: DfE. [online] Available at: https://www.gov.uk/government/uploads/system/uploads/attachment_data/file/502684/OFFICIAL_SENSITIVE_NEET_Brief_Q4-2015_FINAL.pdf [accessed 29 March 2016].

DfE and BIS (2014) 'Additional tables 1: supplementary tables disaggregating NEET estimates from the LFS for 16- to 24-year-olds by; region and gender'. [online] Available at: https://www.gov.uk/government/uploads/system/uploads/ attachment_data/file/ 284202/NEET_Supplementary_tables_16_24.xls [accessed 22 May 2014].

Donnan, S. (2015) 'IMF approves €280m Cyprus bailout payment and praises reforms', *Financial Times*, 19 June. [online] Available at: http://www.ft.com/cms/s/0/34b84450-16c7-11e5-b07f-00144feabdc0.html [accessed 29 March 2016].

Durkheim, E. (1895) *The Rules of the Sociological Method*. London: Macmillan, 1982.

Durkheim, E. (1898) 'Individual and collective representations', in D. F. Pocock and J. G. Peristiany (eds), *E. Durkheim (1965) Sociology and Philosophy*. London: Cohen and West.

DWP (2013a) 'Youth contract'. [online] Available at: http://www.dwp.gov.uk/youth-contract/ [accessed 1 May 2014].

DWP (2013b) 'Youth contract wage incentive – experimental statistics'. [online] Available at: https://www.gov.uk/government/publications/youth-contract-wage-incentive-payments-experimental-statistics [accessed 1 May 2014].

DWP (2015a) 'Youth contract official statistics: April 2012 to May 2015'. [online] Available at: https://www.gov.uk/government/uploads/system/uploads/attachment_data/file/455663/youth-contract-statistics-to-may-2015.pdf [accessed 17 October 2015].

DWP (2015b) 'Unemployment falls below 6% as vacancies hit record high'. [online] Available at: https://www.gov.uk/government/news/unemployment-falls-below-6-as-vacancies-hit-record-high [accessed 8 February 2016].

DWP (2015c) 'Helping young people benefit from the rewards of work'. [online] Available at: https://www.gov.uk/government/speeches/helping-young-people-benefit-from-the-rewards-of-work [accessed 8 February 2016].

Education and Skills Act (2008) [online] Available at: http://www.legislation.gov.uk/ukga/2008/25/contents [accessed 9 September 2016].

EESC [European Economic and Social Committee] (2013) *Opinion on the Youth Guarantee*, SOC/485. EESC: Brussels. [online] Available at: http://www.eesc.europa.eu/?i=portal.en.soc-opinions.27502 [accessed 28 March 2016].

EFA [Education Funding Agency] (2014) *Youth Contract: Delivery Data*. [online] Available at: https://www.gov.uk/government/publications/youth-contract-delivery-data [accessed 22 May 2014].

EFSF [European Financial Stability Facility] (2016) 'About EFSF'. [online] Available at: http://www.efsf.europa.eu/about/index.htm [accessed 29 March 2016].

Elias, N. (1991) *The Society of Individuals*. Oxford: Basil Blackwell.

Elias, N. (2000) *The Civilizing Process: Sociogenetic and Psychogenetic Investigations*. 2nd edn. Oxford: Wiley-Blackwell.

EU [European Union] (2000) 'European Council, Lisbon: Conclusions of the Presidency', 23 and 24 March. [online] Available at: http://www.consilium.europa.eu/uedocs/cms_data/docs/pressdata/en/ec/00100-r1.en0.htm [accessed 2 May 2014].

EU (2005) 'The birth of the European Employment Strategy: the Luxembourg process (November 1997)'. [online] Available at: http://europa.eu/legislation_summaries/employment_and_social_policy/community_employment_policies/c11318_en.htm [accessed 2 May 2014].

Eurofound (2012) *NEETs – Young People Not in Employment, Education or Training: Characteristics, Costs and Policy Responses in Europe*. Luxembourg: Publications Office of the European Union.

Eurofound (2014) *Mapping Youth Transitions in Europe*. Luxembourg: Publications Office of the European Union.

Eurofound (2015) *Social Inclusion of Young People*. Luxembourg: Publications Office of the European Union.

European Commission (2014) 'Youth Guarantee: Commission reviews 18 pilots'. [online] Available at: http://europa.eu/rapid/press-release_IP-14-981_en.htm [accessed 29 March 2016].

European Commission (2016) 'EU Youth Strategy'. [online] Available at: http://ec.europa.eu/youth/policy/youth_strategy/index_en.htm [accessed 29 March 2016].

Eurostat (2015a) 'Youth unemployment'. [online] Available at: http://ec.europa.eu/eurostat/statistics-explained/index.php/Youth_unemployment [accessed 29 March 2016].

Eurostat (2015b) 'Glossary: young people neither in employment nor in education and training (NEET)'. [online] Available at: http://ec.europa.eu/eurostat/statistics-explained/index.php/Glossary:Young_people_neither_in_employment_nor_in_education_and_training_(NEET) [accessed 29 March 2016].

Eurostat (2016) 'Young people neither in employment nor in education and training by sex and age (NEET rates)'. [online] Available at: http://ec.europa.eu/eurostat/en/web/products-datasets/-/EDAT_LFSE_20 [accessed 29 March 2016].

Evans, K. (2002) 'Taking control of their lives? Agency in young adult transitions in England and the New Germany', *Journal of Youth Studies*, 5 (3), 245–69.

Evans, K. (2007) 'Concepts of bounded agency in education, work and the personal lives of young adults', *International Journal of Psychology*, 42 (2), 85–93.

Fergusson, R. (2013) 'Against disengagement: non-participation as an object of governance', *Research in Post-Compulsory Education*, 18 (1–2), 12–28.

Field, F. (2010) *The Foundation Years: Preventing Poor Children becoming Poor Adults. The Report of the Independent Review on Poverty and Life Chances*. HM Government. [online] Available at: http://webarchive.nationalarchives.gov.uk/20110120090128/http://povertyreview.independent.gov.uk/media/20254/poverty-report.pdf [accessed 26 April 2014].

Fishwick, T., Lane, P. and Gardiner, L. (2011) *Future Jobs Fund: An Independent National Evaluation*. London: CESI. [online] Available at: http://www.cesi.org.uk/sites/default/files/publications/CESI_future_jobs_fund_evaluation.pdf [accessed 22 May 2014].

Fletcher, M. (2008) 'Demolition of the Aylesbury Estate – a new dawn for Hell's waiting room', *The Times*, 20 October. [online] Available at: http://www.thetimes.co.uk/tto/life/property/article1768086.ece [accessed 25 May 2014].

Freire, P. (2005) *Pedagogy of the Oppressed: 30th Anniversary Edition*. New York: Continuum.

Furlong, A. (2006) 'Not a very NEET solution: representing problematic labour market transitions among early school-leavers', *Work, Employment and Society*, 20 (3), 553–69.

Furlong, A. and Cartmel, F. (2007) *Young People and Social Change: New Perspectives*. 2nd edn. Berkshire: Open University Press.

Furstenberg, F. (2010) 'On a new schedule: transitions to adulthood and family change', *Future of Children*, 20 (1), 67–87.

Giddens, A. (1973) *The Class Structure of the Advanced Societies*. London: Hutchinson.

Giddens, A. (1984) *The Constitution of Society*. Cambridge: Polity Press.

GLA [Greater London Authority] (2014) 'DC2101EW – ethnic group by sex by age', by email, 19 May 2014.

Gregg, P. and Tominey, E. (2004) 'The wage scar from youth unemployment', CPMO Working Paper Series No. 04/097. [online] Available at: http://www.bristol.ac.uk/media-library/sites/cmpo/migrated/documents/wp97.pdf [accessed 29 March 2016].

Habermas, J. (1984) *The Theory of Communicative Action. Volume 1: Reason and the Rationalisation of Society*. Bolton: Beacon.

Hayward, G., Wilde, S. and Williams, R. (2008) 'Rathbone/Nuffield review engaging youth enquiry. Consultation report', Rathbone/Nuffield. [online] Available at: http://ora.ox.ac.uk/objects/uuid:0df73fda-befd-431d-a1bf-cd53c2493531 [accessed 4 May 2014].

Heinz, W. R. (2000) 'Youth transitions and employment in Germany', *International Social Science Journal*, 52 (164), 161–70.

Heinz, W. R. (2009) 'Structure and agency in transition research', *Journal of Education and Work*, 22 (5), 391–404.

HM Government (2011) *Building Engagement, Building Futures: Our Strategy to Maximise the Participation of 16–24 Year Olds in Education, Training and Work*. [online] Available at: https://www.gov.uk/government/uploads/system/uploads/attachment_data/file/300215/Building_Engagement__Building_Futures.pdf [accessed 22 May 2014].

HM Government (2012a) 'Deputy prime minister speech at CBI Jobs Summit', delivered 27 June. [online] Available at: https://www.gov.uk/government/speeches/deputy-prime-minister-speech-at-cbi-jobs-summit [accessed 17 October 2015].

HM Government (2012b) *Social Justice: Transforming Lives*. Cm 8314. UK: HM Government. [online] Available at: https://www.gov.uk/government/uploads/system/uploads/attachment_data/file/49515/social-justice-transforming-lives.pdf [accessed 3 May 2014].

HM Government (2013a) 'Deputy prime minister announces multimillion pound boost for youth jobs'. [online] Available at: https://www.gov.uk/government/news/deputy-prime-minister-announces-multimillion-pound-boost-for-youth-jobs [accessed 17 October 2015].

HM Government (2013b) *Social Justice: Transforming Lives. One Year On*. Cm 8606. UK: [online] Available at: https://www.gov.uk/government/publications/social-justice-transforming-lives-one-year-on [accessed 3 May 2014].

HM Government (2015a) 'Number of young people NEET falls across the board'. [online] Available at: https://www.gov.uk/government/news/number-of-young-people-neet-falls-across-the-board [accessed 24 October 2015].

HM Government (2015b) 'Number of young people not in work or education falls to 10 year low'. [online] Available at: https://www.gov.uk/government/news/number-of-young-people-not-in-work-or-education-in-england-falls-to-10-year-low [accessed 24 October 2015].

HM Government (2016) 'Prime minister to announce new generation of mentors to help struggling teens'. [online] Available at: https://www.gov.uk/government/news/prime-minister-to-announce-new-generation-of-mentors-to-help-struggling-teens [accessed 30 March 2016].

Honda, Y., Asao, N. and Gotō, K. (2006) *'Nīto' 'tte Iuna!* Tokyo: Kōbunsha. (Don't call them NEETs!)

House of Commons (2012) Work and Pensions Committee. *Youth Unemployment and the Youth Contract: Second Report of Sessions 2012–13. Volume I: Report together with formal minutes, oral and written evidence.* HC151, UK. [online] Available at: http://www.publications.parliament.uk/pa/cm201213/cmselect/cmworpen/151/151.pdf [accessed 17 October 2015].

Huang (2007) 'NEET goes global', *Taiwan Panorama Magazine*. [online] Available at: http://140.130.28.17/courses/flash_course/high/p12.pdf [accessed 30 March 2016].

Impetus (2014) *Make NEETs history in 2014.* London: Impetus – The Private Equity Foundation. [online] Available at: http://impetus-pef.org.uk/wp-content/uploads/2013/12/Make-NEETs-History-Report_ImpetusPEF_January-2014.pdf [accessed 29 March 2016].

Inui, A. (2005) 'Why freeter and NEET are misunderstood: recognising the precarious conditions of Japanese youth', *Social Work and Society*, 3 (2), 244–51.

Isaac-Wilson, S. (2011) 'England's riots look to have hit some young people's prospects hard', *The Guardian*, 26 December. [online] Available at: http://www.theguardian.com/commentisfree/2011/dec/26/riots-youth-prospects [accessed 29 March 2016].

Ishiguro, K. (2007) *Thinking about Younger People's Employment in 21st Century Japan.* [online] Available at: http://www.japanesestudies.org.uk/reviews/2007/Ishiguro.html [accessed 9 June 2014].

Istance, D., Rees, G. and Williamson, H. (1994) *Young People Not in Education, Training or Employment in South Glamorgan*. Cardiff: South Glamorgan Training and Enterprise Council.

Jarvie, I. C. (1972) *Concepts and Society*. London: Routledge and Kegan Paul.

Jayanetti, C. (2010) 'How Connexions has been cut across the country: a spreadsheet of info'. [online] Available at: http://liberalconspiracy.org/2010/09/03/how-connexions-has-been-cut-across-the-country-a-spreadsheet-of-info/ [accessed 22 May 2014].

Jō, S. (2006) *Wakamono wa Naze 3nen de Kaisha wo Yamerunoka? Nenkō Joretsu ga Ubau Nihon no Mirai*. Tokyo: Kobunsha. (Why do young people quit after three years? The seniority-based personnel management system deprives Japan of its future).

Jozwiak, G. (2013) 'Councils seek more power to help young unemployed'. [online] Available at: http://www.cypnow.co.uk/cyp/news/1078105/councils-seek-power-help-unemployed [accessed 2 May 2014].

Krähenbühl, S. and Blades, M. (2006) 'The effect of interviewing techniques on young children's responses to questions', *Child: Care, Health and Development*, 32 (3), 321–31.

Kress, G. (2010) *Multimodality: A Social Semiotic Approach to Contemporary Communication*. London: Routledge.

Leaman, C. (2014) 'YoungMinds vs Launches Today'. [online] Available at: http://www.youngminds.org.uk/news/news/1833_youngminds_vs_launches_today [accessed 3 May 2014].

Lee, N. and Wright, J. (2011) *Off the Map? The Geography of NEETs: A Snapshot Analysis for the Private Equity Foundation*. London: The Work Foundation. [online] Available at: http://www.voced.edu.au/content/ngv51933 [accessed 23 May 2014].

Lees, L. (2009) *The Urban Injustices of New Labour's 'New Uurban Rrenewal': The Case of the Aylesbury Estate in London*. London: King's College London. [online] Available at: http://southwarknotes.files.wordpress.com/2009/12/lorettalees_pptx.pdf [accessed 25 May 2014].

LGA [Local Government Association] and the Centre for Social Justice (2009a) *Hidden Talents: Re-engaging Young People*. London: LGA.

LGA and the Centre for Social Justice (2009b) *Hidden Talents II: Getting the Best Out of Britain's Young People*. London: LGA.

Lincoln, Y. S. and Guba, E. G. (1985) *Naturalistic Inquiry*. Beverly Hills, CA: Sage.

Lister, R. (2004) *Poverty*. Cambridge: Polity Press.

Little, D. (2010) 'Norbert Elias on the individual'. [online] Available at: http://understandingsociety.blogspot.co.uk/2010/04/norbert-elias-on-individual.html [accessed 7 June 2014].

London Councils (2014) 'London Youth Employment Initiative background information – Paper Three'. [online] Available at: http://www.londoncouncils.gov.uk/London%20Councils/20140428YEITFGBackgroundInfoPaper3.pdf [accessed 22 May 2014].

Lopez, J. and Scott, J. (2000) *Social Structure*. Buckingham: Open University Press.

LSC [Learning and Skills Council] (2006) *Learning from Three Local LSC Partnerships Working to Tackle Levels of Young People Not in Education, Employment or Training: Guiding Principles for Policy and Practice*. LSC. [online] Available at: http://dera.ioe.ac.uk/id/eprint/12325 [accessed 3 May 2014].

Luhmann, N. (2012) *Theory of Society, Volume 1*. Stanford University Press.

Lyotard, J. (1979) *The Postmodern Condition*. Manchester: Manchester University Press, 1984.

MacDonald, R. and Marsh, J. (2001) 'Disconnected youth?', *Journal of Youth Studies*, 4 (4), 373–91.

MacDonald, R., Shildrick, T., Webster, C. and Simpson, D. (2005) 'Growing up in poor neighbourhoods: the significance of class and place in the extended transitions of "socially excluded" young adults', *Sociology*, 39 (5), 873–91.

Maguire, S. and Thompson, J. (2007) 'Young people not in education, employment or training (NEET) – where is government policy taking us now?', *Youth and Policy*, (96), 5–17.

Margaronis, M. (2008) 'How police shooting of a teenage boy rallied the "€700 generation"', *The Guardian*, 13 December. [online] Available at: http://www.theguardian.com/world/2008/dec/13/athens-greece-riots [accessed 29 March 2016].

Mason, J. (1996) *Qualitative Researching*. London: Sage.

Maxwell, J. A. (2005) *Qualitative Research Design: An Interactive Approach*. 2nd edn. Thousand Oaks, CA: Sage.

Menuge, A. (2004) *Agents under Fire*. Maryland: Rowman and Littlefield.

Miller, G. and Dingwall, R. (1997) *Context and Method in Qualitative Research*. London: Sage.

Mirza-Davies, J. (2014) *NEET: Young People Not in Education, Employment or Training*. UK: House of Commons Library. Standard Note: SN/EP/06705.

Mirza-Davies, J. (2015) *Youth Contract*. UK: House of Commons Library. Standard Note: SN/6387.

Miyamoto, M. (2005) 'Prolonged transitional period and policy', *Japan Labor Review*, 2 (3), 73–91.

Mooney, A., Oliver, C. and Smith, M. (2009) *Impact of Family Breakdown on Children's Well-Being: Evidence Review*. Department for Children, Schools and Families. [online] Available at: http://dera.ioe.ac.uk/11165/1/DCSF-RR113.pdf [accessed 3 May 2014].

Moore, K. A., Kinghorn , A. and Bandy, T. (2011) *Parental Relationship Quality and Child Outcomes across Subgroups*. Washington: Child Trends. [online] Available at: http://www.childtrends.org/?publications=parental-relationship-quality-and-child-outcomes-across-subgroups [accessed 3 May 2014].

Morrell, G., Scott, S., McNeish, D. and Webster, S. (2011) 'The August riots in England: Understanding the involvement of young people'. London: Natcen. [online] Available at: https://www.gov.uk/government/uploads/system/uploads/attachment_data/file/60531/The_20August_20Riots_20in_20England_20_pdf__201mb_.pdf [accessed 29 March 2016].

Mouzelis, N. (1974) *Back to Sociological Theory*. Basingstoke: Macmillan.

Nadel, S. F. (1957) *The Theory of Social Structure*. Glencoe: The Free Press.

Nakamura, A. (2004) 'Being NEET not so neat for nation's youth'. [online] Available at: http://www.japantimes.co.jp/2004/06/19/announcements/being-neet-not-so-neat-for-nations-youth/ [accessed 3 May 2014].

Newton, B., Speckesser, S., Nafilyan, V., Maguire, S., Devins, D. and Bickerstaffe, T. (2014) *The Youth Contract for 16–17 Year Olds Not in Education, Employment or Training Evaluation: Research Report. Revised September 2014*. Department for Education. [online] Available at: https://www.gov.uk/government/uploads/system/uploads/attachment_data/file/354706/RR318A_-_The_youth_contract_for_16-_to_17-year-olds_not_in_education__employment_or_training_evaluation.pdf [accessed 17 October 2015].

Newton, O. (2009) 'Reducing the proportion of young people not in education, employment or training (NEET)', presentation at the *IES Seminar*, London: 29 October. [online] Available at: http://bit.ly/1iSsPE6 [accessed 3 May 2014].

NIACE [The National Institute of Adult Continuing Education] (2010) 'NEET national research project'. [online] Available at: http://www.niace.org.uk/sites/default/files/documents/projects/NEET-National-Research-Project.pdf [accessed 3 May 2014].

OECD [Organization for Economic Cooperation and Development] (2010) *Off to a Good Start? Jobs for Youth*. OECD Publishing. [online] Available at: http://dx.doi.org/10.1787/9789264096127-en [accessed 29 March 2016].

OECD (2014) '4.7. More young people are unemployed or inactive and not in education nor in training (NEET)'. [online] Available at: http://dx.doi.org/10.1787/888932966409 [accessed 29 March 2016].

OECD (2015) 'Youth not in education or employment (NEET) (indicator)'. [online] Available at: http://dx.doi.org/10.1787/72d1033a-en [accessed on 29 March 2016].

ONS [The British Office for National Statistics] (2011) *Office for National Statistics*. Available at: http://www.ons.gov.uk/ons/guide-method/census/2011/census-data/index.html [accessed 28 May 2014].

ONS (2012) *Labour Market Statistics, February 2012*. [online] Available at: http://www.ons.gov.uk/ons/dcp171778_254579.pdf [accessed 3 May 2014].

ONS (2014a) *Young People Not in Education, Employment or Training (NEET), February 2014*. ONS. [online] Available at: http://www.ons.gov.uk/ons/dcp171778_352770.pdf [accessed 3 May 2014].

ONS (2014b) 'People aged from 16 to 24 Not in Education, Employment or Training ("NEET")'. [online] Available at: http://www.ons.gov.uk/ons/rel/lms/young-people-not-in-education--employment-or-training--neets-/august-2014/rft---table-1.xls [accessed 29 March 2016].

ONS (2014c) 'Statistical bulletin: young people Not in Education, Employment or Training (NEET): August 2015'. [online] Available at: http://www.ons.gov.uk/employmentandlabourmarket/peoplenotinwork/unemployment/bulletins/youngpeoplenotineducationemploymentortrainingneet/2015-08-20 [accessed 29 March 2016].

ONS (2015) *Statistical Bulletin: UK Labour Market, January 2015*. [online] Available at: http://www.ons.gov.uk/ons/dcp171778_390755.pdf [accessed 22 October 2015].

Onwuegbuzie, A. J. and Leech, N. L. (2007) 'Validity and qualitative research: an oxymoron?', *Quality and Quantity*, 41 (2), 233–49.

Oppenheim, A. N. (1992) *Questionnaire Design, Interviewing and Attitude Measurement*. London: Pinter.

Parker, J. (2000) *Structuration*. Buckingham: Open University Press.

Parsons, T. (1960) 'Durkheim's contribution to the theory of the integration of social systems', in T. Parsons (ed.), *Sociological Theory and Modern Society*. New York, NY: The Free Press.

Parsons, T. (1971) 'Comparative studies and evolutionary change', in T. Parsons (ed.), *Social Systems and the Evolution of Action Theory*. New York, NY: The Free Press, 1977.

Patton, M. Q. (1980) *Qualitative Evaluation Methods*. CA: Sage.

Patton, M. Q. (1990) *Qualitative Evaluation and Research Methods*. 2nd edn. Newbury Park, CA: Sage.

Pawson, R. (2004) *Realist Synthesis: Supplementary Reading 8: Mentoring Relationships: An Explanatory Review*. ESRC UK Centre for Evidence Based Policy and Practice. [online] Available at: http://www.kcl.ac.uk/sspp/departments/politicaleconomy/research/cep/pubs/papers/assets/wp21.pdf [accessed 3 May 2014].

Philip, K., Shucksmith, J. and King, C. (2004) *Sharing a Laugh? A Qualitative Study of Mentoring Interventions with Young People*. York: Joseph Rowntree Foundation.

Pickard, J. (2014) 'Flagship youth jobs scheme scrapped', *Financial Times*, July 24. [online] Available at: http://www.ft.com/cms/s/0/97e40d92-1340-11e4-925a-00144feabdc0.html [accessed 17 October 2015].

Pole, C. J. and Lampard, R. (2002) *Practical Social Investigation: Qualitative and Quantitative Methods in Social Research*. Gosport: Pearson Education.

Porpora, D. V. (2013) 'Morphogenesis and social change', in M. S. Archer (ed.), *Social Morphogenesis*. New York: Springer, 25–37.

Preissle, J. (2006) 'Envisioning qualitative inquiry: a view across four decades', *International Journal of Qualitative Studies in Education*, 19 (6), 685–95.

The Prince's Trust (2013) *Youth Index 2013*. [online] Available at: http://www.princes-trust.org.uk/pdf/youth-index-2013.pdf [accessed 3 May 2014].

Raby, R. (2005) 'What is resistance?', *Journal of Youth Studies*, 8 (2), 151–71.

Radcliffe-Brown, A. R. (1940) 'On social structure', *The Journal of the Royal Anthropological Institute of Great Britain and Ireland*, 70 (1), 1–12.

Rahman, K. M. (2006). 'NEETs' Challenge to Japan: Causes and Remedies', *Arbeitswelten in Japan, Jahrbuch des Deutschen Instituts für Japanstudien*, 18, 221–44.

Ray, J. J. (1980) 'How many answer categories should attitude and personality scales use?', *South African Journal of Psychology*, (10), 53–4.

Rennison, J., Maguire, S., Middleton, S. and Ashworth, K. (2005) *Young People Not in Education, Employment or Training: Evidence from the Education Maintenance Allowance Pilots Database*. Department for Education and Skills. [online] Available at: https://dspace.lboro.ac.uk/2134/2460 [accessed 3 May 2014].

Ross, A. (2009) *Disengagement from Education among 14–16 Year Olds*. Department for Children, Schools and Families. [online] Available at: https://www.gov.uk/government/uploads/system/uploads/attachment_data/file/221992/DCSF-RR178.pdf [accessed 3 May 2014].

Rossiter, S. (2009) 'Getting NEETs off the dole and back into learning', *Education Journal*, (118), 37–8.

Russell, L., Simmons, R. and Thompson, R. (2011) 'Conceptualising the lives of NEET young people: Structuration theory and "disengagement"', *Education, Knowledge and Economy*, 5 (3), 89–106.

Russell, L., Thompson, R. and Simmons, R. (2014) *Helping Unemployed Young People to Find Private Sector Work*. Joseph Rowntree Foundation. [online] Available at: http://www.jrf.org.uk/publications/help-unemployed-young-private-sector-work [accessed 6 June 2014].

Sachdev, D., Harries, B. and Roberts, T. (2006) *Regional and Sub-regional Variation in NEETs – Reasons, Remedies and Impact.* Learning and Skills Development Agency. [online] Available at: http://readingroom.lsc.gov.uk/lsc/SouthWest/swr-lsn-neetstudy-2006.pdf [accessed 3 May 2014].

Samuel, H. (2009) 'Riots across Europe fuelled by economic crisis', *The Telegraph*, 1 May. [online] Available at: http://www.telegraph.co.uk/news/worldnews/europe/5258634/Riots-across-Europe-fuelled-by-economic-crisis.html [accessed 30 March 2016].

Schacter, D. L., Gilbert, D. T. and Wegner, D. M. (2009) *Psychology*. New York: Worth.

Schunk, D. H. (2004) *Learning Theories: An Educational Perspective*. New Jersey: Pearson.

Sercombe, H. (2010) *Youth Work Ethics*. London: Sage.

SEU (1999) *Bridging the Gap: New Opportunities for 16–18 Year Olds Not in Education, Employment or Training*. Cm 4405. London: HMSO.

Silvera, I. (2014) 'UK Youth Unemployment: Neet Levels Still "Stubbornly High" at One Million'. [online] Available at: http://www.ibtimes.co.uk/uk-youth-unemployment-neet-levels-still-stubbornly-high-one-million-1438186 [accessed 3 May 2014].

Silverman, D. (1993) *Interpreting Qualitative Data: Methods for Analysing Talk, Text and Interaction*. London: Sage.

Simmons, R., Russell, L. and Thompson, R. (2013) 'NEET young people and the labour market: working on the margins', in *Youth Studies Conference*, 8–12 April, Glasgow, UK. [online] Available at: http://eprints.hud.ac.uk/17187/ [accessed 22 May 2014].

Simmons, R., Russell L. and Thompson, R. (2014) 'Young people and labour market marginality: findings from a longitudinal ethnographic study', *Journal of Youth Studies*, 17 (5), 577–91. [online] Available at: http://dx.doi.org/10.1080/13676261.2013.830706 [accessed 22 May 2014].

Simmons, R. and Thompson, R. (2011) *NEET Young People and Training for Work: Learning on the Margins*. Stoke-on-Trent: Trentham Books.

Simmons, R., Thompson, R. and Russell, L. (2014) *Education, Work and Social Change: Young People and Marginalization in Post-industrial Britain*. London: Palgrave Macmillan.

Simmons, R., Thompson, R., Tabrizi, G. and Nartey, A. (2014) *Engaging Young People Not in Education, Employment or Training: The Case for a Youth Resolution*. London: UCU. [online] Available at: http://eprints.hud.ac.uk/19823/ [accessed 22 May 2014].

Siraj, I., Hollingworth, K., Taggart, B., Sammons, P., Melhuish, E. and Sylva, K. (2014) *Report on Students Who Are Not in Education, Employment or Training (NEET)*. London: Institute of Education. [online] Available at: http://www.ioe.ac.uk/Research_Home/16-Report-students-NEET-RR.pdf [accessed 29 March 2016].

Sodha, S. and Margo, J. (2010) *Ex Curricula*. London: Demos.

Standish, P. (2007) 'Editorial', *Journal of Philosophy of Education*, 41 (3), iii–v.

Stromquist, N. P. and Monkman, K. (eds) (2000) *Globalisation and Education: Integration and Contestation across Cultures*. Maryland: Rowman and Littlefield.

Tamesberger, D. and Bacher, J. (2014) 'NEET youth in Austria: a typology including socio-demography, labour market behaviour and permanence', *Journal of Youth Studies*, 17 (9), 1239–59.

Taylor, M. (2015) '50% rise in long-term unemployment for young ethnic minority people in UK', *The Guardian*, 10 March. [online] Available at: http://www.theguardian.com/society/2015/mar/10/50-rise-in-long-term-unemployed-youngsters-from-uk-ethnic-minorities [accessed 17 October 2015].

Taylor, M., Rogers, S. and Lewis, P. (2011) 'England rioters: young, poor and unemployed', *The Guardian*, 18 August. [online] Available at: http://www.theguardian.com/uk/2011/aug/18/england-rioters-young-poor-unemployed [accessed 29 March 2016].

Taylor, M. C., Bedard, R., Boss, M. W., Evans, K. and Thibault, C. J. (1992) 'Young people's attitudes toward the world of work in three Canadian labour markets', *Canadian Journal of Counselling*, 26 (3), 177–88.

Team Hackney (2014) 'Team Hackney leadership board meeting agenda', 15 January. [online] Available at: http://www.hackney.gov.uk/Assets/Documents/Team-Hackney-Board-Papers-15-January-2014.pdf [accessed 22 May 2014].

Thompson, R. (2011) 'Individualisation and social exclusion: the case of young people not in education, employment or training', *Oxford Review of Education*, 37 (6), 785–802.

TLRP [Teaching and Learning Research Programme] (2008) *Education, Globalisation and the Knowledge Economy*. TLRP. [online] Available at: http://www.tlrp.org/pub/documents/globalisationcomm.pdf [accessed 1 May 2014].

Toivonen, T. (2008) 'The trickier import: should the use of "social exclusion" (*shakaiteki haijo*) be abandoned in Japan?', paper presented at the *81st Annual Convention of the Japan Sociological Society*, Keio University, Tokyo, 23–24 November. [online] Available at: http://www.bristol.ac.uk/poverty/ESRCJSPS/downloads/research/japan/1%20Japan-Poverty,%20Inequality%20and%20Social%20Exclusion%20(General)/Articles%20(Japan%20General)/English/Toivonen%20-%20The%20tricker%20import.pdf [accessed 29 March 2016].

Toivonen, T. (2011) '"Don't let your child become a NEET!" The strategic foundations of a Japanese youth scare', *Japan Forum*, 23 (3), 407–29.

Toivonen, T., Norasakkunkit, V. and Uchida, Y. (2011) 'Unable to conform, unwilling to rebel? Youth, culture and motivation in globalizing Japan', *Frontiers in Cultural Psychology*, 2 (Article 207). [online] Available at: http://journal.frontiersin.org/article/10.3389/fpsyg.2011.00207/abstract [accessed 29 March 2016].

UCU [University and College Union] (2010) 'UCU Policy Briefing January 2010: Young people not in employment, education or training (NEETs)'. [online] Available at: http://www.ucu.org.uk/index.cfm?articleid=4625 [accessed 3 May 2014].

UN (2015) 'Goal 8: Promote inclusive and sustainable economic growth, employment and decent work for all'. [online] Available at: http://www.un.org/sustainabledevelopment/economic-growth/ [accessed 9 November 2015].

UNECE [United Nations Economic Commission for Europe] (2013) 'The measurement of poverty and social inclusion in the EU: achievements and further improvements', Working paper 25. [online] Available at: https://www.unece.org/fileadmin/DAM/stats/documents/ece/ces/ge.15/2013/WP_25_Eurostat_D_En.pdf [accessed 30 March 2016].

UNICEF Office of Research (2014) *Children of the Recession: The Impact of the Economic Crisis on Child Well-Being in Rich Countries*, Innocenti Report Card 12. Florence: UNICEF Office of Research.

UNISON (2011) *UNISON Dossier – January 2011. Con-Demned Jobs: Cuts That Wreck Recovery*. [online] Available at: http://www.unison.org.uk/acrobat/NewUNISONDossierOfCuts.pdf [accessed 4 December 2012].

van Teijlingen, E. R., Rennie, A. M., Hundley, V. and Graham, W. (2001) 'The importance of conducting and reporting pilot studies: the example of the Scottish births survey', *Journal of Advanced Nursing*, 34 (3), 289–95.

Vaughan, R. (2009) 'Top mandarin: 15% of Neets die within 10 years', *Times Educational Supplement*, 7 August. [online] Available at: http://www.tes.co.uk/article.aspx?storycode=6019772 [accessed 3 May 2014].

Vuolo, M., Staff, J. and Mortimer, J. T. (2012) 'Weathering the great recession: psychological and behavioral trajectories in the transition from school to work', *Developmental Psychology*, 48 (6), 1759–73. [online] Available at: http://dx.doi.org/10.1037/a0026047 [accessed 29 March 2016].

Waterman, C. (2007) 'A NEET solution', *Education Journal*, (105), 19.

Weber, M. (1920) 'Conceptual exposition', in G. Roth and C. Wittich (eds), *M.Weber: Economy and Society*. New York, NY: Bedminster Press, 1968.

Wells, G. (1999) *Dialogic Inquiry: Towards a Sociocultural Practice and Theory of Education*. New York: Cambridge University Press.

West, C. K., Farmer, J. A. and Wolff, P. M. (1991) *Instructional Design: Implications from Cognitive Science*. New Jersey: Pearson.

Williamson, H. (1997) 'Status Zer0, youth and the "underclass": some considerations', in R. MacDonald (ed.), *Youth, the 'Underclass' and Social Exclusion*. London: Routledge.

Willis, P. E. (1977) *Learning to Labour: How Working Class Kids Get Working Class Jobs*. Farnborough: Saxon House.

Willmott, R. (1999) 'Structure, agency and the sociology of education: rescuing analytical dualism', *British Journal of Sociology of Education*, 20 (1), 5–21.

Wintour, P. (2012) 'Coalition's child poverty adviser: bring back EMA', *The Guardian*, 18 October. [online] Available at: http://www.theguardian.com/education/2012/oct/18/coalition-child-poverty-ema-1 [accessed 3 May 2014].

Wolf, A. (2008) *Diminished Returns: How Raising the Leaving Age to 18 Will Harm Young People and the Economy*. London: Policy Exchange.

Woodman, D. (2009) 'The mysterious case of the pervasive choice biography: Ulrich Beck, structure/agency, and the middling state of theory in the sociology of youth', *Journal of Youth Studies*, 12 (3), 243–56.

Woodman, D. and Wyn, J. (2013) 'Youth policy and generations: why youth policy needs to "rethink youth"', *Social Policy and Society*, 12 (2), 265–75.

Yates, S., Harris, A., Sabates, R. and Staff, J. (2011) 'Early occupational aspirations and fractured transitions: a study of entry into "NEET" status in the UK', *Journal of Social Policy*, 40 (3), 513–34.

Index

www.ingramcontent.com/pod-product-compliance
Ingram Content Group UK Ltd.
Pitfield, Milton Keynes, MK11 3LW, UK
UKHW020142290926
15471UKWH00004B/649

9 781350 093768